Paul Kagame and Rwanda

Paul Kagame and Rwanda

Power, Genocide and the
Rwandan Patriotic Front

COLIN M. WAUGH

McFarland & Company, Inc., Publishers
Jefferson, North Carolina, and London

Maps by Phillip Green.

LIBRARY OF CONGRESS CATALOGUING-IN-PUBLICATION DATA

Waugh, Colin M., 1955–
   Paul Kagame and Rwanda : power, genocide and the Rwandan
Patriotic Front / Colin M. Waugh.
      p.   cm.
   Includes bibliographical references and index.

   ISBN 0-7864-1941-5 (softcover : 50# alkaline paper)

   1. Kagamé, Paul, 1957–   2. Rwanda — Politics and government.
3. Rwanda — History — Civil War, 1994 — Atrocities.
4. Genocide — Rwanda.   I. Title.
DT450.437.K34W38   2004
967.57104'31'092 — dc22   2004017525

British Library cataloguing data are available

On the cover: Rwandan refugees arriving at Kibiriti port, December
1996 (UN/UNHCR/L. *Taylor*).

Manufactured in the United States of America

McFarland & Company, Inc., Publishers
  Box 611, Jefferson, North Carolina 28640
    www.mcfarlandpub.com

To Alastair and Isabel

ACKNOWLEDGMENTS

The idea for this book grew out of a conversation with Jennifer Stoddart, whose creative sense of the possibilities for the subject as well as her early encouragement got the project under way. During the research stage, access to the resources of the United Nations' IRIN service and the help of Joanne Clark in particular opened doors and added valuable material. For their work in reviewing and criticizing early drafts of the manuscript, I would like to thank both Katharine Mann-Jackson and Alyson Smith for their detailed attention and helpful suggestions. Professor Alan Goodall provided useful contacts for my interview schedule in Kigali.

Inside Rwanda, I benefited from the close cooperation of several members of the communications, protocol and media staff of the Presidency in Kigali, and the hospitality of Professor Silas Lwakabamba at KIST, while doing my research in the capital city. In organizing and conducting my daily work schedule, the quick thinking, local knowledge and reliability of Albert Ntaganda helped make an otherwise difficult program run smoothly. To him and the other Rwandans who provided assistance and information for this book, I extend my grateful thanks.

CONTENTS

PREFACE

In late April of 1994, as hundreds of thousands of Rwandans were being killed in their homes, fields and villages or trying to flee from the torrent of death that engulfed their country, very little was known about their plight in the wider world. Few who understood what was happening and were in a position to help were motivated enough to champion the cause of humanity in a small country in the heart of Africa. Most of the western nations with the resources and logistical means to come to Rwanda's aid had become involved in the continuing crisis in the former Yugoslavia, and if there was an interest in Africa, it was focused on the conduct and outcome of South Africa's first post-apartheid elections. There had long been predictions of bloodshed on the road from white minority rule to democracy in that country, and the international community was anxious to see a peaceful electoral process to secure the transition of power to the country's black majority leaders.

It was while sitting with colleagues in a small town in Mpumalanga Province, eastern South Africa, on the morning after Nelson Mandela's resounding victory at the polls on April 28, 1994, that the news of the unfolding genocide in Rwanda was first brought home to me. As a worker for an international agency based in neighboring Mozambique, what I knew of Rwanda was gleaned from reading week-old newspapers and by listening to occasional radio broadcasts. I had only a sketchy appreciation then of what was happening a few thousand miles to the north, in a country I had never seen and whose social, political and geographical landscape for me was unknown.

A group of us sat together drinking coffee and watching the morning mist clear over the rolling hills that rise from outside Nelspruit, the provincial market town that lies near the lower end of Kruger Park. We listened to a brief news bulletin about Rwanda on the BBC, barely able to understand the cataclysmic events that were unfolding in what for us was

an unfamiliar, unfrequented and hitherto becalmed corner of the continent. Another guest at the hotel, a visiting election observer from the
United Nations, had just come off duty from her night shift monitoring
the vote counting process in one of the area's polling stations. She turned
to me and with a note of scorn in her voice, predicted: "That's where *you'll*
be going next." I glanced back at her, wondering what reply to make to
this presumptuous international civil servant on a short-term monitoring
trip to Africa. Finally I could only manage a scowl of disbelief at the very
thought of ending up working in an obscure zone of terror in such a
diminutive nation, seemingly lost at the center of the African continent.

Before the end of that year I was on a plane to Kigali, the Rwandan
capital, traveling to participate in a series of meetings to plan an international effort aimed at assistance to the displaced and returning populations affected by the genocide. I was employed then as an official
responsible for Rwanda in an agency called the International Organization for Migration, and it was the first of several trips I would make to the
country over the coming few years.

Arriving in Kigali in late 1994, only five months after the end of the
genocide, the mood was not at all what I had expected to encounter. There
were no signs of violence, let alone dead bodies in the streets or any such
evidence of recent human carnage. Despite a shattered infrastructure and
a decimated population, I distinctly recall a certain sense of optimism,
almost a lightness in the mood of the Rwandan people I met in my first
few days of that initial voyage.

A short time later I understood that many of these upbeat African people I had been meeting were, like me, visitors to the country, most of them
Rwandan Tutsis who had been in foreign countries for decades and some
of whom were now visiting their homeland for the first time as adults.
Others had never even seen the land of their parents' birth. For both groups
it was a tremendous experience, a time of discovery and exploration as well
as an historic opportunity for reunion and renewal.

If there was something of the surreal about the celebratory mood
among the newcomers during those first months after the genocide in
Rwanda, there was to be a slow, hard and painful adjustment to a new
reality for the vast majority of their compatriots for many years thereafter.

For the next two years I was involved as an outsider in the business
of humanitarian assistance to the country, a representative of the international community. I was part of a community which had, in the minds
of ordinary Rwandans as well as by the standards of its own lofty ideals
and undertakings, abdicated its responsibilities during the holocaust of
April–July, 1994.

In the years following the genocide, some of my international colleagues who had been present just prior to Rwanda's Apocalypse may have wished that the one million dead would soon fade from the attention of the world, as had the victims of the Armenian genocide of 1915 in Turkey, or the millions of Ukrainians starved to death in peacetime under Stalin's regime, or in the other unremembered genocidal atrocities of the twentieth century.

However, entering the stage in the traumatic and controversial aftermath of a civil war superimposed upon a genocide, Rwanda's new generation of leaders did not behave as many outsiders had expected. Although initially presented with a paucity of options, they were not prepared to settle down to waiting for handouts and running another African backwater whose development had just been retarded twenty years by a preventable calamity. The Rwandan Patriotic Front (RPF), which took power in July of 1994, was not ready to go back to the end of the queue and accept the strictures of the international community, which had spurned the nation in its plight before and during the months of unrestrained mass murder in 1994. Although an unlikely cast of characters for the task of government, many appearing to be more Ugandan in their speech and upbringing than representatives of their native Rwanda, the RPF and its military commander in chief, Paul Kagame, were as different as they were determined.

With a philosophy hewn more from the hinterland of Africa's rift valley than the boarding schools and academies of Europe, little Rwanda's new leaders had their own agenda to pursue and Paul Kagame soon became its embodiment, figurehead, and later the country's first Tutsi president since independence. He rose to power in a country that at first had almost no allies, but that later won the respect and backing of powerful international friends.

I spent much of the decade after the genocide traveling and working in different countries in Africa. By the time this book was written, I had been to over twenty nations on the Forgotten Continent. Dividing my time between assignments for international agencies, financial and publishing work, as well as private research, I came across governments, business people and politicians in a rich variety of lands with a diversity of styles of administration.

In setting out to write an African political narrative, I had to choose which of the countries I had come to know was the one with the most worthwhile story to tell and the most potent message to deliver. Rwanda quickly emerged as the best-qualified candidate. In my mind, there were three irresistible reasons for this.

Firstly, the experience of the genocide makes Rwanda unique at least in terms of modern African history. It is a fact of human nature that there is a fascination with violence and death among readers, television viewers and cinemagoers. Violence is the stuff of countless action films, TV crime thrillers, wartime documentaries and big screen productions. Sometimes the more gruesome the violence the more compelling the reading or the viewing. Genocide is a particularly atrocious form of violence, a repugnant crime, an extreme form of persecution and an act of mass murder all rolled into one horror story to whet the appetites of the most compulsive of audiences.

Yet while the European wars, the Nazi genocide against the Jews, or more recently the struggle for power in Vietnam have absorbed those with a fascination for humanity's darker side, somehow when it comes to Africa, everyone turns the other way. I wonder still if Rwanda's story will become like the accounts of those other little-known periods of mass terror in far-off countries which soon become confined to a small section of the "History — Rest of the World" shelves of the bookstores.

In our modern global society where the most developed, most literate nations are also rapidly becoming the most multiracial, events such as Rwanda's genocide should not be confined to the bottom shelf in the basement.

However, this work is not principally about the genocide, although the events surrounding the tragic months of 1994 in Rwanda inevitably occupy a prominent place in any account of the country's modern political era. The second reason for my choosing to produce a chronicle of current Rwandan politics is because of the alteration from the accepted norm of post-conflict recovery and development in Africa that this unusual country represents.

Rwanda, although among the world's poorest nations, is run according to a formula that doesn't quite fit the mold familiar to the western reader with a passing interest in sub–Saharan Africa. In addition to civil war, poverty and disease, novice western readers are given to associating African societies with corruption. In this respect, Rwanda begins to break away from the conventional model, although like most states its record is far from unblemished. Nevertheless, corruption is not endemic in Rwanda in the way that it is in much of the rest of the world, or in many countries in Africa itself.

I recall vividly an incident in 1995 when, driving northwards from Kigali on a Sunday afternoon with a colleague in my four-wheel-drive company car and having just completed an illegal shortcut to reach a turnoff to my destination, I was stopped by a Rwandan officer who had observed the maneuver. After checking my license and identification and scrutinizing the vehicle, he informed me that I would have to come back to the police station the following day to retrieve my documents, quite an inconvenience as I had by now driven far from my base. I told him that I could not agree to this demand and a standoff then ensued.

Remaining patiently seated in the car, I talked to the soldier about our respective hometowns, sports, languages and the like, while he held on to my license and I declined to agree to returning on Monday to retrieve it. My colleague suggested a small bribe to break the impasse, which I at first resisted, then later agreed to, offering the price of a few sodas, perhaps a day's pay for the young Rwandan serviceman.

As I anticipated, he rejected the offer and proceeded to carry on the conversation for another 15 minutes, this time asking about cars, the organization I worked for and other personal miscellany. The light was fading and our urge to capitulate mounted by the minute, but now we had neither monetary nor moral leverage over this determined recruit who refused to be bought.

Suddenly, when it seemed that only our surrender could break the deadlock, he leaned closer towards the car and looking straight at me, said, "You know, you are very disciplined," and handed me back my license without emotion. I later learned that this was a fair compliment from a young member of Rwanda's armed forces and one which he had not chosen to utter by coincidence.

The intrinsically ordered nature of Rwandan society stems in part from the tradition and history of its people but also, in recent times, it is in good measure due to a leadership which has reinforced a natural tendency through authority as well as example.

The story of Paul Kagame's ascent from junior officer in a foreign guerrilla army to the presidency of Rwanda is the story of how this leadership, this authority and this reassertion of traditional "Rwandanness" came about in a country that had known only fear, division and clan-based nepotism for many years. The personality of Paul Kagame and his centrality to the evolution of a different type of modern African state is the third reason for my choice of modern Rwanda in producing this document of an African political landscape.

Kagame's story is also that of a battlefield general and a politician who was often described in the past as "secretive" or "mysterious" and who was given neither to public displays of emotion nor to unnecessary discussions with members of the foreign media. I wanted to ensure that Kagame's views, often contested, were as much part of this record as the descriptions and conclusions that I came to through my own reading and research or from listening to the opinions of others.

Being neither an accredited journalist from a major news organization nor an "insider" with Rwandan connections, the process of arranging interviews with President Kagame was a lengthy and frustrating one. Unanswered letters and faxes, unreturned e-mails and phone calls were the staple diet of responses to my early attempts at access. Nevertheless, as in all endeavors, with a measure of persistence some helping hands were finally extended and soon the formalities towards arranging my presidential encounter were under way.

Once focused on the idea of my project, albeit for the very brief time that could be afforded from an exacting schedule, the president participated in the interview process with remarkable relish, particularly when the opportunity arose to recount experiences from the early days of his career. Advisors who were present at the sessions commented afterwards that they too had been made aware of new details from their chief executive's early life that came as revelations about the person to whose service they consecrated most of their daylight hours.

While much of the early work for this book was carried out in libraries, through consulting internet archives and in talking to people living outside Rwanda, the journals kept from my visits during the 1990s are the source of much of the anecdotal material that is included. While avoiding personal references in the text itself, I have nevertheless tried to open up a number of topics with relevance beyond the Rwandan experience for the reader's reflection.

Important among these is the comparison between the "validity" of the victims' cause in an African country like Rwanda as justification for subsequent actions by the authorities to ensure that the experience of the genocide was never repeated.

While the words and actions of the international community have suggested otherwise, the case exists for a more flexible assessment of a leadership that has been accused of atrocities, human rights violations and the plunder of its neighbors' territories. To assist with the necessary mental transition, comparisons are drawn between the challenges of post-genocide reconciliation and reconstruction in modern Rwanda and the aftermath of World War II and the Jewish holocaust. I invite the reader to consider the philosophy, actions and strategy of Paul Kagame and his government in an African context as well as suggesting an altered judgment of his record other than against purely western benchmarks. Reading this book without making just a little of this perceptive adjustment might result in a lost appreciation of the saga of Kagame and Rwanda and its relevance for future relations between the African continent and the outside world.

Colin Waugh
August 2004

1

EXODUS AND EXILE

Escape from Gitarama

Across the fields of Nyarutovu houses burned, cries rang out, people ran across hillsides and fled down roadways, desperately trying to escape from a mayhem of arson and pillaging that had reached their commune in Gitarama Prefecture, 40 miles west of the Rwandan capital Kigali. In 1959 Paul Kagame, born into a Tutsi family, was only three years old when his village in Ntambwe commune was attacked. Because of his family's race, they risked becoming victims of the outbreak of lawlessness that was spreading across sections of the countryside, in which Hutu gangs were targeting Tutsi civilians.

Local peasants armed with machetes, clubs, spears and a few rifles were moving around the hilltops, from village to village, setting light to homes and evicting or killing their residents. Their actions were condoned by the local authorities and in most areas where such attacks occurred, no attempt was made by the Belgian-led army or the police to protect the residents, who had no option but to flee for their lives. The attackers moved through each community, working in relays of around ten men each, emptying houses of their inhabitants, then beating and sometimes killing their victims, before moving on to the next village. The groups' leaders rallied them by blowing whistles as they went along, in the trademark signal to others to prepare to join in the campaign of burning and eviction.

Paul Kagame and his family were forced to abandon their home when they became threatened by the mounting tide of sectarian violence. Learning one day that a gang of looters was approaching their house, they hurriedly bundled their belongings together and left quickly, never to see their home intact again. Shortly afterwards their house was emptied of the remaining valuables and razed to the ground by looters. Years later Kagame would revisit his birthplace only to find an almost empty hill and just one

7

or two older survivors of the massacres which had followed to bear witness to the horrors of that day.

From Ntambwe, the family fled their commune for nearby Nyanza,
where they spent two weeks, before continuing northwards to Paul's
mother's birthplace of Mutara, near the Ugandan border. Much of the
countryside was still not safe, however, and the attacks were becoming
more widespread as the Rwandan "revolution" which began in 1959 continued. In the following years extremist elements from the Hutu ethnic
majority rampaged more widely through the countryside, continuing and
heightening their campaign of violence, looting and arson.

Family Life of Fugitives

From a family of six children, Paul Kagame was the youngest and the
only surviving son, his brother Joseph having been killed in a car acci-
dent. His four sisters, Mars, Cathy, Béatrice and Jeanne, split up shortly
after their flight from Gitarama; Paul was separated from two of them for
many years. Jeanne and Cathy stayed behind in Rwanda in 1961 and were
brought up by another family related to theirs—they remained in the
country until 1973, finally leaving for Burundi, then Zaire and eventually
Italy, where Cathy was later married. The family was to be scattered across
central Africa and beyond as part of a pattern so typical for many victims
of the changing social and political times in the region.

Paul Kagame's father, Deogratius, was born in Gitarama. Related to
the royal family of Mutara Rudahigwa, he had enjoyed a close association
with the king in his early career. A property and cattle owner, he led a comfortable life by Rwandan standards of the day. His wife, Asteria, was very
closely related to the queen and so the family had access to the benefits of
a position in traditional Rwandan society. However, unlike most Tutsis of
his position, Kagame's father was not a chief, not because he could not have
become one but "because he didn't like it himself," Kagame recalled his
father telling him in later years.[1] In 1951, Deogratius went into business
independently, distancing himself further from the traditional cattle-keep-
ing and property-owning roles of an aristocrat of the day.

He became involved in agricultural and other businesses and by the
time the persecutions began, Kagame's father was a successful businessman still associated with but not dependent on the monarchy for his position in Rwandan society. As such, when the mood in the country turned
violent beginning in 1959, he would have been targeted along with other
leading Tutsis for arrest and harassment by the newly empowered Hutu-

led administration. He therefore left Gitarama for Burundi early in 1959, spending some time there and in Zaire, before returning to northern Rwanda to rejoin his family.

There was, however, little prospect of any return to security for the foreseeable future and so in 1961, Kagame's father, after reuniting with his household in Mutara, decided to move across the border to Uganda, the country which was to become their family home for the next three decades.

Once inside Uganda, with the money he had been able to bring with him, Deogratius was able to rent a house in Kamwezi, immediately across the border from Rwanda. Then later the family joined with other groups of Rwandans who were streaming across the border during those years and followed them further into Uganda's Ankole Province, where refugee camps had by then been set up for the exiles. After some time, the family moved again, going further north and finally arriving at another refugee camp called Nshungerezi, in Toro District, where they settled in mid–1962 and stayed for the rest of Paul's childhood years.

Early Refugee Experiences

Refugee life in Uganda for Rwandans fleeing ethnic persecution in the early 1960s was hard: refugee camps, for those who were able to reach them, were poorly equipped and infrequently supplied and many of those Rwandans seeking refuge did not survive the early months of exile. Eventually, some poorer land was allocated by the local Ugandan authorities to the Rwandans to cultivate, but many ended up working as cheap labor for the local farmers in order to make ends meet. Later, the United Nations High Commission for Refugees (UNHCR) helped to establish more permanent refugee settlements, providing food and non-food items, which went part of the way to sustaining the livelihood of the refugees.

By 1964, according to the UNHCR, 336,000 Rwandan Tutsis had fled their country to seek refuge in neighboring lands. The majority, around 200,000, went to Burundi, with 36,000 fleeing to Tanzania, 22,000 to Zaire and 78,000 going initially to Uganda.[2] Actual numbers, including those not registered by the UNHCR, were almost certainly higher; others have estimated, for example, that a further 100,000 unregistered Rwandans went to resettle independently in Uganda over the following several years. In all, seven refugee settlements were founded in western Uganda between 1962 and 1966, and over time many of the refugees were able to support themselves by cultivating food and in a few cases by continuing their traditional cattle-rearing way of life.

For the next quarter of a century, successive waves of persecution and conflict inside Rwanda brought the total numbers of Tutsi refugees in the region to between 400,000 and 600,000 or around half of an estimated total Rwandan Tutsi population of just under one million in 1990.[3]

Student and Outsider

Despite the early hardships, the Rwandans exiled in 1959 and the subsequent years gradually began to integrate into Ugandan society, learning English and speaking less and less French, the language of their former colonial masters. Soon many came to see themselves as Ugandans in practical terms, and as the months of exile turned to years, then decades, much of their direct association with the motherland began to diminish. No matter how long they stayed, however, those affected by the strife in Rwanda were never granted Ugandan citizenship. At the same time, political conditions at home remained unfavorable for a safe return, leaving the exiles in Uganda, who probably numbered over 150,000 by 1966, condemned to a state of long-term limbo.

Paul Kagame attended primary school in Toro District where he learned English in a class of refugees, before moving to a Ugandan state school in Ntare from the age of nine, where he finally began to mix with the local population. He performed well and was at the top of his class in the last year of primary in Ntare. Even at this early age, his academic achievements were already causing administrative problems for the authorities of his adoptive land. According to regulations, the top three students in the class qualified for a grant to go on to secondary school; however, since he was not Ugandan, Paul did not qualify, leaving the authorities in the difficult position of having to award the grant to a student with inferior marks or deny him access to the school.

To avoid the issue, he was initially refused a place, until financial help could be found from elsewhere. Luckily, Paul Kagame was able to benefit from the aid of a refugee assistance network established in different countries in Europe, which provided sponsorship, through a friend of his father in Belgium named Yves Genin. In this way Paul was able to complete his secondary schooling in Uganda; Genin maintained his close relationship with Rwanda and later became the Belgian ambassador to Kigali during Kagame's term of office as president.

Paul's academic performance was not atypical of his generation of young Tutsi refugees, who unlike their Rwandan cousins, the economic migrants to the region from an earlier era, showed both an appetite and an aptitude for learning and qualifications. After graduation, many of the new refugees in Uganda would move away from their homes and villages

Paul Kagame seated second from right, with classmates in 1972 at Ntare school in Uganda. (From the personal collection of President Paul Kagame.)

in the refugee districts to seek fresh advancement in the larger towns such as Kampala, the Ugandan capital, and Mbarara, while some went to Nairobi or left Africa completely, going to Europe and North America.

Many among the early Banyarwanda and indigenous Ugandan community resented the success of the newcomers, as Paul Kagame's schoolday experiences illustrate. This bitterness extended to economic life too, as the progeny of the "'59ers," as the new arrivals were known, soon overtook their neighbors in material status. A 20-year-old refugee, Silas Mukankusi, interviewed in the late 1980s, commented: "When we arrived, the nationals offered us jobs in their gardens. That's how we got food and made ends meet. But by 1972–73, we were employing them. That's why we are at loggerheads. They can't understand how we passed them."

Although the young Rwandan Tutsis had no material advantage to start with, their parents were used to an elevated status in their homeland and this may have contributed to the drive for academic achievement which they displayed. Christine Majagari, a 25-year-old, summed it up: "We had no land, so we had to move with our heads. Our heads were our only capital."[4]

Because of the ill feelings which this above-average achievement often generated, the exiled Rwandan students like Kagame growing up in Toro in the early 1970s increasingly encountered social difficulties as well as financial hardship. Children from the local western Ugandan group, the Banyankole, harassed the young Rwandans, often reminding them of their outsider status, and these feelings of alienation were to carry on into adult life for many of the refugees.

Another graduate of Ntare school who was to become Kagame's mentor and political inspiration was a Banyankole Ugandan called Yoweri Museveni, some twelve years Kagame's senior, a political activist and already a determined opponent of the way the authorities were running his country. Museveni came from the Hima ethnic group, which was closely related to the Tutsis, and he sympathized with the Rwandan exiles from his home region. He soon befriended Kagame, later influencing him to join in political and military opposition to the Ugandan regime that was oppressing both their native tribes.

By 1972, following the *coup d'état* against President Milton Obote staged in the previous year by his army chief, General Idi Amin, more serious changes were also occurring at the national political level. Many of the foreign teachers, who were mostly British, were being forced to leave the country, in order to be replaced by Ugandan nationals. Such measures served only to emphasize the isolation of outsiders and added to the obstacles which they faced.

For Kagame, however, influential friends were not far away. His mother, Asteria, was a sister of the late king's wife, Rosalie Gicanda. King Mutara Rudahigwa had died in Burundi in 1959[5] and his successor, Kigeli V, returned to Kampala in 1972 and was able to offer moral if not material support to his relations in exile. However, not all exiled Rwandans were monarchists, and as Kagame's father had somewhat distanced himself from the royal court, there was less of a link with the monarchy than during the early years in Rwanda. Furthermore, a foreign king in Uganda was not entitled to any special privileges, especially during the two regimes of the republican socialist president Milton Obote. Kigeli's stay in Uganda was cut short by the changing political situation and he soon sought exile outside the region, ultimately settling in the United States, outside Washington, DC.

Among the children of the '59ers, not all were as fortunate as Kagame in gaining access to education in their host country. In many cases, refugees would change their names to gain places in schools, as outsiders were often identified and prevented from enrolling. As tuition was in English, some would try to adopt a local name from the Ankole region of western Uganda,

King Charles Mutara Rudahigwa and Queen Rosalie Gicanda, at the royal residence in Nyanza, 1958. (From the personal collection of President Paul Kagame.)

in order to be granted access to classes. "I felt very bad when I changed my name," said one refugee student. "But if you didn't the headmaster would not offer you a place." But then they would live in fear of being exposed if another student chose to address them in front of the class in Runyankole, the local language.

The psychological impact on many of the young students was heavy, as the enforced denial of identity under threat of persecution only compounded their feelings of vulnerability and a rootless existence. Even those who joined the army or the civil service after school were never granted Ugandan passports. It was this continuing disenfranchisement, exacerbated in the early 1980s after Milton Obote returned to power and began a campaign of expulsions of the Banyarwanda, that contributed so strongly to the lingering desire of many to make a stable return to Rwanda. On the one hand, life in Uganda was hard and nothing was ever permanent for the refugees, thereby pushing them to want to return. On the other hand, and because of their chronically temporary existence, the inaccessible homeland became idealized in the minds of many, creating a pull factor attracting them towards a land which most of them had never even known.

However, despite his position of relative advantage in early life, even Kagame would never have found a place for himself in the upper echelons of Ugandan society. He later explained: "Professional advancement was restricted for Rwandans in Uganda. There were limitations on our progress. They would still have considered Kagame a Rwandan and have said that he cannot go beyond a certain point, because he is a Rwandan." But, to underline the proud and deep-rooted desire for return held by many of his compatriots, Kagame went on to describe their feelings: "[Most of the Rwandan refugees] would never have accepted Ugandan citizenship even if the Ugandans wanted to grant them their nationality.... I wanted to be a Rwandan."[6]

Extremist Influences at Home, a New Alliance in Exile

As an unsympathetic ruler once more took the reins of power in Kampala, at home in Rwanda the exclusion of Tutsis from much of public life had all but been institutionalized. In Rwanda in 1964, nearly all the remaining Tutsi politicians had been purged from office at the same time as massacres of thousands of their fellow countrymen were being carried out. From that time on, Tutsis stayed away from politics, although many were able to continue working unharassed in the private sector, on the unwritten understanding that they would not attempt to meddle in public affairs.

Furthermore, the Rwanda of the 1960s and early 1970s had few allies in the region. Having been created and preserved thanks to Belgian sponsorship and support, there was no possibility of joining in the socialist or anti-colonialist movements of the day that were blossoming in neighboring Tanzania, for example. Burundi had become a kind of "apartheid" state, with a Tutsi minority army maintaining hegemony over its Hutu majority population. Meanwhile Uganda, upon which Rwanda was dependent for its main road connection for international commerce, was involved in its own tribal struggles and internal feuding between factions.

Rwanda at the time was ruled by Grégoire Kayibanda, who had taken over as the first Hutu president of Rwanda just before the country's official independence from Belgium in 1962. In the early 1960s he had conducted purges of Tutsis, both from public office and of ordinary citizens in reprisal massacres against Tutsi insurgency attacks. His hold on power began to slip, however, and in 1972–73, Kayibanda orchestrated another round of persecutions to try to shore up his own domestic power base.

He conducted another purge of the small remaining number of Tutsis holding higher public office, while tightening enforcement of the quotas on the positions which they were allowed to hold in academia, the professions and local government. The new measures were not greeted with as much popular support from Hutus as he had hoped, however, and the tactic failed to bring him back into favor in the country at large.

In 1973, Juvenal Habyarimana,[7] the commander in chief of the armed forces, overthrew Kayibanda in a bloodless coup; two years later Rwanda became a one-party state under Habyarimana's Mouvement Révolutionnaire National pour le Développement (MRND). In 1978 a new constitution was promulgated and elections were staged in which he was the only candidate.

Habyarimana came from Gisenyi in the northwest and as such, his takeover represented a long-awaited opportunity for the Hutu clans from that region to reassert what had historically been their regional group's relative dominance in the Rwandan hierarchy. His wife, Agathe Kanzinga, came from an even more influential northern Hutu dynasty which had continued to rule its territory until late in the period of colonial takeover and subsequent Tutsi ascendancy. She steadily grew in power and was relied on by her husband for intelligence and support in critical matters of state. Latterly, she came to preside over what was referred to as "Le clan de Madame," her own clique which many regarded as the real power behind Rwanda's presidency.[8]

Calm Beginnings to Habyarimana Rule

Initially, Rwandans, including the country's disenfranchised Tutsi minority, greeted the arrival of Habyarimana to power in Kigali with a measure of relief. One of the first declarations made by the new president was that the security of the Tutsis in the country would be guaranteed. For many years, this commitment was largely upheld, and although the quotas were less strictly enforced, Tutsis continued to play very little role in the public life of Habyarimana's Rwanda. By 1980, for example, there were only two out of eighty Tutsi members of parliament and one Tutsi cabinet minister out of thirty. In local administration, there were no Tutsi *bourgmestres* or prefects throughout nearly all of the 1980s. Thus, while they were largely left in peace in the early years of Habyarimana's rule, the Tutsis were essentially second-class citizens whose only real option for advancement lay in going into the private business world in Rwanda or taking their chances with their cousins in exile abroad.

In an attempt to provide self-help following the fall of Amin and the looming threat from Obote, in 1979 the Tutsi exile community in Uganda formed the Rwandese Refugee Welfare Foundation (RWWF). Soon the humanitarian RWWF became the more politically ambitious Rwandese Alliance for National Unity (RANU), which was formally established in 1979. As the name suggests, RANU stood not only for an improvement in the Tutsi refugees' lot in Uganda, but also for an end to the politics of division and persecution based on ethnicity. These themes were to remain central to the guiding ideology of RANU and its successor movement for the next twenty years when they ultimately led the exiled diaspora and democratic opposition back to power in Kigali from 1994 onwards.

Lure of the Homeland

Through all his childhood years, Kagame had never been able to return to Rwanda, but soon the young Rwandan student felt a growing curiosity to know more about the land of his birth. Approaching adulthood, as the social and looming professional consequences of being a foreigner in Uganda became apparent, he began asking his parents about what it was that they had done to become refugees and why their situation continued to be as it was.

The desire to know and to understand soon became the desire to go and see for himself, and so in 1977 Kagame arranged through contacts from his school to go to Rwanda and explore the homeland, to see the places and to know more of what had effectively become a forbidden territory for the young exile. Although he knew he still had relatives in Rwanda, particularly those on his mother's side who were related to the queen, he was unsure of the feasibility of reaching them from Uganda prior to visiting. Instead, by contacting older students from his own Ugandan secondary school who had families in Kigali and who had gone back to live, Kagame was able to arrange to come and stay with them, ostensibly planning just to spend a few days in Rwanda before returning to Uganda.

Upon arrival, however, he quickly linked up with his own family, then extended his contacts and decided to stay on to go around and travel more thoroughly in the country and to deepen his newfound knowledge of the land of his birth. Walking all around Kigali, often taking taxis to outlying villages and visiting different friends, the young Kagame moved around the country during two months in 1977. In this way, he made the acquaintance of the real Rwanda and he soon knew many things about Rwandan life which his fellow exiles in Uganda could only hear about from others or guess about from distant childhood recollections.

After returning to Uganda, in 1978 Kagame came again for another visit to Rwanda, this time not taking the chance of crossing the border directly, but first going through the southwest into Zaire and from there passing through the Rutura area to Goma then crossing into Rwanda by the road to Gisenyi. Even in the relatively stable early years of the Habyarimana regime, the risk of being arrested as the exiled son of a family with prominent relatives could have entailed danger to a lone traveler. The longing for a return to Rwanda and the desire for exploration was something even Kagame could not logically explain: "I wasn't sure what I was doing, I wanted to know something and perhaps to build on that.... It wasn't too dangerous ... not yet, maybe they didn't bother about me, as I wasn't threatening in any sense — just a student, simple, going about on my own.... Although if someone had found out about me, known who I was, from a refugee camp in Uganda and the family I came from, it could have been very dangerous — you had to be very careful then."[9]

One of the reasons for the risk that was entailed in traveling around Rwanda during those times was the strict control by the authorities on its own citizens' movements around the country. On the national identity card, in addition to the all-important *ubwoko,* or ethnic designation, every citizen had to state his or her address; traveling far from one's home was discouraged and moving house without the necessary permission was not allowed. Rwandan society in the early years of Habyarimana's rule was tightly controlled although the restriction on freedom was relatively benign and well intentioned at that stage.

The regime was serious and expected its people to be the same. Habyarimana was intent on developing his desperately poor agricultural country, and there was no time or place for dissent or political debate. After several years in office, the Rwandan president made his views clear to a French journalist soliciting his views on the issue: "...as far as I am concerned, I have no hesitation in choosing the single party system," he said.[10] Until 1981, Rwanda had not even had a parliament; but when one was finally established in that year, it was given the non–political-sounding title of Conseil National de Développement (CND), as if to emphasize the seriousness of the country's needs and the priorities of its economy at the time.

Despite or perhaps because of the climate in Rwandan society during those years, the underlying interest in politics and career motivations of Paul Kagame were born of those early visits. Although he maintained that his agenda at the outset had been one of innocent curiosity, had the observations and experiences of those two visits in 1977 and 1978 been formative on his political thinking and ambitions for the future? "Absolutely," he said, "it was after all the origin of that mission, as it was going on I improved my [political] ideas."[11]

On the second visit to Rwanda, Kagame stayed with different hosts, finding friends and sympathizers from among the returning student diaspora in eastern Europe who were also eager to return to live and work in the homeland, despite the developments since their departure. The students who Kagame was able to contact had been at university in what was then communist Czechoslovakia, invited, like many young Africans in the 1970s, by the authorities to study there and hopefully appreciate the benefits of a socialist education. The thinking of the hosts, then, apart from the philanthropic goal of cooperation with the Third World, was that the students would come to know the communist system through their education, possibly later on working upon returning home to promote a similar political ideology in their own countries of origin.

However, because of the connections of the Union Nationale Rwandaise (UNAR) in the early 1960s with socialist backers and the former's opposition to the "democratic" Hutu takeover of Rwanda, these students found themselves less than welcome on trying to return home from the Eastern Bloc. The group which Kagame encountered in 1978 in Kigali had forced their return home after being officially denied permission to enter the country. Some were then arrested by the authorities and sent to prison.

One such detainee who became Kagame's host for his stay in Kigali in 1978 was a former student nicknamed "Clever," a Rwandan graduate from Czechoslovakia who was later released and found employment in the Ministry of Health. Doubtless sympathetic to the touring exile from Uganda because of his own experiences, Clever took Kagame into his house in Kigali and despite the possible risks of re-arrest from being discovered with a well-connected young exile, they stayed together for much of his 1978 visit.

By the time of Kagame's return to Uganda in late 1978, however, a new situation was developing in his country of exile, as an armed struggle against Idi Amin was gaining momentum and a new phase of persecution for many of the Rwandans in that part of the host country was about to begin.

Politics in Exile: Obote, Amin and Museveni

The world which faced the young Paul Kagame and his peers in the 1980s in Uganda was full of uncertainty and at times fraught with danger. In addition to the second-class status which the Banyarwanda were accorded within Ugandan society, regional and ethnic rivalry among other groups during the post-independence period had a heavy bearing on national politics and ultimately determined the fate of the country's system of government as well as the identity of its rulers.

Under British colonial rule, Uganda was divided into a number of kingdoms including Buganda, which includes the capital Kampala, and Ankole to the southwest, where Yoweri Museveni grew up. In 1966 Buganda's ruler Freddie Mutesa was titular president of the country, and the prime minister at the time was Milton Obote. Mutesa and Obote were rivals for power in the newly independent country, ultimately leading to the king expelling Obote and his government from Bugandan territory. Obote responded by sending in the army and exiling Mutesa, then abolishing the kingdoms and declaring Uganda a republic in 1967.

The main power base of Obote's UPC (Ugandan People's Congress) was in the north and the east of the country as well as among the Bairu people of Ankole Province in the west of Uganda. His suspicions of the rival Bugandans as well as the Banyarwanda in Toro and particularly in Ankole led to a campaign of ethnic persecutions starting in the late 1960s. The Bahima of Ankole Province were an aristocratic, Catholic group not unlike the Rwandan Tutsis and were socially and politically opposed to their Bairu ethnic neighbors.

When a radical, Protestant, pro–UPC Bairu group took power in Ankole, their ethnic rivals, including the Banyarwanda Tutsis of the region,

found themselves targeted for reprisals. In addition to removing the Banyarwanda from government jobs, there was harassment at the local level
with expulsions from land and theft of cattle and property of the victim
groups who were characterized as "foreigners" by pro–Obote propagandists.

When General Idi Amin took power in Kampala in January 1971, at
first most of the refugee community welcomed him as offering a change
from Obote's persecution. One of his early measures was to arrange for
the return to Uganda of the exiled Rwandan *mwami* Kigeri from Nairobi.
But the Rwandans in Uganda soon found that they were little better off
under Amin than they had been under Obote. In September 1972, when
the deposed president attempted an armed return from Tanzania, Amin
accused the Kigali authorities as accomplices and, paradoxically, the Rwandan exiles inside Uganda were again targeted as scapegoats.

However, in 1973, following Juvenal Habyarimana's *coup d'état* in
Kigali, Amin recruited Rwandan exiles into his secret service, the State
Research Bureau. Here the Rwandans gained a reputation for ruthlessness
and violence, which would later become a pretext for persecuting the exiles
more brutally, after Amin was overthrown by the Tanzanian army in 1979.

Following Amin's expulsion, an interim government was formed in
which Yoweri Museveni became Minister of Defense, giving him a foothold
on the ladder of power in Ugandan national politics for the first time.
However, Obote had also returned from exile and when elections were
held in December 1980, he returned to power in what was widely recognized as a sham ballot.

One of the maneuvers of Obote's UPC during the run-up to the elections had been its campaign to ban all Banyarwanda from voting. Ultimately, large groups of ethnic Rwandans, including many who had been
in Uganda since before independence and who had voted in 1961 and subsequent ballots, were prevented from participating in the December poll.
In reaction to the rigged vote, many of Obote's defeated opponents in the
election, most notably Yoweri Museveni, soon began to prepare for a continuation of the struggle by arms.

Thus, by early 1981, Museveni had gone into the bush to fight against
Obote's UPC regime and the anti–Kampala campaign of his National Resistance Army (NRA) was launched. His first raid against the government
took place at Kabamba in Luwero District on February 6, 1981, and among
his small band of dissidents numbered Paul Kagame and another Rwandan exile, Fred Rwigyema, Kagame's only compatriot in Museveni's attacking force on that day. Kagame and Rwigyema had already become followers
of Museveni in the late 1970s and had joined the small resistance organi-

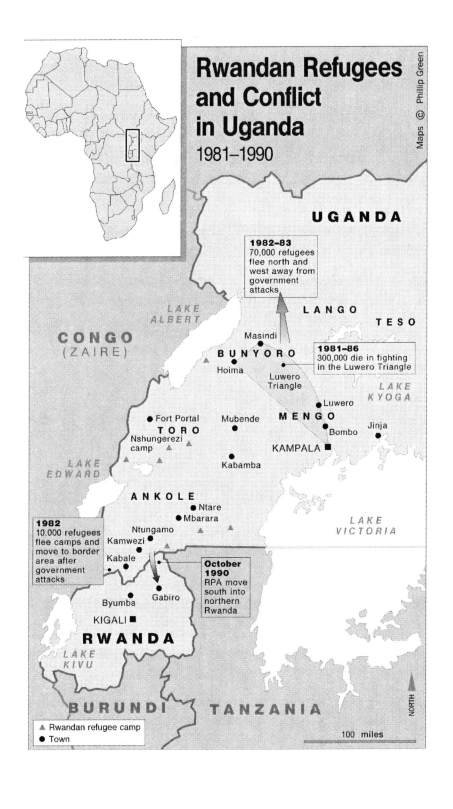

Rwandan Refugees and Conflict in Uganda
1981–1990

Maps © Phillip Green

UGANDA

1982–83
70,000 refugees flee north and west away from government attacks

LANGO

TESO

LAKE ALBERT

CONGO (ZAIRE)

Masindi

BUNYORO
Hoima

1981–86
300,000 die in fighting in the Luwero Triangle

Luwero Triangle

LAKE KYOGA

Luwero

MENGO

Jinja

Fort Portal
TORO
Nshungerezi camp

Mubende

Bombo

KAMPALA ■

LAKE EDWARD

Kabamba

ANKOLE

Ntare
Mbarara

LAKE VICTORIA

Ntungamo
Kamwezi

1982
10,000 refugees flee camps and move to border area after government attacks

Kabale

October 1990
RPA move south into northern Rwanda

Byumba
Gabiro

KIGALI ■

RWANDA

LAKE KIVU

BURUNDI

TANZANIA

NORTH

▲ Rwandan refugee camp
● Town

100 miles

zation which was formed in 1978 in Tanzania to help overthrow Idi Amin. The Front for National Salvation (Fronasa) eventually fought alongside the invading Tanzanian army which overthrew Amin in 1979.

The northern Ugandans who made up the core of Obote's power base lumped all his enemies together, for propaganda purposes, referring to them as 'nyarwanda, a derogatory term with racist overtones which served as a combined insult for Banyarwanda, whether old or new, as well as Banyankole or Bairu, and which could include Ugandan citizens in their eyes just as easily as true Rwandan refugees.

By 1982 in Uganda, Milton Obote's regime was becoming increasingly repressive and together with its Bairu UPC–youth movement allies in Ankole, in that year he embarked on a propaganda campaign as a prelude to a wave of attacks against the refugees in western Uganda. The *Uganda Times,* the official government newspaper, in its issue of January 11, 1982, set out the government stance against the Rwandans: "Most atrocities during Amin's era were committed by refugees ... refugees have been found to flirt with terrorists in Luwero District and are responsible for the unrest there.... If refugees, particularly those from Rwanda do not reciprocate our hospitality, Uganda may order their government to build camps for them ... alternatively we shall tell them to go."[12]

In October of that year attacks against the refugees began in earnest, with evictions, beatings, rape and looting across the area of the Banyarwanda settlements being carried out on a massive scale. In addition to pleasing the UPC's allies and displacing its potential opponents from the province through the wholesale intimidation of a population that had been settled in an area for some 20 years, it seemed that the main object of the attacks was to dispossess the Rwandans of their cattle. By the end of the spate of attacks, which took place in 1982, an estimated 45,000 cows had been stolen, over 70,000 people uprooted and some 16,000 homes destroyed.

Many of the victims of the Obote persecutions fled towards the Rwandan border, where a number succeeded in crossing back over to escape the pro-government gangs that were pursuing them. Others fled towards the older refugee camps, but many soon became trapped as the Kigali authorities deployed their border guards to prevent further returnees from arriving. About 10,000 people became trapped in a two-kilometer-wide strip of land just between the two countries.

The Rwandan Tutsi exiles were thus placed in the impossible predicament of not being allowed back into their own country of origin nor to stay in safety in their adopted home of some 20 years' residence. The trapped Rwandans soon began to die of malnutrition and disease and only an international outcry forced action to come to the aid of the refugees who were wanted by neither Kampala nor Kigali. Their position recalls the plight of tens of thousands of European Jews in 1945–1946, who in the wake of the Second World War, fleeing a continent which had offered them only persecution and death for over a decade, boarded ships for Palestine only to be held up outside their destination and in some cases turned back again towards Germany while both the conquering powers and colonial authorities in Palestine struggled uncomfortably to determine their fate.

Despite official pronouncements from Obote after October 1982 that the perpetrators of the expulsions would be punished, nothing happened and in the following year a further 19,000 Banyarwanda in the south of the country were evicted. In the following years, Banyarwanda residents in Luwero were severely victimized, as were migrant Tutsi cattle keepers in Teso and Lango, Obote's home province, to the northeast of the country.

In closing its borders to their own nationals, the Kigali authorities sent an even stronger and more ominous message about their future intentions towards the Tutsi exiles in Uganda and elsewhere. Habyarimana's official stance regarding the accommodation of returnees was that the country was "full up"— that there was simply not enough land to support the existing population, let alone to sustain tens of thousands of "new" arrivals.

Despite the overriding unacceptability of the policy of a regime which turns back its own nationals facing danger at the hands of foreign tormentors, in the 1980s in Rwanda there was indeed an increasing demographic and economic case to support the "full-up" scenario which allowed Habyarimana to at least buy some time if not find support for his plan to delay the return of the Ugandan Tutsis for as long as possible.

No Room Left in Rwanda

Historically, Rwanda was a lush, fertile kingdom which attracted immigration in the early centuries of its existence. With these influxes and a rapid birthrate similar to other east African countries, its population density was always high by regional and international standards. At the beginning of the period of the Tutsi exodus in 1959, the country's population was 2.6 million, rising sharply to 7.4 million by 1989. In a country of only 26,000 square kilometers, just a little larger than New Hampshire, it has a density per square kilometer of 284 persons.

This compares with around 19 persons per km^2 in the Democratic Republic of Congo, 110 per km^2 in France and around 27 per km^2 in Texas. With a population surviving on Third-World agricultural incomes and only one serious export crop, coffee, whose price plummeted on world markets in 1989, it was easy to argue that there was very little space or means to support over 100,000 "newcomers" despite their nationality of origin.

In this way President Habyarimana officially informed the world that such was the state of his country's economy and its capacity to absorb returning exiles that he could not undertake to bring back the Tutsis at that time. To appease international critics he did, however, agree to conduct a survey in 1988, jointly with the Ugandan authorities, of the status, numbers and migration intentions of the exile caseload, to determine their wishes concerning repatriation and with a view to facilitating return of (it was hoped) the relatively few selected refugees who would want to come home to Rwanda.

None of these reluctantly taken measures could conceal the fact that Kigali's true agenda was increasingly influenced by the hard-liners within the ruling MRND whose objectives were explicitly ethnically based and had little or nothing to do with demographics or the absorption capacity of the Rwandan economy. The signal to the remaining Uganda-based Tutsi diaspora was clear: if prevented from returning home and constantly at risk of being evicted from their adoptive land, in resolution of the crisis, what other option could remain for them but to resort to force?

A senior member of the RPF, himself born in Uganda, described the choice facing the young Rwandan men and their families: "You could either go into exile or go into the bush," he said. "Recruitment into the NRA was an almost automatic choice for most of us at that time."

Intelligence Training for Rebellion

Kagame spent the early years in Museveni's NRA as an officer charged with information gathering in the countryside, a vital requirement for a guerrilla army which had to remain concealed while knowing the maximum about its more powerful enemy's movements and intentions. He often received assignments to go off on reconnaissance missions either alone or with one or two other officers, to assess potential targets or learn details of enemy strength and military operations. What brought the young Major Kagame of the NRA to become involved in intelligence work for the NRA? Remembering the early times of the Ugandan insurrection, he recalled:

> During such a situation of guerrilla warfare as when we were starting
> the war in Uganda, you find when you start as a small number ... it
> requires collecting a lot of information, a lot of intelligence work ...

and then of course it later builds up into a military experience, where you start fighting battles and so on ... so we used to have to go out through jungles, for 200 kilometers at a time, alone or in small groups, often being away for two weeks, maybe three weeks before you come back. It was because the situation demanded it that I got involved with this kind of activity."[13]

From being a specialist in intelligence matters for six years with the NRA, Paul Kagame rose to become head of military intelligence in Museveni's army following Milton Obote's overthrow in 1986.

His training did not end with the NRA's victory in Uganda, however, and in 1986 Kagame doubtless sought to strengthen his skills and sharpen his ideology for the struggles to come. It was still the era of the cold war and many African rebel movements were molding themselves on the guerrilla principles of Maoist revolution, receiving support and training from international socialism's most famous backers. The NRA's founder and leader, Yoweri Museveni, accepted assistance and training from a variety of backers, socialist and otherwise, while himself remaining at the head of a more pragmatic kind of revolutionary movement, more suited to change and grassroots political awareness in Africa. Rather than following in the Marxist footsteps of other prominent African rebels such as Robert Mugabe and Mozambique's Samora Machel, who had been in the front line of anti-colonialist struggles in the preceding decade, Museveni charted his own revolutionary path, not falling into the trap of becoming an obvious proxy for either side of the cold war superpower struggle for influence in the Third World.

As a result of this web of international political relations, with the war over in Uganda, Kagame and other officers who had fought in the NRA were soon sent overseas to build on their skills, and they often ended up in far-flung and diverse locations around the globe. "When the war ended in Uganda," Kagame explained, "Museveni was trying to build institutions, the army, the police and other institutions and he was seeking help and he asked different countries ... such as Libya and some other African countries to help to train people. So it happened that after the war in Uganda they were selecting people, they took about 70 people just out of the bush ... I was picked and I went for nine months to Cuba, but there was no special connection.... Some were trained by North Korea, China or other countries that offered the further training that they needed."[14]

The overseas training which Uganda's new ruler believed was essential for his program of nation building served to sharpen the skills but also to open the eyes of some of his brightest young officers, among them the Rwandans who had successfully led his fighting units to victory in 1985.

With the fighting over in Uganda, these ambitious military leaders nevertheless remained exiles with unfought battles of their own still ahead of them. The soldiers of the Rwandan Tutsi diaspora in Uganda soon came to galvanize the existing exile associations in the region into a proactive movement dedicated to overturning the regime in Kigali and establishing a very different type of government in their homeland.

2

REBEL MOVEMENTS

Early Armed Resistance — Inyenzi Attacks

Rwanda's political scene was in a state of upheaval in 1959, the year when Paul Kagame and his family were forced to flee from their home in Gitarama. Although still under Belgian administration, internally a revolutionary transfer of power was already under way in the country's institutions. As independence drew nearer and the ascendant Hutu leadership tightened its grip on local and then later on national government, most Tutsis in positions of public office or of an educated background were able to read the writing on the wall. Although some initially tried to accept their drastically diminished status within the new arrangements, most realized that the door of access to power had now slammed shut in their faces and that the path of peaceful participation no longer made sense.

There were those who chose exile and a new life as refugees in a foreign land, but there were also many Tutsis who decided on a course of active armed resistance against Grégoire Kayibanda's regime. Operating from outside Rwanda's borders, the Tutsi dissidents began to organize and seek support for a campaign of insurgency, intended to destabilize the new Hutu government and possibly regain some of their recently forfeited leverage in the running of the country's affairs.

The largest group of Tutsi exiles to flee following the initial attacks by Hutu gangs went to Burundi and it was from there that the first armed opposition by the exiles was launched against the government in Kigali. The guerrillas who opposed the regime of President Kayibanda nicknamed themselves *inyenzi* (the cockroaches), according to some because they operated under cover of darkness.[1]

The *inyenzi* were, however, splintered and disorganized, with varying political aims. Some favored the restoration of the monarchy, while others were left-leaning and sought help from the socialist states that had supported UNAR in the political struggles prior to independence.

Between 1961 and 1966 a dozen or so *inyenzi* attacks were carried out from outside Rwanda's borders, but after each incursion the Kigali authorities and their Belgian-backed army meted out harsh reprisals against Tutsi civilians inside the country. Thousands were killed in this way for very little gain on the part of the insurgents. The closest that the invaders came to overthrowing the regime was in 1963 when a particularly bold raid from the south succeeded in overcoming initial resistance from the government forces and reached to within 20 kilometers of Kigali. At that point, however, the Rwandan army brought its superior numbers and heavy weaponry to bear against the invaders and dispersed their attack. There followed a severe purge of the remaining Tutsis from positions in government and the authorities unleashed their most vicious attacks yet against civilians.

The wave of killings that followed the 1963 *inyenzi* attack shocked international opinion, although very little was done to intervene or to sanction the government in Kigali for its brutality. Kayibanda, however, tried to defuse the situation by first admitting publicly that "hundreds" had been killed in the unrest and then promising to prosecute the organizers of the attacks on civilians. Bloody reprisals continued however, prompting the British philosopher Bertrand Russell, in the February 6, 1964, edition of *Le Monde*, to describe the situation as a "holocaust" of proportions "not seen since the extermination of the Jews" in the 1940s. In a similar vein, Vatican Radio in a broadcast at the time said: "Since the Genocide of the Jews by Hitler, the most terrible systematic genocide is taking place in the heart of Africa."[2]

This type of public outrage further alerted the world to the consequences of the strife and directed the attention of the church in Rwanda itself to resist the bloodshed which was taking place within its own community. Between December 1963 and January 1964, an estimated 10,000 Tutsi were killed in Rwanda and the last of the Tutsi politicians still in office were systematically eliminated.

Both due to the bitter pain of reprisals and their lack of lasting military impact, the *inyenzi* attacks petered out by 1966, and although violent persecution against prominent Tutsis continued, there ensued a period of some two decades when most ordinary Tutsis were left alone in the relative economic and social stability which lasted until the mid-1980s. Many in the diaspora created by the upheavals of revolution and independence settled down to a pattern of life in exile, and UNAR as a movement faded from the scene, unable to influence events for the time being and no longer able to resist the changes at home which had by now become a fact of life.

Fanning the Embers of Resistance

As the years of exile went by, adjustment to life outside Rwanda took different forms for different communities within the Tutsi diaspora. Some managed to rebuild their lives in their adoptive countries and regained a measure of normality which allowed them to slowly forget about a return to the homeland, while others continued to struggle for survival, living a rootless existence and often in hazardous conditions, such as was the fate for many of the refugees in Uganda.

In the late 1960s one attempt at reconciliation between the diaspora and the motherland took the form of the Association Générale des Etudiants Rwandais, an effort at fostering dialogue between young Rwandans of all backgrounds but with a view to reform within the country as well as reconciliation of the feuding groups both inside and outside Rwanda's borders. After 1973, however, when Juvenal Habyarimana came to power and began what he called his "moral revolution" bringing with it promises of reforms, the movement lost momentum and disappeared from the scene.

Another group that found its way to Uganda and campaigned for the right of return, while rejecting the pro-monarchist stance of the early UNAR opposition, was composed of middle-class Tutsi exiles from teaching, local administration and other professions. The so-called *Imburamajo* ("the lost ones") set up a movement in 1972–73 but ultimately suffered when Idi Amin took power and invited *mwami* Kigeli to return to Uganda. The king managed to convince Amin that his Rwandan compatriots would threaten security in the country and shortly thereafter Amin crushed the movement.[3]

Yoweri Museveni's NRM — Template for African Resistance

As a young guerrilla officer Kagame had thrown in his lot in the 1970s with Yoweri Museveni, whose emerging rebel movement was the most likely of the competing groups in Uganda at the time to be supportive of the Rwandan Tutsi community in exile. Following Museveni into Tanzania in 1978 when Fronasa was formed to fight against the regime of Idi Amin, Kagame remained loyal to him in the interim government of

1979–80 in which the Ugandan rebel leader briefly held the post of Minister of Defense. When Museveni failed to be elected president in 1980, Kagame and his former schoolmate Fred Rwigyema signed up for Museveni's newly formed NRA, which went into the bush to launch its struggle against the second Obote regime. Rwigyema had left Uganda in 1976 to join the anti–Amin guerrilla movement, going first to Mozambique[4] and later joining forces with the Fronasa Ugandan rebels based in Tanzania.

From its birth, the NRA was a different kind of rebel army from many that had been seen on the African continent since the beginning of the post-colonial period. Although it drew strong support from the regions of Uganda where tribal persecution was at its worst, Museveni sought to avoid creating an army of one group which would struggle to win power and reassert its dominance over another, thereby restarting the cycle of resentment and counter-resistance.

Neither was his movement a front for the takeover by a neo-colonial despot, intended to create a client state and serve foreign masters in exchange for personal gain, such as was the case with Zaire's Mobutu. Nor again was the National Resistance Movement (NRM), the political wing of his rebel army, to be cast in the mold of its Marxist-Leninist, anti-colonial predecessors such as most of the front-line states of southern Africa that had been involved in the struggle against apartheid.

It is true that in 1967, like many of the generation of aspiring leaders of newly independent African states, Museveni had studied in the University of Dar es Salaam, an institution where President Julius Nyerere's socialist philosophy helped set the tone for the political curriculum. But Museveni was also willing to embrace certain capitalist economic principles for development purposes, while not subscribing to the template multi-party democracy that powerful western donors were seeking as part of a standardized package of aid — a package which frequently included privatization and budgetary restraint in order to obtain credits for development projects.

However, Museveni was a champion of a new brand of African political movement and he rejected the idea of a western-style imposed democracy. Years after taking power, he said: "I don't really think the Europeans have the capacity to impose their will again. I don't think that America or anybody will dominate Africa anymore. They may cause destabilization, but they cannot reverse the situation if the indigenous forces are organized. By the sheer force of Africa we shall be independent of all foreign manipulation."[5]

In politics, the NRM sought to create an inclusive, national political community, in contrast to the privatized partisan states of Obote and

Amin. In areas under the NRM's control, local chiefs were replaced with resistance councils, which explicitly canvassed the support and promoted the participation of formerly excluded ethnic groups, women and youth.

Not the Time for Parties

After taking power, Uganda became what Museveni liked to call a "No-Party Democracy"— he believed in democracy for the election of the country's leader (he later won presidential elections in 1996 and 2001) but not in the politics of opposition parties. Political parties, he argued, in the African context are all too easily identified with "groups," which in turn quickly fosters tribal division and instability. He banned any form of political party being established or holding rallies outside the capital for this reason, although his own NRM could always freely recruit and campaign across the country. This was both consistent and fair, Museveni would argue, because the NRM is a "movement," not a political party.

Whatever the merits or shortcomings of Museveni's political philosophy, in the early years the involvement of the wider community in politics dovetailed well with a military strategy based on insurgency. Dependent on the loyalty of the population in the countryside, the economic crisis plaguing Uganda in the early 1980s also helped to bolster support for his cause and make the NRM's struggle into a "People's War" against state oppression, which Museveni had long sought to establish as the image and mission of his movement. In tandem with the creation of a national political community, during the insurgency years the NRM built its ideological support through a process of popular political education, something which the country's former leaders had never implemented.

This experiment in inclusive popular government against the backdrop of fighting a war of resistance which Museveni conducted undoubtedly shaped the thinking of his military lieutenants and in particular the young Rwandan officers at his side who were now cutting their political as well as military teeth. Paul Kagame and Fred Rwigyema would draw strongly on the thought leadership of Yoweri Museveni, and when the time came for struggle in Rwanda, the NRM model provided the inspiration for a change of government through force in Uganda's southern neighbor.

The practicalities of winning a war against a ruler with strong regional and tribal support nevertheless set the NRA's priorities in the early years of the campaign against Obote. At first, the majority of Museveni's initial recruits were Baganda, formerly subjects of the king of Buganda and opponents of the Obote Republic. However, because of his Ankole provincial power base and its high proportion of sympathetic Rwandan exiles, Museveni could be portrayed as a "Rwandan" by the Kampala authorities and their Bairu allies in the southwest of the country. By issuing propaganda of this nature Obote was able to discredit Museveni in the eyes of many of his countrymen and at the same time convince Ugandans that the struggle against the NRA was a noble and necessary fight to put down a "foreign-engineered plot."

The first action of the resistance struggle took place in February 1981, with the attack on the government barracks at Kabamba. Moving out from their base in the so-called Luwero Triangle,[6] Museveni's small band of rebels raided the Kabamba Police Military School in an attempt to steal the valuable guns and ammunition which his young army needed. Unfortunately, the soldiers defending the barracks prevented the attackers from breaking into the armory, which was their primary goal. Although they succeeded in seizing eight government vehicles and some small arms, the bold mission failed, for example, to secure any of the rocket-propelled grenades which the insurgents needed to become a more effective threat.

Nevertheless, the lightning raid had a psychological impact on the government troops and succeeded in convincing Kampala that the attacking army was becoming something more powerful than just a handful of bush guerrillas. During the following years, the rebels carried out further sporadic raids from their bases in the countryside, where the local populations as well as the Rwandan refugees were often sympathetic to their cause and willing to provide cover and sustenance to the fighters between their bouts of action.

A successful counteroffensive by the government in 1982–83 sent the rebels fleeing northwards and was followed by massive reprisals against the local population and the refugees. During this counteroffensive, it is estimated that over 30,000 were killed and 1.5 million new refugees were created. Many of the orphans created by the government's bloody revenge became the young *kadogos*, the child soldiers who would later swell the ranks of the NRA, helping the adults by acting as scouts or bodyguards until they were sixteen, when the children could become real soldiers in the main fighting force. In the face of the government offensive, the NRA retreated, desperately short of guns and ammunition: the entire army in that year had no more than 400 guns shared among 4,000 "troops" and had no choice but to retire and regroup.[7]

In order to strike an objective inside government territory, they would often march for several nights, surviving only on the sticks of sugar cane or cassava that the local farmers could provide. For longer missions, when available they also took dry rations such as corn and meat, but food was often scarce during the early campaigns and the resulting fatigue and indiscipline among the recruits was a recurring problem.

During these lean years of his movement, Yoweri Museveni strove to build morale and strengthen the ideology of his followers, not only in order to build an effective military force, but also to explain his philosophy to the ordinary people in the countryside whose support he needed. His alternative approach to the issues of economic security, growth and development departed from much that had been taught and accepted about his continent and his region, but years later the same basic philosophy came to be hailed by many in the west as a new model for African economic success.

Roads to African Development

In Uganda, as in much of the Third World, the key economic challenge according to Museveni, is intractable rural poverty and the persistent inability of the population to achieve human and economic development. While the historical domination of man by nature is a challenge which the advanced countries have largely been able to overcome, drought, famine and disease still loom large on the list of problems to be solved in Africa before true progress can occur. Museveni pointed to the legacy of the additional externally imposed burdens brought on by a feudal approach to agriculture, by colonial development and by slavery.

Well after independence, the peasant farmer was still trying to produce the same cash crops for export which the former colonist had cultivated, to provide income from exports, or to satisfy the needs of the mills and factories in Europe and America. However, instead of growing tea, coffee and cotton, much as the foreign exchange inflows which these brought were important for financial development, the ordinary rural communities failed to produce the basic foodstuffs which they themselves needed.

Economic development first requires a sufficient local market in which to sell produce, without which it is pointless to develop output beyond the minimum for survival. But a market requires roads, first and foremost, in order to bring the goods to the customer. Museveni pointed to the wrong priorities of post-colonial development: the approach which had been taken was to allocate resources to education in the countryside and to install other infrastructure such as telephones when what the local economy really needed was basic physical communications instead. As he put it, with such priorities there is no point in being able to increase output but then only being able to telephone your customers to tell them you are unable to deliver the goods to them because of a failing road network.[8]

Compounding these inappropriate development choices was the attitude of the people towards their own human progress. In the feudal and colonial systems, ordinary people looked to the government to provide the solutions to their problems: if they were hungry, they asked to be fed. In exchange they followed the orders of the chief or king, whose own goals were often the pursuit of sectarian rivalries or self-enrichment.

The key to escaping this familiar African paradigm of underdevelopment propounded by the NRM was to encourage people to seek solutions to their own financial problems through taking action in society or in the marketplace. The way forward was to reject the aims of a tribal chief whose interests were by their nature at odds with the ordinary citizen according to Museveni. The politics of group interests were at the heart of Uganda's problems and the poverty and socio-economic dependence of the peasants forced them into following rather than participating in the running of their community's affairs.

The mobilization pattern adopted in the countryside consisted initially of winning over a sufficient number of people in a village to join the movement; from there a village resistance council would be formed, which in turn joined a parish resistance council, which sent representatives to a county council and then district resistance council; and at the top of the pyramid of the organization was the National Resistance Council, completing a comprehensive executive network while at the same time giving local representatives power over their own affairs. This structure in itself constituted a revolution in Uganda, since it directly replaced the colonial system of administration under which Uganda's rulers continued to operate, which was essentially built on patronage from the central government and selection of local officials by tribal preference or to facilitate corruption. As well as being revolutionary, the NRM's approach was comprehensive, far reaching and effective: "...in local government the NRM dismantled the institutions of chieftains, stripped the chiefs of legislative, judicial and executive power and placed these powers in the hands of the resistance councils (RCs). Chieftaincy had been one of the long-lasting legacies of the colonial and post-colonial state, which by making the people accountable to state officials had turned upside down the democratic principle that state officials should be accountable to the populace."[9]

Beyond its revolutionary administrative dynamism the national resistance network also supported the military effort, with the local populations sensitized through their village resistance councils to the required tasks in their area. Other than the maintenance of civil order, these included helping to feed and shelter the NRA fighters, manning roadblocks in areas under NRA control and providing intelligence to the military command.

At the same time as he mobilized his troops for the first task at hand, the overthrow of the Obote government, Yoweri Museveni also worked to disseminate the elements of his political thinking on government and economics to his country people to prepare them for a new kind of society when his movement would take power. In the countryside he steadily gained support; and among the Banyarwanda community, his following grew rapidly. Museveni imparted his ideology to the young officers who followed him into battle in the mid–1980s, many of whom in turn soon found themselves in positions of government, or in the case of the Rwandans, carving out the building blocks of their own rebel movement and philosophy.

A Survival Call to Arms

As Yoweri Museveni's National Resistance Movement began its operations from the Luwero Triangle in 1981, young Rwandan men who were being harassed and threatened with eviction increasingly saw nothing to lose in joining with the rebels. Not only was it probably safer for them than remaining at home as potential victims of attack but also as the guerrilla war progressed, rebels were able to move their families to areas in Luwero where their troops could offer protection against the forces of Obote's Uganda National Liberation Army (UNLA).

As the NRA and its Rwandan allies organized their campaign in the Luwero Triangle, reprisals against civilians in the area (most of whom were Baganda) as well as the intensity of the propaganda campaign against the rebel movement heightened sharply. The population of the Triangle, some 4,500 km^2 in area, contained about 20 percent Banyarwanda, but in some settlements in the area the proportion is estimated to have been as high as 40 percent. By the end of the fighting in 1986, the International Committee of the Red Cross estimated that over 300,000 people in the Luwero Triangle had died in the five-year conflict and that at least half of the population of the area was unaccounted for.

The Obote propaganda machine denounced Museveni and his NRA as being "Rwandans," thus continuing the momentum of the "outside threat" assertion to mobilize the local population against the rebels. The NRA was also accused of recruiting inside the refugee camps and promising Ugandan citizenship to those who joined their number. Most of the Rwandan exiles were not that interested in Ugandan nationality, however, and usually the causes of self-preservation or outright revenge were motivations enough to bring them to join Museveni's guerrilla army.

By the time the NRA captured Kampala in January 1986, it had become a force of some 14,000 men, as many as 4,000 of whom were Rwandan. Building on the similar but unresolved grievances of this latter faction, the popular army of Yoweri Museveni would soon spawn an offshoot, a rebel movement with the Ugandan resistance story ingrained into its experience but with the Rwandan Tutsi cause still burning at its heart.

Foundations of a Rebel Movement

It was in parallel with these NRA guerrilla attacks, which were carried out initially with very little participation from the broader exile community, that the Rwandese Refugee Welfare Foundation (shortly afterwards RANU) began to gain support as Obote continued his reprisals against the civilian population. As it had been created by Rwandans exiled in Uganda, RANU's leaders knew that their members were bound to be targeted by the regime, and so the organization soon established its headquarters in Nairobi. In practice it operated underground for a number of years, building a network of autonomous cells and drawing support from among the different Tutsi communities in east Africa and overseas. With membership from all over the diaspora, including North America, Europe and several African states outside the Great Lakes region, a regional structure was established, with an annual RANU Congress including regional chairmen, representatives of interest groups and the professions, as well as a political bureau with a 26-person executive committee (which was intended to be composed of over 50 percent Hutus) and later, a military high command.

In the wake of the brutal 1982 attacks, young Rwandan men began swelling the ranks of RANU and the organization prepared to become both more active and more militant in support of the refugees' aims. The first response of many was to join Museveni's NRA, in which they played an important role, particularly in the difficult period which ensued after the rebels were forced westwards out of the Luwero region in 1984. For those like Kagame, who were looking to the long term, the skills and experience gained while fighting in the NRA were not merely a useful by-product of a struggle for survival and a mutual hatred of Obote; a Uganda under the control of the NRA could provide an invaluable base for the time when the exiles turned their eyes towards the real prize — the removal of the repressive Habyarimana regime in Kigali and a return of the Tutsi community to Rwanda.

Minimalist Agenda for Maximum Support

As many of RANU's members were conservative, Catholic and not highly educated, the revolutionary ideology of some of its founders was not easily palatable to them. Many of the rank and file equated socialism with atheism and were far from comfortable with the ideals behind a radical movement whose leaders had admired the struggles of Mao Tse Tung and Che Guevara and some of whom were inspired by the thinking of Pan-Africanist visionaries from elsewhere on the continent. Furthermore, there were many who still supported a return of the monarchy, which was counter to RANU party policy, but in its early days the movement could not afford to alienate any group, as it was striving to build as broad a base of support as possible.

In trying to expand the movement, RANU initially adopted a strategy of working with the educated and established members of the diaspora, with a view to using their influence and resources and drawing on their expertise to build the movement. This method proved unsuccessful, however, as not surprisingly many of those who were approached, particularly professionals and business people who had made it to developed countries, did not want to risk their positions. By joining up with an embryonic rebel movement in Africa, no matter how much they might have identified with its members or sympathized with its objectives, they could lose the social and material security which they had achieved in their countries of exile.

A new strategy was then adopted by RANU's Political Bureau, which at its 1985 Congress conceived a task force under Tito Rutaremara, to try to tap the popular support of ordinary refugees from around the region.

Rutaremara, a senior figure and one of the intellectual fathers of the organization, had first been exiled in Uganda like many of his compatriots. He succeeded in going to France to study in the 1970s, but when he tried to renew his passport to return in 1981, the Ugandan embassy in Paris refused, leaving him stranded in Europe while his comrades continued to organize without him. The Ugandan government had blocked his entry, already identifying him as a member of RANU and therefore a potential opponent of the regime. He continued to remain in contact and collaboration with his Rwandan allies, however, and shortly after the NRA began its armed struggle, he became an "external" member of Museveni's rebel movement, before finally returning to Uganda to reestablish himself as a key player at the center of developing the ideology and strategy of RANU.

Rutaremara recalls the challenge which RANU faced in the mid–1980s: "Until that time, it was a movement of intellectuals, of young educated Rwandans in exile," he explained. "The challenge we faced was to create a dynamic mass movement, involving the whole population. We discussed how to do this, wrote papers and suggested strategies, until the decision was taken to deploy the task force in 1987."[10]

The approach which Rutaremara's task force took involved sending out young supporters, often members of the student community to the various refugee camps and settlements where the future grassroots membership of RANU could be found. Over a five-month period between July and November of 1987, the volunteers sought out members of the diaspora not just in Uganda but in all the countries in the region where Rwandans were in exile. They took with them RANU's message, recruiting new members for the movement's ranks and at the same time soliciting the views of the refugees, in order to build consensus, popular appeal and cohesion in the party's political agenda.

Refugees were canvassed on their ideas, desires and opinions and the results were compiled and studied by the executive of the organization with a view to setting out its future strategy, aims and procedures. Rutaremara was among those who drafted papers which were brought before the RANU Congress in December of that year and which ultimately were adopted as the guiding principles and operational constitution of the movement.

The result of this rare example of direct democracy and popular consultation at work in an African refugee context was the adoption of a pragmatic and minimalist RANU agenda, but one which was nevertheless consistent with the founders' long-term principles of national unity, social cohesion and disciplined government. At the heart of RANU's mission statement was the Eight Point Plan which it adopted at its 1987 Congress, which called for the achievement of the following aims: *national unity, democracy, the creation of a self-sustaining economy, an end to the abuse of public office, establishment of social services, democratization of the security forces, a progressive foreign policy and an end to the state-induced creation of refugees.*

Most of these objectives, contained in what appeared to be an ambitious agenda to say the least, were not spelled out in great detail, as in the short term the most important goal for RANU was to maintain the unity and momentum of the alliance. The emphasis was on the "non-political" nature of the party in the sense that the leaders stressed the common aims of all in their capacity as Rwandans, not as socialists, monarchists or adherents of any potentially contradictory ideology. Mass mobilization and the imperative of gaining representation in the ascendant military movement of the day were the overriding objectives. Indeed, from 1983 until Obote's fall in 1986, RANU's paramount short-term aim could have been more succinctly described as "getting our men into the NRA."

At the 1987 RANU Congress, operational guidelines were drafted for the conduct of the movement's activities and in addition, a personal code of conduct was established, confirming the commitment of the organization to principled behavior and self-discipline among its membership.

At the same 1987 forum, RANU also adopted a new name to reflect its nascent militancy and mobilization: from that time onwards the movement became the Rwandan Patriotic Front (RPF). In their own Kinyarwanda language, the founders of the RPF dubbed themselves the "Inkotanyi," which henceforth became the popular name of the movement in battle and in politics, through military campaigns to peacetime elections. With Museveni now securely in power in Kampala, in 1988 the RPF moved its headquarters back to Uganda and in the following year Fred Rwigyema became its president. Rwigyema was the natural choice as leader of the new movement, with his extensive experience from liberation movements in several countries; an energetic, popular man and also an easygoing character, he was both respected by his political peers and liked by the ordinary troops he led on the battlefield.

As so many of its leaders had cut their political and ideological teeth in the NRA, it is to be expected that the constitutional declarations of the RPF would be closely modeled on those of its Ugandan mother movement. But to what extent did Museveni's thinking on popular involvement, resistance and economic progress give the Rwandans the template upon which to found their newly launched Patriotic Front? Tito Rutaremara points out that although many of their key ideas were largely the same as those of the NRA, they were also the ideas of the RPF, as it was the same people who had helped to form both movements. But there were important differences, too, regarding the phases of politicization of the membership and the mobilization of popular involvement. "The RPF and the Nicaraguan Sandinistas were the only movements that started out with the political education and awareness of their members, moving to their armed struggle at a later time," declared Rutaremara. "The NRA and most other guerrilla movements in recent times began to fight in the countryside first, then developed their political ideas as they fought, or afterwards, which is different from what we did in the RPF."[11]

Into Government in a Foreign Land

The NRA victory in 1986 was a psychological boost for the Rwandan Tutsi diaspora, many of whose members now believed that, with their strong participation in the successful rebel movement, there was a secure place in a new homeland for them. Others, emboldened by military success, felt that this was the time for an armed conquest of Rwanda and began plotting along these lines. Their premature efforts at hijacking NRA units to help carry out an attack were thwarted, however, and those conspiring to foment an invasion were detected by Ugandan military security and many were redeployed to fight in the continuing campaign by anti–Museveni groups in the north of the country, to keep them out of harm's way.

For those Rwandans who were willing to leave the issue of a return to Rwanda aside, however, because they felt that Uganda was now theirs under President Museveni, there was to be disappointment too. Although the Banyarwanda had played an important role in the NRA military victory and were often the best and most experienced of the soldiers, they soon encountered resentment from among the Ugandan population. During the campaign, Yoweri Museveni had offered citizenship to any of those who had fought alongside him in the NRM, but by the late 1980s he began to renege on this promise, even for some of the most highly ranked Banyarwanda in his administration.

The Baganda of the Kampala capital area, whom the Rwandans had helped liberate from Obote, were a particularly well-established business community. Seeing the sudden rise to success of the new, often brash Rwandan insiders, many began to feel resentment at Museveni's willingness to have such a powerful outside presence in the running of their country's affairs.

The two most prominent Rwandans in the NRA, Paul Kagame and Fred Rwigyema, both reached high positions in the Museveni administration following the end of hostilities. Kagame became acting head of the NRA's military intelligence and Rwigyema rose to the rank of Major General in the NRA and Army Chief of Staff, then later Deputy Minister of Defense.

By 1988, Museveni found himself in a position of being torn between conflicting interests: on the one hand, the Rwandans in his army were some of the best soldiers and the most trustworthy (not being citizens they would be unlikely to try to seize power from him in Uganda), but on the other hand, their strong presence in key government posts and in the economy was seen as an embarrassment and a political liability. Furthermore, without being aware of specific plans, Museveni knew that the Rwandans in his army, as well as being increasingly powerful, also had their own agenda beyond the wholehearted support of his NRM.

At the same time, the anti–Rwandan lobby was gaining momentum

Major Kagame (far right) on military training in the United States at Fort Leavenworth, Kansas, in 1990. (From the personal collection of President Paul Kagame.)

in the Kampala parliament, which still contained elements strongly opposed to Museveni's NRM agenda. Kampala's senior national legislative body, the National Ruling Council, sought to bar Rwandans from land ownership and attempted to remove them from the armed forces. This added to the already powerful Ugandan "push" factors driving the Tutsi exile community towards a return to their homeland as well as the better-known "pull" factors of restoring their rights, position, and property as well as securing the protection of their ethnic cousins inside the country's borders.

Opposition factions continued their campaign against what they saw as the excessive prominence of Rwandans in the national government and finally Museveni caved in to their pressure, ordering the removal of Major General Rwigyema from his position as Army Chief of Staff in November 1989. Paul Kagame was also relieved of his duties as head of military intelligence in Kampala and was dispatched to the U.S. for a training course at Fort Leavenworth, Kansas. Both of these redeployments were engineered as part of an attempt by Museveni to sideline his embarrassingly influential Rwandan lieutenants whom the Ugandan leader felt were perhaps planning to make a move of their own from inside his national territory.

Keeping in Touch with Rebellion

The two leading Rwandan rebels were neither surprised nor deterred by Museveni's strategy; Kagame and Rwigyema conspired to keep a grip on their followers and their movement by not letting the Ugandan authorities dispatch both of them outside the country at the same time. As Kagame described it, to send both of them overseas would be to "cut off the head of the organization," so they secretly agreed between themselves that Fred should stay in Rwanda whatever the circumstances. Museveni had originally planned to send Rwigyema to the United States and Kagame to Nigeria, but that would have broken up the leadership:

> They wanted to disrupt our activities by sending us on courses and keeping us out of the country ... in 1989 their plan was that Fred would be sent to the USA but he refused, saying he had family problems. Museveni did not accept that, he said if you are not going, then Kagame is going. I had actually just got married that same week, when they told me, on a Friday, you are leaving next Monday. So I said no problem and on the Monday I left for the USA ... I knew that if I refused I would have ended up in jail. They would have known something was going on if I said no and so I said yes I would go ... and I told Fred in any case you stay and organize and I'll join you later. I kept in touch with him on the phone each week and I knew of the progress of our forces...[12]

So it was that Fred Rwigyema stayed in Uganda while Kagame and others left. Nevertheless, Rwigyema had lost his position as Ugandan Army Chief of Staff, considerably diminishing his influence and that of his countrymen in the new Ugandan political arena. For many of the Rwandans in Uganda in 1989, who were feeling that their hosts and recent allies in the NRA were increasingly ungrateful for the contribution they had made in the struggle against Obote, the removal of the respected and popular Fred Rwigyema was the final straw. If the regime that they had fought alongside in order to gain freedom from persecution could no longer return the loyalty shown by its Army Chief of Staff, a long-time personal friend of the president, what hope was there for ordinary Rwandans in the long term to establish their lives and earn their livelihood in this country?

In short, despite the seeming change of fortunes for the better for the refugees in Uganda, a new set of pressures was pushing the Rwandan Tutsi community towards a return to their homeland by late 1989. The situation in exile combined with an increasingly repressive climate at home vis-à-vis the Tutsi minority now pointed to the only remaining means of effecting that homecoming: through an armed invasion using the military resources at their disposal from the Ugandan army of which they were already a part.

Timetable for Conflict

President Habyarimana, fully aware of the growing strength of the RPF in Uganda, finally agreed to take steps towards addressing the long-standing issue of his country's Tutsi refugees. In late 1989, he had agreed to internationally brokered talks in conjunction with neighboring heads of state and the UNHCR, aimed at surveying refugees' intentions, a move intended to lead to selective repatriations of Tutsis from Uganda in mid–1990. Moreover, by now political conditions on the Rwandan side of the border were deteriorating, reducing the Rwandan president's room for maneuver at home, just as his regime was coming under increasing pressure from abroad.

The economy had turned sour, with the collapse of coffee prices and the recurring threat of famine due to droughts and consequent crop failures; there was social unrest and increasing infighting between political clans. There were frequent and arbitrary arrests in the country, following which people were often carted off to re-education camps for "immoral behavior" such as selling condoms or loitering in the streets of the capital in the hope of finding work.[13]

Moreover, Habyarimana's one-party state was showing increasing signs of being under the influence of extremists. Opposition by his party's hard-liners towards the concept of multi-party democracy, which foreign donors were beginning to clamor for, gave the RPF what they saw as a valid excuse for using force, even if Kigali continued to deny the existence of the mounting state-tolerated violence and discrimination carried out against the country's Tutsi minority.

However, on the other side of the border the lip service being paid by Kigali to refugee repatriation and inclusive government was seen as being too little too late. The RPF was increasingly skeptical about the value of the talks in bringing about real change in the refugee situation of the Tutsis. The internationally brokered discussions envisaged a kind of selection process to allow certain refugees to return whilst others would have to stay and be "absorbed" by the host country in which they found themselves. In a last-ditch effort to prevent hostilities, presidents Museveni, Habyarimana and Mobutu Sese Seko of Zaire met in mid–September 1990 in Kampala but they failed to establish common ground for a solution.

Kagame criticized the repatriation talks for their irrelevance to those who were actually affected: "It wasn't going to work because it wasn't involving the people who actually had the problem," he said. I didn't see how Habyarimana and Mobutu were just going to sit down with each other and decide how to deal with it their own way.... Maybe they would come out and say these ones will go and these ones will stay and be absorbed ... and they can just shut up ... so I might be told to stay without my own consent ... and then I would have to stay but without my full rights ... then the Ugandans would just say that he is one of the ones who has been absorbed ... but I would be there as a second-class citizen and a foreigner."[14]

As well as the pressure being felt by the '59ers and other Rwandan exiles to find a more secure home, Museveni was by now more willing to risk international opprobrium in the short term to solve what for him was a long-term and mounting domestic political problem. Thus an imminent departure of the Rwandans, armed or otherwise, could only help to ease the pressures that the anti-immigrant lobby inside his own country was increasingly bringing to bear on him.

On Museveni's side, pressures were clearly mounting from international quarters as well. His new government still relied heavily on foreign aid to survive, and the NRA was by late 1986 already fighting a war in the north and east of the country against the remains of Obote's forces, now regrouped and renamed as the Ugandan People's Democratic Army. In order to secure the economic assistance which he so badly needed, Museveni had signed up to a program of economic liberalization and free market reforms which brought close scrutiny from the IMF and international donors, notably the United States. Washington was making it increasingly clear that support for rebel movements bent on invading neighboring countries would not be looked on with favor, so whatever plans and maneuvers the Rwandans might be embarking upon inside Uganda were, in theory at least, strictly without the knowledge and backing of the NRM administration in Kampala.

Indeed, the more militant Rwandan elements could quickly become a liability for Museveni if allowed to gain too much power inside Uganda, hence his seeming change of loyalties in sidelining old allies under the international pressures and economic exigencies of the times.

The military preparations which the Rwandan exiles were starting to make by early 1990 were regarded in two lights by the Ugandan president: on the one hand, he could not be seen as allowing his territory to be used as a staging ground for the overthrow of an established neighboring government, potentially making him responsible for throwing the entire region into military conflict and humanitarian turmoil; however, on the other hand, a successful invasion by the Rwandans of their homeland would inevitably mean their departure from Uganda on a permanent basis, something which would solve a long-standing domestic political and social problem for his administration. The Ugandan president therefore watched with a blinkered eye, but also with an ambivalence born of self-interest, as preparations went ahead for the long-expected military showdown between the RPF forces based in his country and those of the neighboring state of Rwanda.

Changing pressures on the Ugandan government as well as developments inside their homeland both had an important bearing on the timing of the Rwandan faction's next move. President Habyarimana was increasingly anxious about the possibility of an imminent attack from the north and had begun to ask for international support to deter the potential aggressors.

The Ugandans knew that something was going on, too, and by mid–1990 they were working against the Rwandans, preventing them from getting organized. Time was running out, and there was a sense of increasing urgency in the RPF leadership for action.

While invading Rwanda to strike against the Habyarimana regime to force change was the military objective, according to the then Major Kagame it was in fact the developments in Uganda which had the ultimate bearing on the decision to make a move: "The timing and the feeling to start something was based on what was happening in Uganda," he explained. "If we had taken a longer time they would have had an opportunity to disorganize us, sending us for courses, displacing us from one place to another. Therefore we would have lost control over the Rwandese forces that we had operating in the army. That is how we decided to act very quickly irrespective of the odds ... that were really strongly against us. But we knew if we had taken much longer it would have been really problematic."[15]

3

THE INVASION OF 1990

The RPF Attacks

Colonel Fred Rwigyema assumed command of the splinter group of the NRA that was due to carry out the invasion in the closing months of 1990. In fact, a defection from the ranks of the Ugandan army had to be engineered and therefore secrecy was maintained until the last minute. The small band of Rwandan exiles, most of whom were veterans of the armed struggle against Milton Obote's regime, was ready to break from the regular Ugandan army to attempt an invasion of its homeland. They chose Ugandan independence day, October 1, as their moment to attack, which gave Rwigyema the excuse that he was moving large numbers of troops out of their positions in preparation for a military parade on the holiday. The Rwandan force moved southwards towards the border, assembling around the town of Kabale, and by the evening of September 30, their force was in position.

Crossing the frontier at Kagitumba from Uganda on the afternoon of October 1, 1990, the RPF invading force, which numbered over 4,000 men, initially had the advantage of surprise and made rapid progress southwards. They were able to take the northern market town of Gabiro with very little difficulty, but the advancing rebels soon became overstretched and were cut off from their supply lines and contact with potential reinforcements closer to the Ugandan border.

French Intervention

Although more numerous, the Rwandan government army, the Forces Armées Rwandaises (FAR) was less disciplined and certainly less motivated than the RPF,[1] but they had been receiving substantial military support from Belgium and more importantly from France. The French had long backed the Habyarimana regime, and indeed the Rwandan president was a personal friend of François Mitterand. Officially not present on the ground, the French military were inside Rwanda in the form of advisors and intelligence and communications specialists and also assisted the FAR with logistics and strategy, while not actually going so far as to pull the triggers of the Rwandan government army's weapons.

Following the initial few days' thrust southwards, the RPF's luck began to run out quickly and the invading force was beset with misfortunes on all sides. Fred Rwigyema was killed leading his army on only the second day of the attack, leaving the force temporarily leaderless. Worse still, the French had not been slow to react and within days had sent reinforcements to bolster the FAR on the battlefield as well as stepping up shipments of materiel and munitions to the Kigali regime. The FAR were able to regroup and laid an ambush for the RPA advance force around Gabiro, sending the invaders fleeing back northwards and westwards by the end of October.

It quickly became clear that the French contingent, ostensibly dispatched to protect and evacuate its own and other foreign nationals, had a much farther reaching purpose to its mission. The first 150 French paratroopers who arrived in *Opération Noroit*, as it was known, were already on the ground by October 4 and, together with the 300 reinforcements that were sent later, ended up staying in Rwanda for three years, while their Belgian counterparts, also sent to protect their own nationals, managed to finish their job and return home after only three weeks.

Kagame Returns from the United States

At the time of the invasion in 1990, Paul Kagame, then a major in the Ugandan army, was still attending the command training course in the United States, at Fort Leavenworth in Kansas. He had been inside the U.S. for over three months at the time of the attack and so did not participate directly in the final preparations for war, although Rwigyema and the other commanders in Uganda had kept him regularly briefed on their plans.

His U.S. military hosts were taken by surprise when the Ugandan major finally approached them to say he was going to return to Uganda to join an army that had just invaded Rwanda. "Most of them didn't know who I was," said Kagame, "although they could have known from when my papers were processed when I departed from Kampala, they could have seen my background…. But they didn't know until I told them I was Rwandan and I said to them that this is going on and this is how I am linked to it

Paul Kagame at his wedding to Jeanette Nyiramongi, June 1989, in Uganda. (From the personal collection of President Paul Kagame.)

and that is why I want to go.... They couldn't understand why I wanted to leave such a prestigious military institution to go back and fight in the bush..."[2]

Kagame went quickly about his departure. Asking to be discharged, he went to the school and asked to clear all his bills and said he was leaving. The Fort Leavenworth administrators were taken aback, Kagame recalled. "They couldn't understand all that. The senior commander in charge of the college got confused ... as I was supposed to be here as a Ugandan then I was leaving as a Rwandese....[3] They thought maybe I was crazy or something ... but I could see they were not really understanding what I was talking about."

While the buildup of the Rwandan faction within the Ugandan army in preparation for a return was an open secret, the timing of the invasion was determined by outside events and the pressures that the Rwandans were beginning to feel from inside Uganda. The difficulty of keeping informed and in touch with battleground developments made the opening days of the offensive tense ones for Major Kagame. But within weeks of the news of Rwigyema's death, Kagame returned and made his way to the front lines in northern Rwanda, assuming control of the invading RPF forces from that point in the struggle onwards.

He was able to return to Kampala by late October and upon arrival at the airport was immediately met by RPF officers still operating inside Rwanda. "We just picked him up at the airport and took him straight to the border," said a fellow intelligence officer who later became a senior security chief in the government in Kigali and who wishes to remain anonymous. There was no time spent nor trouble taken on the part of the Ugandans to prevent the defection of one more of their elite officers to the front in the Great Lakes region's latest civil war.

The RPF military offensive was in total disarray by the time of Kagame's return from the United States. In addition to their defeat on the battlefield, the security consequences for the Rwandan Tutsis remaining inside the country were arguably even more disastrous, as Habyarimana could now claim the need for an internal roundup of opponents citing the self-defense of the country as justification for his actions.

Internal Repercussions

Indeed, the opportunity to do just this was seized on the night of the 4–5 October, when the sounds of machine gun fire could be heard all around Kigali, as a fierce gun battle appeared to be taking place. The news of course made it to the international media, which by now had tuned in to events in Rwanda as a result of the invasion of less than a week before. In fact, after sustained shooting throughout the night, mysteriously there were no wounded arriving at the capital's hospitals.

By the following morning, it transpired that there had not been one single casualty from the "attack" on the capital. The whole charade had been orchestrated by the authorities as a pretext for the clampdown, arrest and elimination of their enemies and suspected *ibyitso* (collaborators, of the RPF) whom they had been watching for months. The lists of those to be arrested had been prepared well in advance and by the end of the sweep of its opponents, the regime had detained thousands of suspects, some 90 percent of whom were of Tutsi ethnicity.

On the propaganda front another harmful repercussion for the RPF was that negotiations between the government and the opposition had been making progress and according to some were at the point of reaching an acceptable conclusion. The RPF could therefore be accused of having been *against* peace, or otherwise why would they have attacked just at the moment of resolution of the crisis except to preserve themselves and their self-conferred mission as military liberators of the homeland?

The Habyarimana regime had in fact agreed to a schedule for the return of selected Rwandan Tutsi refugees during the months prior to the outbreak of hostilities and was due to begin repatriations in November 1990. Once underway, such a program would have severely eroded the momentum behind the military preparations and indeed the whole rationale for the RPF's campaign. According to this interpretation, the timing of the attack had to be brought forward, despite its being executed by what was a lightly armed and ill-prepared guerrilla army, facing an opposition fighting on its own territory with heavy weaponry and superior numbers.

On the other side of the border, the intention to attack Rwanda had hardly been a secret either, but in some ways it allowed Habyarimana to carry out his purge of opponents with justification and under cover of the confusion of war. The staged fighting in Kigali and subsequent roundup of thousands of opponents which took place on October 4, for example, could hardly have been carried out with only three days' advance planning. Thus in terms of the Kigali regime's internal security strategy, the attack was something which served a valuable purpose and, gambling on a French intervention to secure victory, Habyarimana could take the calculated risk of allowing an invasion to happen.

The military involvement of the French in Rwanda from 1990 onwards is a contentious issue, and varying explanations have been offered for the seemingly disproportionate role played by France in a country which had little economic importance and no strategic value to French global interests. The Rwandan situation, it seems, warranted military intervention on behalf of an embattled regime with few supporters and a questionable human rights record, let alone any evidence of making progress towards democracy.

Some commentators explain the obsession with Rwanda as stemming from the need to maintain the self image of a neo-colonial France, with an aging President Mitterand at its helm, paranoid about an incursion of English speakers from "Anglo-Saxon" Uganda. France's cultural *cause célèbre*, namely the defense of *francophonie* whether in North America, the Caribbean, in remotest Oceania or in deepest central Africa, has rarely needed further justification, at least to its domestic electorate. Furthermore, its 1990 Rwanda involvement could be presented to observers in the west as an intervention to stop an invasion of a sovereign nation and stave off civil war in the developing world where it had traditional influence, if any further excuse should be needed.

A sounder basis for the intervention could perhaps be found in the military cooperation agreement signed between France and Rwanda in 1975, which remained in force at the time of the October 1990 attack and which indeed lasted right up until the United Nations arms embargo against the country in 1993. Official French military support for the Kigali regime had reached a level of over 50 million francs (around $8m) per annum by that time, which in addition to the weaponry and funds reaching Habyarimana's forces from France through unofficial channels represented a serious commitment to keeping his dictatorship in power.

Other less admirable motivations have been suggested as the true reasons for the excessive level of French concern that the MRND, the party of the government, remain in power in Kigali. One is that Paris was using Kigali as a conduit for its arms sales to Iran, Syria and elsewhere in the Middle East. Related and not insignificant was the fact that President Mitterand's son, Jean-Christophe, was head of the Cellule Africaine (the Africa Unit) in the French foreign ministry and was a known arms dealer, actively operating from Rwanda throughout the period.[4]

Whatever the main motivation behind the French actions, it is true that, following the fall of the Berlin Wall in 1989 and the mood of pan-global democratic ideals which enjoyed a renaissance at that time, Paris had declared that its future support of African (and other Third World) regimes would henceforth be contingent on progress towards democracy. Habyarimana had met Mitterand at the Franco-African summit in La Baule early in 1990 and an agreement was reached between the two men pledging France's strengthened commitment to military (and doubtless personal) support, in exchange for Kigali making the "right moves" for international consumption in the democratic arena.

Zairian Involvement

A further element of military support for the Habyarimana regime was the intervention of President Mobutu of Zaire. The end of the cold war made Mobutu strategically redundant in the eyes of the west, and the Zairian kleptocrat had been eager to find a new role to improve his image on the international stage and divert attention from problems at home. The opportunity to join battle on the side of France's old ally in the region was therefore ideal and the Zairian troops fought alongside the FAR at the front in the war against the RPF.

Unfortunately, the 1,000 or so soldiers of the supposedly elite Zairian Presidential Guard turned out to be so ill-disciplined in their conduct that they quickly became an embarrassment to Habyarimana. Looting, raping and terrorizing the Rwandan population (of both ethnicities) in the areas to which they were deployed, their presence became intolerable and after a few weeks at the front the Rwandan president had to ask for them to be withdrawn.

The French contingent did not officially engage in combat, although observers at the time said that their leader, Lieutenant Colonel Chollet, officially an "advisor" to the Chief of Staff of the FAR, was regarded by combatants as the commander in chief of military operations on the government side.[5] Furthermore, highly placed intelligence sources in the RPF at the front claimed to have clear photographic evidence of French commandos in action in northern Rwanda.[6]

Rebuilding the RPF

Although a military and propaganda setback in the short term, the birth of the RPF as a fighting force undoubtedly marked a milestone in the struggle of the expatriate Tutsi community to retake their country by force. Following defeat in the 1990 war, from their Virunga mountain bases just inside Rwanda's borders, Kagame set about the task of reorganizing, retraining and recruiting for his army, which he was rapidly to transform into a formidable fighting force for the military campaigns which lay ahead.

With personal prestige and extensive contacts among the Tutsi diaspora internationally, not only was Major-General Kagame[7] to re-engineer and reinforce his army on the northern fringes of Rwanda over the coming months, but he was also to prove a highly effective fund-raiser among the Tutsi diaspora of businessmen in Europe, North America and elsewhere. Despite remaining in essence an armed rebel movement until 1994, as the political arm of the RPF took substance and form over the years, so did Kagame become its figurehead, politically as well as militarily.

Many of the remnants of the attacking force from the October 1990 war took refuge in two locations inside Rwanda: the Akagera Forest in the east of the country and the mountainous Virunga region in the north, famous among zoologists and western tourists for its gorilla population. From these two refuges and in particular from its bases in Virunga the RPA continued a campaign of harassment of the Rwandan army and succeeded in seriously disrupting economic activity in the north of the country.

Although a good deal of the RPF's military supplies came from Uganda, President Museveni was careful to not be seen by the international community as fomenting civil wars among his neighbors, as some 60 percent of his country's GNP at the time came in the form of loans and grants from overseas. The RPF was, however, able to take advantage of another recent development in geopolitics at the time, the 1989 collapse of the Soviet

Union and its satellite republics in Asia and eastern Europe. Many of the newly liberated ex–Soviet republics were now resource-strapped but at the same time found themselves bequeathed with armed forces and weapons arsenals as the legacy of their former totalitarian regimes. In many cases they set about flooding the international arms market with these now useless (to them) military materiel to raise the cash which they desperately needed for the development of their fledgling market economies.

The RPA as well as numerous other African governments and rebel movements were able to take advantage of this arms glut and for years to come around the continent, a common sight was Soviet- or east European–manufactured weaponry deployed in sub–Saharan civil wars, materiel which had found its way there through the international arms market to Africa's military leaders and their armies.

RPF Harassment and FAR Reprisals

In the meantime, however, inside Rwanda the repercussions of the October invasion and each subsequent incursion by the RPF were becoming increasingly painful for the Tutsis remaining there. Reprisals against Tutsi civilians were swift and ruthless, with entire communities being systematically slaughtered amid denials of involvement by the Kigali government.

The authorities would travel to a community in advance and tell the local peasantry what their work was to be for the following day. Instead of the usual agrarian tasks, they were to kill all the Tutsis in that area, according to lists distributed by their foremen and supervisors. Used to following community leaders' instructions in the execution of the required communal work details, known as *umuganda*, they set off to the houses and the fields to seek their victims, many singing or drumming in the traditional fashion of the Rwandan peasant worker.

Because of the advance planning, the nature and the mechanics of these massacres, in many ways it was during this phase that the Rwandan genocide truly began. In its organization and execution and by its hallmark of efficiency and emotionless methodical implementation it was in every way except its magnitude a dress rehearsal for the 1994 slaughters.

But already by early 1991, the newly regrouped RPF led by Paul Kagame was ready to launch another major action. Kagame selected as his target the northwestern town of Ruhengeri, for both psychological and logistical reasons. Firstly, it was the home region of the Hutu ruling elite who made up Habyarimana's inner circle and would therefore send a strong

message to the country's political leaders that the RPF was a force that had
to be included in the ongoing negotiations. Secondly, it was the only major
center in the country that the rebels could hit from their bases in the
Virunga mountains without the FAR having time to send the necessary
reinforcements to defend it.

Attacking the town on January 24, the RPA forces scored a lightning
victory, and Ruhengeri was quickly under their control. In addition to its
strategic importance, the town was also the site of the country's largest
prison, with over 1,000 prisoners, many of whom were political detainees,
among them key RPF sympathizers. Upon striking the city, the rebels were
able to liberate all the prison inmates, despite their warders having been
given strict orders to kill them in the event of an attack.

The RPA retreated again quickly from Ruhengeri, in a hit-and-run
style of attack that was to become its trademark for this phase of their
campaign. However, in the by now established pattern, reprisals against
the local Tutsi population were not long in coming. Throughout that year
organized massacres of Tutsis in and around Ruhengeri were to claim hundreds of lives, making the bold raids of the expatriate Tutsi RPA into
pyrrhic victories for many of the ordinary Tutsis still inside Rwanda, con-
tinually at the mercy of the Hutu militias' backlash.

Major-General Kagame (white suit) at the signing of the peace agreement brokered by the OAU at Nsele, Zaire, in March 1991. (From the personal collection
of President Paul Kagame.)

International Pressure on Kigali

During this period, President Habyarimana was conducting an increasingly difficult balancing act between grandstanding for peace on the international stage on the one hand, by fulfilling his commitment to international backers to move towards multi-party democracy, and on the other, maintaining the confidence of his increasingly hard-line domestic power base, composed of a bloodthirsty core of community execution squad administrators.

All this was having to be managed against the backdrop of a rapidly deteriorating economy, hastened by the successful campaign of disruption being conducted in the northwest of the country by the RPF. Indeed, Habyarimana tried calling cease-fires with the RPA during 1991, but usually his own FAR broke them after a very short time, only using the breathing space afforded by each agreement to organize assaults on the rebels in their mountain hideouts.

After one such cease-fire in March 1991, the FAR launched artillery attacks into the Virunga mountains to try to dislodge the RPA. The attack failed, as the insurgents took cover in the bamboo foliage and sheltered from the shelling in the valleys and mountain overhangs. A second, much larger artillery attack was launched in November 1991, also in breach of a cease-fire agreement, and again the bombardment failed. This time the psychological impact on the government side was much greater as it now knew that it could not banish the invading forces from its national territory through military means alone.

From that time on, the RPA was able to move out of its remote bases and capture and hold territory in the north of the country, notably the prefectural capital of Byumba, an important market town and significant population center.

Regional Diplomatic Efforts

On October 14, 1990, Belgium sent its prime minister, Willy Martens, together with his foreign minister and minister of defense, to meet with representatives of the warring parties in Nairobi. Further meetings were held in Tanzania and Uganda as well as with the Organization of African Unity (OAU) based in Addis Ababa and including representatives of the regionally influential Communauté Economique de Pays des Grands Lacs (CEPGL). President Hassan Ali Mwinyi of Tanzania was among the most active forces for moderation in the region and was able to guide the parties towards issuing a number of declarations and communiqués in the following weeks, intended to lead to peace and a solution of the underlying problems of the war.

Beyond regional discussions, the United States and France in particular were playing their respective peacemaking roles during this period, jointly with the involvement of the United Nations. Although they kept each other more or less informed, Washington and Paris conducted their negotiations with Kigali and the RPF in parallel rather than as any kind of tripartite effort. In view of existing economic, military and linguistic associations it is not surprising that the U.S. efforts were most effective in trying to restrain Uganda's Museveni from continuing to give support to the rebel army while France was more able to bring influence to bear on Juvenal Habyarimana's regime and the FAR.

During this time an additional important peace track was pursued through influential members of the Rwandan diaspora in Europe and North America. On the Hutu side, there were powerful overseas Rwandans with close connections to Madame Habyarimana's *akazu*, the MRND or both who took up contact with western diplomatic actors in attempts to influence or mediate in the discussions. At the same time there were RPF sympathizers among the Tutsi diaspora who used their positions in business or international affairs to try to support the rebel arguments in the negotiations. Particularly on the Tutsi side, several of the RPF's new leaders were being drawn directly from overseas during this period, from Belgium, the United States, Canada and elsewhere. Among these were Patrick Mazimpaha, Vice Chairman of the RPF, who had been a geologist living in Canada, and Jacques Bihozagara, who had become the RPF's representative in Brussels.

Calls for Multi-party Democracy

The Kigali government had been increasingly under pressure to establish a multi-party democracy in the months prior to the October 1990 invasion. However, while France was nominally one of the western powers calling for democratic institutions and a multi-party system, in reality Paris did not use its military presence on the ground to influence its client government. The drift towards internal extremism that was occurring during the early 1990s therefore continued unabated.

Despite the political deadlock, 1991 and early 1992 saw the setting up of a number of "opposition" parties, many of which were ineffectual or posed no political threat to Habyarimana's MRND. In fact, at first a series of front parties were set up by him with no real program and with the sole objective of providing a façade of opposition and serving to confuse the international community.

Some parties which emerged could, however, be described as forming a genuine opposition. The PSD, the Social Democratic Party, with its power base in the liberal university town of Butare, Rwanda's ancient capital city, was a force for moderate non-racist opposition, as was the PL — the Liberal Party — which drew support from around the country, typically from the middle class and the Tutsi business community. The PL was in fact the only major opposition party with substantial Tutsi support. The clerically aligned CSD (Christian Democrats) were also reincarnated, to capitalize on the country's long-standing ties with the Catholic church through which they could expect to draw political support from outside the country. The MDR (Mouvement Démocratique Républicain), a major force from the time of independence, was also revived and even the ruling MRND was reinvented. Opportunistically and in the spirit of the times, Habyarimana's party was rebranded, adding a second "D" to its acronym, thereby becoming the Mouvement Révolutionnaire National pour le Développement et la Démocracie (MRNDD).

The CDR (Coalition pour la Défense de la République), however, with its overtly racist agenda, was a real and radical force, and its creation and controversial inclusion in the newly legitimized multi-party system in March of 1992 could hardly be characterized as a stabilizing factor in the future evolution of the country.

The Rise of Extremism

While these parties did come into existence in more than name, Habyarimana's strategy was still based on absolutism. At the same time, the unofficial movements were gaining power, too, and the steady flow of arms into the country allowed the *interahamwe* to become an increasingly lethal force. The FAR was also recruiting rapidly, rising in strength from around 5,500 men at the time of the October 1990 war to over 30,000 by the end of 1992.

Arms shipments to the government were paid for mostly by France, either directly or indirectly. At times the volume of shipments became too great for the *Elysée* to authorize without causing controversy and so intermediaries had to be found. The most popular conduit countries were Egypt and apartheid South Africa, through which the French arranged for shipments in excess of $5 million each to be sent during the 1990–92 period, often with the guarantee of France's state-owned bank, Crédit Lyonnais.

Furthermore, many of the ruling MRNDD's actions and pronouncements were short-term and intended purely for external consumption. For example, in response to international fears that ethnically based extremism was reaching dangerous proportions, the president made a speech in early November of 1990 in which he announced that the *ubwoko*, the system whereby every person's official records showed his or her ethnicity, was to be revoked. This measure was met with approval in the overseas press, but when the time came for implementation by the Ministry of the Interior, the initiative was quietly quashed, and ethnic delineation by ID cards and documents was maintained from then on and all through the preparations for the genocide.

Although the Kigali regime was to a large extent playing games with the international community and its French patrons, this should not be allowed to obscure the fact that during this period there was in reality an active internal opposition to the Habyarimana-dominated Hutu state that Rwanda had become. Thus when talking about the period that immediately preceded the genocide in Rwandan politics, it is not accurate to describe the struggle as a Tutsi RPF versus Hutu MRNDD two-sided affair.

Internal Opposition and the RPF

Thus in addition to countering the RPA, the Rwandan president was dealing not only with a moderate opposition on one side but also an increasingly militant extremist wing within his own party, as well as the CDR, who were growing in strength and in the sympathy they received from the populace with every successive RPA border incursion. In reality, by early 1993, all opposition parties in the Rwandan system had effectively split into two wings: those advocating a version of Hutu power and those rejecting it.

A further complicating factor was the relationship between the RPF outside the country and the opposition Hutu parties inside Rwanda. In as much as both were opposed to the dictatorial regime of Habyarimana and the MRNDD, it might have been thought that they would form a combined front against the Kigali regime. In fact the situation was quite the opposite. The RPF was frequently denounced by opposition leaders as a party of "quasi-foreigners" and, for example, MDR manifesto documents of the early 1990s already used the derogatory term *inyenzi*—cockroaches— to refer to the RPF, scarcely an indicator of commitment to reconciliation.

The RPF, because of its origins, was mostly led by its Uganda-based core members, as has already been described. As negotiations loomed, however, and as a chance of a settlement leading to a share in government for the RPF neared, the party was increasingly at pains to include high-ranking Hutus in its leadership, to give at least some semblance of being a non–ethnically based movement.

Thus in the faltering and deceptive transition to democracy that ensued in the 1991–92 period, there truly was a three-cornered struggle continuing apace: Hutu extremists gaining influence, bent on eliminating all Tutsis and distrustful of the moderate wings of their own parties; RPF Tutsis outside the country actively opposing the government and rapidly arming to take on the FAR and the extremist militias; and a totalitarian government in the capital trying to oppose both internal extremists and RPF outsiders with international support, feigning democracy and inclusivity for its increasingly skeptical outside audience.

Propaganda and the Growth of the Militias

Meanwhile, at grassroots level on the domestic front, Hutu youth groups were becoming increasingly militant and were transforming themselves into the racist militias that would later form the front lines of the genocidal attack squads in 1994. Many of these had their origins in soccer supporters' associations, dating back to the 1980s, and at the outset were not unlike such gangs from anywhere else in the world.

However, with the worsening economy and mounting unemployment, many found racist extremism an attractive outlet for their frustrations and energies and they joined in pro–Habyarimana rallies and "civil defense" training sessions. These latter sessions would include activities such as techniques of arson, grenade-throwing and machete practice on human dummies. The two best-known militia groups to emerge were associated with extremist youth wings of political parties. The MRNDD spawned the militia known as the *interahamwe* or "those who work together" and the CDR sponsored the creation of the *impuzamugambi*, "those with a common purpose."

The machinery of extremist propaganda was also building momentum during 1991 and 1992. The official national radio station, Radio Rwanda, took a new step forward towards the propaganda of hate when in March of 1992 it began to broadcast news of the discovery of a "Tutsi plot" to attack Hutus throughout the country. The announcement was followed by a renewed outbreak of massacres of Tutsi civilians.

By this time, the opposition had begun to organize demonstrations against Habyarimana, which provoked increasingly desperate tactics from his supporters in response. The only hope for the MRNDD to maintain its grip on power and to unite Hutus generally was through attempting to implicate the wider population in the massacres and terrorist attacks which were occurring throughout the country. Through a mood of solidarity through guilt, the government hoped to refocus attention on the outside RPF threat and prioritize the imperative of eliminating their domestic Tutsi collaborators, the hated *ibyitso*.

Power-sharing

By March of 1992, however, with the MRNDD's survival options running out, the intervention of the international donors was finally brought to bear more forcefully. The Habyarimana government agreed to the creation of a power-sharing cabinet, which was sworn in on April 7, 1992, with Dismas Nsengiyaremye (MDR) as prime minister and representative of the largest opposition party. The new foreign minister, Boniface Ngulinzira, was also from the MDR, as was Agathe Uwilingiyimana, who became the education secretary. Representatives from the PSD, PL and other parties were also allocated key ministerial posts. Although the new cabinet tried to reverse many of the extremist policies of their predecessors in the MRNDD, they frequently met with opposition when it came to implementation, particularly from the civil service, who were often hard-core MRNDD cadres.

Furthermore, the gradual progress being made towards peace did not please many elements who had relied on the status quo not only for their claim to power but also for their livelihood. Many soldiers in the FAR had not been paid for months and with the prospect of a negotiated settlement, they became increasingly concerned about demobilization. In May 1992 the army mutinied in Ruhengeri and Gisenyi, areas where they had the support of the local authorities, and several thousand soldiers went on a rampage of burning, looting and killing.

Meeting the Opposition — Cease-fire and the Launch of Arusha

On June 6, 1992, the main opposition parties took a gamble and, risking alienation of the Hutu majority at home, they met with the RPF in Brussels to conduct peace talks. Believing that there was a chance to be brought into the process through negotiations, the RPF then called an end to hostilities in the expectation of a peace accord following the talks and their being included as a partner in a new power-sharing government. On July 14 a cease-fire was signed and the first steps towards the formal peace process were taken in Arusha, Tanzania.

The MRNDD commitment to participation in the RPF/opposition-initiated peace process turned out to be yet another Habyarimana ploy to secure a few more months of breathing space and a chance of receiving some further donor support. Despite his commitments in the international arena, by October 1992 the president of Rwanda was making a speech for a domestic audience in which he referred to the peace agreement as a mere "piece of paper," after which hostilities against the RPF in the northwest quickly resumed. Furthermore, throughout the talks, the campaign of internal persecution and violence by the *interahamwe* continued, with a particularly brutal slaughter of hundreds of Tutsis in the Kibuye area being carried out in late October 1992, just as delegates were returning from the signing of an accord in the Arusha peace process.

This was to become the pattern for the coming year as the RPF would continue its campaign of harassment in between cease-fires, from its bases in the north of the country, while Habyarimana would play for time at home and negotiate abroad and the Hutu Power and *interahamwe* extremists organized and executed their "warm-up" genocidal attacks against Tutsis inside Rwanda.

Throughout the marathon sessions of the Arusha peace process, both sides carried on rearming heavily, with the RPF and the FAR using their different international connections to procure the materiel they needed. A December 1993 CIA study estimated that some 40 million tons of small arms originating in Poland reached Rwanda through Belgium in the 1991–93 period. Between 1992 and 1994, Rwanda took delivery of 581,000 machetes and other farming implements from China which were procured by local companies, most of which had no prior involvement in the import of agricultural tools.[8]

The rebels developed their own military supply lines, too, and both sides continued the recruitment process into their respective armies. The RPF, which had numbered only 4,000 men when it had first crossed into Rwanda in October 1990, had an estimated strength of 20,000 by the end of 1992, although this was still only half the size of the newly reinforced FAR.

Despite the outward show of diplomacy and commitment to peace negotiations, the internal reality was one of preparations for war. Cynicism about the prospects and distrust of each side's respective motives marked the entire process, and the reluctance to disarm was evident to observers on the ground if not to those from outside who participated in shuttle diplomacy to and from Arusha.

During the final stages of the Arusha discussions, a key problem to emerge was the security of the required RPF representatives who would come to Kigali to participate in the Broad-Based Transitional Governemt (BBTG). Kagame insisted to the UN that they would have to have protection, or they would refuse to come at all. The UN leaders, under Special Representative of the Secretary-General Jacques-Roger Booh-Booh and Force Commander General Roméo Dallaire, insisted that protection could be given only by UN forces.

Kagame refused to accept this, telling the UN representatives: "...no way, you cannot send our people, our whole political leadership to Kigali, without our own protection, added to the United Nations or whatever other force, otherwise we can't go." Kagame continued to argue this point with the UN, ultimately refusing to compromise: "General Dallaire and Booh-Booh tried to convince me that they could give them protection and I told them ... finally I told them to go to hell, it's not going to happen. Either we don't go and that's the end of the story, or if we have to go we go with our own force." He described it as "a make or break issue" and later on the UN leaders agreed. "So now the issue became how many would go ... we started with a brigade and then later brought it down.... Finally it became 600 men."[9]

With agreement on this key issue and a resolution of the other remaining obstacles to agreement, the signing of the final Arusha Accord took place in October 1993, leading to the deployment of an international peacekeeping force, the United Nations Assistance Mission to Rwanda (UNAMIR). However, rather than being the final step in the completion of a process towards peace as its international backers had hoped, the Arusha signing in reality marked one of the closing acts in a long, drawn-out diplomatic charade by two adversaries who had already embarked on a near-certain path to war.

4

OFFENSIVE AGAINST GENOCIDE

No Turning Back from Conflict

In anticipation of an imminent transfer of power under the Arusha peace agreement between the Habyarimana government, the opposition parties and the RPF, Paul Kagame, Pasteur Bizimungu and Jacques Bihozagara arrived in Kigali on December 28, 1993. They were the three nominees who would take up the ministerial posts which had been allocated to the RPF under the Arusha Accords.

On the military side, the month before, the first contingent of UNAMIR soldiers had begun to arrive, and the 600 RPF troops provided for in the last of the agreements, signed on August 3, 1993, took up their station in Kigali's parliament building, the Conseil National de Développement (CND).

However, extremist elements in other opposition parties blocked implementation of the power transfer and President Habyarimana seemed unable or unwilling to bring about the changes, scheduled for February but postponed due to the impasse. Kagame, in frustration, returned to the RPF headquarters at Mulindi, while the opposition banged their heads together and tension in the capital mounted on a daily basis.

As the weeks passed, Kagame used the time to bolster his army through further recruitment and the acquisition of much-needed small arms through Uganda. But the extremists were rearming too, and distribution of guns and machetes inside the country was occurring at a frenetic pace. The UN special envoy, Jacques-Roger Booh-Booh from Cameroon, stated publicly that he was incapable of stopping the rearmament, and Belgian foreign minister Willy Claes flew to Kigali to inform the president that there was no room left for further delay.

The atmosphere inside the country and in Kigali in particular became one of menace and fear, spurred on by continual and unrestrained hate broadcasts from the Radio Télévision Libre des Mille Collines (RTLMC). In the capital's Gikondo quarter, threats against Tutsi residents became so intense that scores of people simply started to leave their homes to escape the imminent and violent end that they were by now certain awaited them if they stayed.

On February 21, the day before the rescheduled inauguration ceremony of the Arusha power-sharing executive, known as the Broad-Based Transitional Government (BBTG), Félicien Gatabazi, the Social Democratic Party's executive secretary, was assassinated on his way home at night and the country soon erupted with tit-for-tat killings. Rival political leaders and dozens of ordinary civilians were murdered or wounded in the rioting which ensued. At this moment the long-expected generalized massacre which had been predicted by many could easily have broken out.

Somehow, however, Habyarimana continued to hang on, presiding over a country poised on the edge of a precipice, staggering from one near catastrophe to another. Meanwhile, his neighboring countries' leaders and international sponsors grew more vociferous and increasingly impatient in their calls for him to implement transfer of power to the BBTG.

A last-ditch meeting was set up on April 6 in Dar es Salaam by Tanzania's President Ali Hassan Mwinyi, attended by leaders from Uganda, Kenya, Burundi, the UN and other international brokers of the peace process. Under extreme pressure Habyarimana at last agreed to move to the implementation of the previously agreed power-sharing arrangement. It was on his return to Kigali that night, together with Burundian president Cyprien Ntaryamira and their advisors, that his French Mystère Falcon jet was shot down, just before landing in Kigali, killing all on board and unleashing the massive outpouring of Rwandan blood that in a matter of days became the genocide of the Tutsis.

Throughout the closing acts of this unfolding tragedy, the RPF leadership maintained a low profile, while continuing to point to the root causes of the accords' non-implementation — intransigence by the executive and resistance to power-sharing by internal extremists. For the most part, however, Major-General Kagame and the RPA appeared to remain calm in their twin bases in Mulindi and at the CND building in Kigali, while in practice preparing for what was now a near-inevitable military showdown with Rwanda's government forces.

The RPA Provoked to Action

Over the night of April 6/7, roadblocks were thrown up in and around Kigali and targeted killings of opposition leaders began. Most notable among the first of those who died trying to escape was the prime minister, Agathe Uwilingiyimana, an MDR moderate. It was while attempting to escort her to safety that ten Belgian paratroopers were captured, disarmed and later butchered by government forces, an action which led a few days later to the withdrawal of the entire Belgian contingent from UNAMIR. The commander of the 2,700-strong UNAMIR force, Canadian General Roméo Dallaire, called for urgent reinforcements for his troops and an immediate change of mandate from the existing passive "peacekeeping" role to one that would allow it to intervene to save lives.

Later that night, with the president and his advisors dead and many government ministers out of the country, an assortment of extremist leaders gathered together to form an "interim government." Chief architect of the process of putting together the new administration that night was Colonel Théoneste Bagosora, who helped craft the shape of the successor regime behind closed doors, while at the same time orchestrating the campaign of massacres against civilians going on outside.

Throughout that night, Bagosora was in regular contact with his operations commander in Gisenyi, where the killing had begun almost immediately following the presidential plane crash. His army chief in the northwestern town, Anatole Nsengiyumva, telephoned Kigali at regular intervals to advise him of which sections his men had "cleared" and how the massacres were proceeding in each sector under his command. During his talks with the UN and Kigali diplomats, at which Bagosora was ostensibly discussing the establishment of an interim government, he reportedly had to frequently excuse himself to keep updated on the progress of the first day of the genocide.[1]

Initially, the RPF remained impassive as Major-General Kagame monitored the situation. In the first day of fighting, the deputy commander of the FAR, General Gatsinzi, who was not part of the extremist plot, ordered his soldiers to help put an end to hostilities and prevent the militias from extending their killing spree. However, some among his forces had already joined in the killing, and the Presidential Guard was also acting in support of the militias.

Tito Rutaremara, stationed in Kigali with the 600 RPF troops in the parliament building, also delivered an unambiguous threat: if the killing did not stop, he said, his troops would be forced to attack. Kagame called Dallaire from Mulindi on the morning of the 7th saying that his people inside the capital were at risk and steps must be taken to protect them as well as to safeguard the lives of the politicians who had been placed under arrest. "...I asked him what was happening and what we were expected to do ... as I learned from our people who were sending us information that they were picking people from houses and killing them and also attacking members of the general public," information which Kagame shared with Dallaire. "He said I should wait, that the UN was doing its best and that they think they have the situation under control.... As if that was not bad enough he suggested that I come there and together we should try to deal with the problem."[2]

Gatsinzi had asked the UN commander to contact the RPF to obtain a cease-fire. Perhaps on day two of the genocide there was still a real chance of ending the slaughter if the RPF and FAR commanders could be brought together to stop the fighting. Kagame's response was to propose combining forces to create safe havens for civilians. He initially suggested the dispatch of a battalion who could join forces with government troops to stop the killing. He felt at the time that such a joint effort would prove irresistible and the "renegade forces," as he called them, would disperse when faced with a show of multilateral solidarity.

However, Dallaire was wary of this proposal, as his tolerance for losses among his UN peacekeepers was much less than those he imagined the Rwandan units were willing to sustain. "I needed troops from a third party," Dallaire said." A strong UN force to stop the killings was absolutely essential."[3] Furthermore, the reports that some of the RPF contingent had broken out of the CND building and that both sides were now killing civilians tainted Kagame's offer, and Dallaire preferred to continue to ask his UN headquarters in New York for a neutral backup to his contingent. He also focused on trying to get Kagame to come to Kigali, to negotiate a cease-fire.

Kagame for his part remained skeptical about the proposal to enter into talks, however.

General Roméo Dallaire, UNAMIR force commander, at press conference in Kigali, September 1994 (UN/DPI photo 185722/M. Grant 1063 L).

So I told him that I thought that that was not a good proposal at all. I said it's not the right time and the place for me to come. I kept in touch the whole day ... then I got more information from our people, I learned that [the militias] had taken different leaders in Kigali, some were being killed and so on ... and when it came to 1 P.M. I asked him, 'What do you expect us to do? ... what is the UN doing about it?'"... Then he actually insisted that I come and told me he was meeting with Bagosora and Gatsinzi and other leaders ... and I said again it's the wrong time ... I'll never come there to meet them." Dallaire offered to come with two helicopters, to bring him to Kigali with a UN escort for protection, but Kagame said: "...some of those people may not care if it's the UN, they can still shoot you down."[4]

Then by 3 o'clock, Kagame was receiving more intelligence about how things were getting out of hand. He called Dallaire again: "...either the UN stops that, or we might have to intervene ... and specifically to save our own people who are caught up in that situation ... so we didn't agree. An hour or so later I learned that they [the FAR] had brought forces to attack and they were digging trenches outside the parliament building. ...I told Dallaire, 'It doesn't make sense to keep listening to you and to keep arguing with you," Kagame threatened. "'...I am actually going to prepare to send forces and rescue our people ... we are coming, just take note.'"

The following day, Kagame ordered his RPF forces to move south to relieve the pressure on his embattled Kigali brigade. Fighting for each position in turn, with frequent and effective use of mortars, the RPF slowly gained ground, but the well-armed and heavily equipped FAR fought back doggedly, only slowly giving up ground to the advancing rebels. It would ultimately take the invading force until late on the 11th of April to reach Kigali to relieve their garrison in the CND building. With the news of the RPF attack from the north, the remainder of the FAR under the moderate General Gatsinzi could no longer resist the call of the extremists. They yielded to the pressure from the hard-liners, joining in the massacres of civilians in support of the militias. So for nearly four days, the 600 RPF soldiers in Kigali were isolated and had to face the full weight of the Presidential Guard, the FAR and the militias, until their comrades could reach the capital.

The push towards Kigali was only one part of a well-planned offensive by the RPF, which involved three main thrusts across an 80-kilometer front, breaking out from positions in the northern demilitarized zone. One arm swept rapidly down the eastern side of the country, close to the Tanzanian border, before separating, with some units turning in to join the battle for the capital and others moving farther south to capture

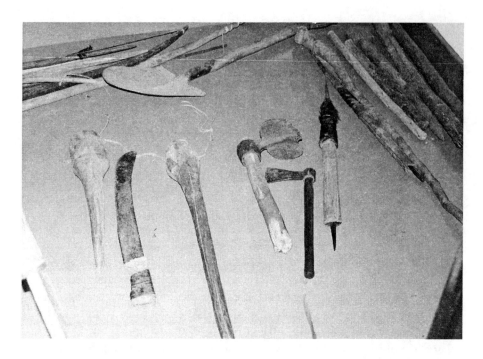

Examples of the types of weapons used in the genocide, from Gisozi Genocide Museum, Kigali.

Kibungo and Rusumo later in the month. On the western flank, after taking Byumba, other divisions pushed towards Ruhengeri and engaged the FAR in the west and northwest, thus splitting the government forces which were at least three times more numerous than the RPF.

As the RPF swept with lightning force across the countryside, its troops began to discover massacre sites and encountered victims fleeing with machete wounds to their heads and bodies, the first evidence for many in the invading force of the trauma which had been unfolding behind government lines. Large numbers of Tutsis took refuge in areas cleared by the RPF as safe havens while the main force moved onwards.

Campaigning Against Continuing Massacres

In the center, the strategy was not to make an all-out assault on Kigali initially, as the potential losses to a lean fighting force could not be risked at the beginning of the war. Therefore, after joining up with the entrenched battalion at the parliament building and having captured part of the city, Kagame ordered his troops to consolidate their positions rather than going for an all-out offensive at once. For almost three months the front line in the fighting ran through the middle of the capital, with RPF and FAR facing each other in places at not more than 100 meters' distance.

Whether forcing the pace of the advance to secure the capital could have saved more civilian lives is uncertain, as the genocide in Kigali had already largely occurred by mid–April. In addition, although tactically adept and with early successes under its belt, the RPF fighting force was still heavily outnumbered and Kagame was mindful of conserving his force for battles elsewhere. Whatever the balance of the argument, from the purely military point of view, the early RPF strategy worked well in securing a large swathe of the country in a matter of weeks. The imperatives of achieving military victory and ending the genocide had to be addressed simultaneously, according to the RPA's commander in chief. "If you saw how we moved, it was trying to deal with both aspects," said Kagame. "But we were very thin on the ground, having to deal with too many places over a very large area in such a short period of time ... so the immediate thing was to move to Kigali, joining with our forces at the parliament building, also continuing to increase the force in there, so it could fight better within Kigali, so it could save people with whatever force we had on the ground and deal with whatever confrontation we had to deal with..."[5]

Dallaire himself summarized the dilemma following a meeting in early April 1994 where he asked Kagame what his strategy was with regard to saving civilians: "I asked Kagame why he wasn't going for the jugular in the opening days of the war," the UN commander recalls. "He ignored the implications of my question ... he knew full well that every day of fighting on the periphery meant certain death for Tutsis behind RGF [FAR] lines."[6]

In the countryside the RPF tried to weaken the government troops on all fronts so that they could not have the latitude to simultaneously carry out massacres behind their battle lines. At the same time, the rebels were taking on the militia groups in the places where they were killing people and providing safe corridors out of the government-held zone for those Tutsis who were trying to escape. As they pushed forward into different areas, the advancing RPF troops sometimes arrived in time to stop killings that were going on, other times coming just too late, discovering fresh bodies as they entered a village where the *interahamwe* or the FAR had already completed their massacres.

The pace of the offensive was exacting on the rebel fighters at the beginning of the campaign. "That first week our people had to fight almost 24 hours without a break ... it was one day after another," Kagame recalled.

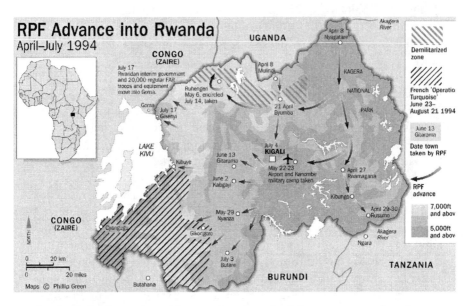

"Nobody had any sleep, I remember everybody's eyes were red.... I spent about four days myself without having an hour of rest, only stopping to have a glass of milk or something small to eat, but that whole first week nobody had even a single moment to rest."[7]

The interim government fled the capital already on the 12th of April, moving to Murambi outside Gitarama and then later, as the RPF's advance continued, to Gisenyi in the northwest. They left only their armed forces in Kigali under the command of General Augustin Bizimungu as Gatsinzi had by now been relieved of his post and banished southwards to Butare, sidelined from the command for his earlier conciliatory actions towards the rebels.

On the international stage, all was confusion at the UN in New York, as the Security Council increasingly received evidence of massive civilian killings in addition to the reports of fighting between government and rebel armies. Each of the major countries with an interest in the conflict had its own agenda to advance at the world body, with some on the Security Council arguing for deployment of reinforcements, others for a total pullout of the UN and still others again demanding a cease-fire before taking further decisions. All agreed on the first priority of sending forces quickly to evacuate the thousands of French, Belgian, American and Italian nationals trapped inside the country. However, after this had been completed, the discussion steadily moved towards the ultimate decision to make a partial withdrawal of UNAMIR from Rwanda in the face of a situation so desperately out of control and in which the UN felt it had neither the mandate nor the resources to cope.

The rhetoric of inaction in New York was in stark contrast to the unfolding nightmare on the ground. On April 21 General Dallaire formally requested reinforcements, insisting that with a force of just 5,000 men he could save thousands of civilians' lives and bring much of the killing to an end. His assessment and recommendation were however, all but ignored and on the same day the Security Council voted to reduce UNAMIR's strength by 90 percent, to a mere 270 men, while Secretary-General Boutros-Ghali continued to call for a cease-fire and a resumption of negotiations.

Meanwhile, the public stance of the new Rwandan government towards the genocide from the night of April 6 onwards would be that it was a natural reaction of the Hutu population in their outrage at the killing of their president by the RPF and their Tutsi collaborators.

By May 23 the airport and nearby Kanombe military camp fell to the RPF, which reduced the intensity of fighting in Kigali. The RPF continued to push southwards and westwards during June and soon the end of government resistance was in sight, although massacres of Tutsis continued in many cases as the FAR and militias retreated westwards.

Controversial French Intervention

In late June, with the hand-wringing at the UN still under way and serious attempts at intervention having been all but blocked by the Clinton administration, with the UK and Belgium also in support of non-intervention, an initiative billed as a humanitarian expedition was finally proposed, financed and dispatched by France. It came as a great relief to many on the Security Council that something was finally being done by somebody. Despite its highly suspect profile as a long-standing supporter of the Habyarimana regime, France received the assent of the UN in a resolution to establish a "humanitarian zone" in the southwest of the country, and on June 23 the first troops of an expeditionary force of 2,500 men began to arrive in Rwanda through Goma airport in eastern Zaire.

Although the French *Opération Turquoise* had been internationally sanctioned, the RPF leadership was strongly opposed to its enemy's old international backer appearing on the scene at the eleventh hour just as its victory was almost complete. In fact, the genocide was almost over by late June and the French forces actually had difficulty in finding people to protect. In the far southwest at Nyarushishi camp near Cyangugu, a group of some 8,000 fleeing Tutsis were protected, although the French force was unable to save smaller groups of victims who were still being massacred in the open countryside by the retreating militias.

Furthermore, the RPF had not expected the French "humanitarian" mission to be so well armed and equipped: the force which Paris sent ultimately included 100 armored vehicles, heavy mortars, fighter bombers, helicopters, ground-attack planes and Mirage reconnaissance aircraft. Far from being a deployment with humanitarian relief as its principal aim, the *Turquoise* deployment was a formidably equipped and well-supported fighting force, especially by central African standards.[8]

Indeed, the original pretext for the French intervention faded from importance within days of their troops arriving on Rwandan soil. In a short time what had originally been approved as a purely humanitarian mission then became an operation to establish a "safe zone." The French forces set about securing a huge chunk of Rwandan territory in the southwest, totaling almost a quarter of the country, which then became known as the *Zone Turquoise*. Despite what amounted to a potentially offensive military presence, the official French stance remained that their actions were driven by humanitarian motives. In early July the prime minister of the day addressed the UN, stating that France "has sent its soldiers out of

A makeshift camp for displaced persons in the French *Zone Turquoise*, July 1994 (UN/DPI photo 186770/J. Isaac 1059L).

a moral duty to act without delay in order to stop the genocide and provide immediate assistance to the threatened populations."[9]

However, the retreating Hutu Power government was almost ecstatic at what it saw as last-minute reinforcements for their own army as well as a protective shield to allow many of their leaders to escape through the *Zone Turquoise*, away from the clutches of the RPF. In the final weeks of fighting the FAR often tried to lead and provoke the French into clashes with the RPF, which could result in their "humanitarian" army being forced onto the offensive. Furthermore, many of the hawks in the French military were spoiling for a fight with the RPF, which they still thought of as something of an upstart army needing to be taught a lesson.

The RPF itself was now concerned that their total victory was in jeopardy and wasted no time in trying to minimize the amount of territory that the French could control. They moved to take Butare in the first week of July, then continued to push westwards where they at last came into contact with the French forces. The closest to a real confrontation that the RPF was to have with the Europeans took place outside Butare at the beginning of July as the rebels were approaching the city. Kagame received a message from the French through General Dallaire instructing him that his troops should not enter the city, where some French soldiers were already stationed. Kagame replied that he knew that people in Butare were being killed and he didn't see the French protecting people there. Dallaire then warned the RPF leader that if his forces came into the city, it would mean confrontation with the French. Kagame, however, was unmoved: "As we parted I told him, 'You can go and tell the French to expect us.' I could see that Dallaire was visibly worried…. He thought there was going to be a confrontation and that we were going to get a bloody nose … I told him we are in the business of fighting so for us it's not anything to have to go and deal with the French."[10]

Around 5 the next morning the RPF entered Butare and just as they were arriving they found that the French were leaving. However, in case there had been any confrontation, Kagame had also stationed a large force on the other side of the town, on the road to Gikongoro, the route which the French were due to take. As the long French convoy of jeeps and trucks was leaving Butare, Kagame's forces stopped them with the intention of checking to see that there were no militias or government leaders trying to escape by hiding inside their vehicles.

"I remember that the French wanted to fight, to force their way across our roadblock," Kagame recalls. "Then they realized that their whole convoy was in an ambush. One of their soldiers who had pointed his gun at us was told that his force was in trouble…. They were told to put their guns down, so they were forced to abandon it and they had to obey and let us search their trucks. It was a convoy of about 25 vehicles. We found one soldier who tried to run, and they shot him dead ... and we picked out a few other people who we suspected were *interahamwe* trying to escape with the convoy...."[11]

Although relations continued to be tense between Kagame and the French command and the two forces came close to confrontation again on one or two occasions, after the Butare incident and the final defeat of the FAR in the northwest two weeks later the French contingent and the RPF managed to avoid engaging each other until the end of *Opération Turquoise* in late August.

With the swearing in of Pasteur Bizimungu as president of a newly appointed Government of National Unity with Paul Kagame as his vice president on July 19, a new chapter in the history of Rwanda was formally opened and the incoming authorities began the long struggle to rebuild from the ruins of genocide.

Resistance at Bisesero

Although the genocide of the Tutsis took place in almost every corner of the countryside, in houses, open fields and numerous public buildings where groups of fleeing civilians sought refuge from the killers, very little resistance to the murderers was offered by their victims, unarmed and helpless as most of them were. For the most part, those who were slaughtered in the genocide had to try to run and hide, or pretend to be already dead in the hope that the killers would leave them. Those who became trapped and were no longer able to run could only wait for the end and pray that they would be finished off quickly, sometimes paying to be killed by a bullet rather than enduring a long and painful death by machete blows.

One major exception to the pattern of defenselessness and desperation stands out in the annals of the grisly period of the genocide, however. The resistance put up by thousands of mostly unarmed Tutsis at Bisesero in Kibuye Province in the west of Rwanda constitutes a memorial in itself to the determination of one major group of the population to not become victims. Kibuye, a lush, mountainous region, was one of the areas of Rwanda with the highest proportion of Tutsis, approaching 50 percent in much of the province. In previous times of ethnic violence, its Tutsi inhabitants had successfully beaten off attacking bands of Hutus by rallying together on their hillsides and showing resistance to the enemy, rather than merely becoming their passive victims.

Vice President Kagame at his swearing-in ceremony in July 1994, Kigali. (From the personal collection of President Paul Kagame.)

With the beginning of the killings in April 1994, an effort was once again made to do just that. Large numbers of Tutsis gathered together on the hills of their community to seek safety in numbers and to make the most of the few weapons which they had to defend themselves against the militias. Mostly, however, they had only farm tools and stones in their feeble armories against the killers' grenades and guns.

On Bisesero's hillsides, the Tutsi inhabitants of the area initially banded into groups and succeeded in beating off the first waves of attackers, although always at great cost in lives to themselves. Each attack claimed hundreds of victims compared to the much smaller casualties on the militias' side. The desperate strategies adopted in battle included trying to mix in with the enemy at close range so that they could not use their firearms, while at the same time attempting to target those who had guns which could be captured for use against them in future assaults.

The struggle on the hillsides of Bisesero continued throughout May and into early June, and the remaining defending Tutsis steadily became weak from their wounds, or from hunger and exposure. In the end, the vast majority only succeeded in postponing their death by a month or so and in the process caused enormous and prolonged suffering to the survivors in their own community.

Still, the women continued to gather stones to throw at the *intera-*

hamwe and often men and women would struggle side by side on the hill-sides as they were cut down together by the murder squads. In the end, those who were too weak to resist could only attempt to hide and hope not to be discovered, or in a last desperate encounter with the *génocidaires*, try to rush towards the ones who had guns, to at least secure a swifter end.[12]

Tragically, due to its distant location in the west of Rwanda, Bisesero was one of the last areas to be liberated by the RPF in 1994. The French troops of *Opération Turquoise* reached the area first, but this did not always mean safety at last for the encircled Tutsis. Kagame called what happened there a "terrible scandal" with the French action in appearing then disappearing at the height of the killings.

> The French came and camped across Lake Kivu in Bukavu and in other areas of Congo. They then crossed the lake and came to Kibuye and we thought they had come to save people who were being killed. They actually came to villages, talked to people and even met some of the people who were resisting and told them to come out of hiding ... then after that they just boarded their boats again and went back over to the Congo. The FAR and *interahamwe* then came back and killed a number of them.[13]

In a final cruel twist for the defenders of Bisesero, some *interahamwe* sympathizers even sought to trick those in hiding by telling them that the French had arrived and that the killing was over and thereby lure them out towards the roadside, after which they called on the militias to come back to those areas to finish off their remaining victims.

Forces of Destruction — Internal and External

The fall of Kigali on July 4, the flight of the FAR from Gisenyi into Zaire on July 17 and the swearing in of the new government in Kigali on July 19 were the key events which marked the end of a tumultuous period in Rwanda's history of which the genocide was the tragic climax. As they fled, the FAR and the militias coerced a great mass of the Hutu population into going into exile with them. In total, some 3.2 million Rwandan Hutu refugees were created between April and July of 1994, mostly ending up in camps in Zaire, Tanzania and Burundi.

The frenzy of mass murder which was unleashed on the night of April 6, 1994, stunned the world into inaction and later, as details emerged, staggered international onlookers by its swiftness and magnitude. In just over

Skulls and other human remains of genocide victims, in Gisozi Genocide Museum, Kigali.

100 days an estimated one million Rwandans died, according to the International Committee of the Red Cross, one of the few international organizations that remained active in Rwanda throughout the slaughter. Although other observers have reported that the number who died was much lower and the estimate of around 800,000 dead appears regularly in publications and media items referring to the genocide, the one million figure has been confirmed as likely both by the UN Rwanda Emergency Office (UNREO) and by actual figures calculated later by the new Rwandan authorities themselves after the bloodshed had ceased.[14] What is not disputed is that the vast majority of the dead were Tutsis, killed in a countrywide systematic slaughter aimed not at intimidating them as a group, not at forcing them into exile, but in a willful, organized attempt at their total elimination as a race from Rwanda.

If the forces which led to the orgy of bloodletting in Rwanda in 1994 were first and foremost ethnic in nature, beyond that the factors which provoked genocide were also economic, demographic and geopolitical in different measures and at different stages over a period of almost a century of the country's history.

For those inclined to lay blame on the outsiders who managed Rwanda's affairs in earlier times, it is true that the seeds of violent conflict were already sown by the country's former colonial masters. First the Germans but more particularly and acutely the Belgian colonists took a system characterized by an unusual and delicate balance of feudal coexistence and strained it to the breaking point. They did this through their decision to steadily reverse their traditional support for the Tutsis, built up over forty years, ultimately replacing it with unconditional support for the Hutu ethnicity from 1959 onwards.

Although the crashing of gears which this culturally misaddressed and developmentally mistimed U-turn brought about led to violence, dislocation and hardship for a generation of Tutsi exiles beginning in 1959, it did not lead immediately to wholesale genocide. However, through the reinforcement of injustice and by acquiescing in the power of the Habyarimana regime's exclusionist society, the seeds of future conflict were undoubtedly sown.

Three decades after its independence, Rwanda's demographic upsurge made reconciliation less and less likely as the Kigali regime declared that the country was "full up" and there was no room for returning refugees. The plunge in the world prices of cash crops, coffee in particular, spelled further trouble for a country trying to quell the mounting demands of extremism while at the same time sharing an ever-decreasing national pie among an increasing number of mouths.

The population of Rwanda in 1959 was 2.6 million; at the August 1991 census it had grown to 7.1 million, by early 1994 it was already over 7.7 million and demographic projections at the time put the 2000 population at over 10 million. Against a plummeting GNP and an increasing proportion of scarce resources going toward military expenditures, the stable but artificial paradise of the Rwanda of the 1970s to mid–1980s was doomed to implode.

As for outside geopolitical influences, the winds of change favoring independence that were sweeping across Africa hastened the call for a republic and hence the need to replace the monarchy and its elite which had held sway for centuries over Rwanda's land of a thousand hills. The cold war forced different western nations into accepting and cultivating new client states practicing standards of human rights that would be unacceptable in their own societies. In Africa, however, the priority was influence and ideology, not internal rights, and so rulers with otherwise questionable records were bestowed with military aid and political muscle all in the name of maintaining their solidarity with the appropriate first-world ideology — or in the case of Rwanda and France, loyalty to a curiously powerful language-based alignment.

Why Hutu, Why Tutsi, Why Rwanda?

Not all of the root causes of Rwanda's descent into apocalypse can be blamed on colonization, the population explosion and outside imposed influences. Many other small African nations suffered from similar problems in the late twentieth century, and while some endured civil wars and ethnic conflict, none underwent the same wholesale genocidal explosion that Rwanda experienced.

Looking elsewhere for parallels, one might point to Sierra Leone, where disaffected youths and rebellious army dissidents combined under the leadership of Foday Sankoh's Revolutionary United Front (RUF) to wreak terror and mayhem through a small country plagued by a long tradition of corruption in government. Sierra Leone's civil wars of the 1990s were largely fuelled by the potential for protagonists to share in the spoils of the country's considerable mineral wealth, none of which, however, could be said to exist in Rwanda. In that situation, too, the country's European masters undoubtedly left scars on the social landscape, but the British could never be said to have attempted to engineer major changes in Sierra Leone's social and ethnic hierarchy during their years of colonial rule.

Paradoxically, in neighboring Liberia, a country which never had been formally colonized by a European power, closer parallels to the Rwandan experience are to be found. Africa's oldest republic, created in 1847 with American sponsorship but not tutelage, was effectively governed for a century and a half by a Christian ruling class of like geographic origins but different ethnicity from indigenous Liberians. In the twentieth century, the Americo-Liberian settlers who based themselves mostly in the country's coastal towns ran one of the region's quite successful economies for decades, mostly for their own benefit and that of the foreign corporations that they invited to invest there.

But in Liberia in the 1950s and 1960s, as in Rwanda, the children of peasants and laborers from Liberia's interior increasingly began to visit the coastal settlements of their republic and saw the houses and lifestyle and education of their compatriots. Calls for a share in the economic spoils were not far behind and in the absence of real democratic change in the country, an indigenous Liberian, Sergeant Samuel Doe, took power by force in 1980. Once in the state house in Liberia's capital, Monrovia, for a decade Doe sought to reverse the long-standing grip on power and patronage which the Americo-Liberian economic aristocracy had held. In this respect his role and actions were not unlike those of Habyarimana and Kayibanda before him, in asserting the rights of the hitherto disadvantaged Hutus in Rwanda.

But by early 1990, the year when the RPF first launched Rwanda's civil war in earnest, the forces of reaction also overtook Liberia and a new version of the old coastal elite was brought back to power in Monrovia through an invading rebel movement. Charles Taylor and his National Patriotic Front were welcomed by some as peacemakers, but after arranging to be "democratically" elected in 1997 he increasingly turned from civilian government to what he knew better, sponsoring civil war in neighboring countries with a wealth of resources to boot.

Lastly and perhaps most pertinently, an image of what Rwanda could have become lies in its former twin kingdom to the south, the Republic of Burundi. However, in Burundi the Tutsis had managed to hold on to power after independence. Even after the country elected a Hutu president, Melchior Ndadaye, in 1993, the army was always under Tutsi control and indeed it was an extremist army faction which kidnapped and murdered Ndadaye later that year. Following the assassination, widespread attacks against Tutsi civilians occurred, which were followed by equally brutal army reprisals against Hutus, but all-out inter-community warfare never erupted on the scale which Rwanda experienced in 1994.

In the Burundi case, not only was ethnic side-taking by the patron European powers and its institutions less pronounced, but the diplomacy conducted by the international community was also more inspired and skillful than in Rwanda. In Bujumbura, Ahmedou Ould Abdallah of Mauritania, the UN Special Representative, struggled during the 1990s, ultimately with a degree of success, to keep the two communities from veering down the path to mutual destruction while Rwanda descended into the abyss.

Similarities in the mechanisms of violence and their propagators among the above three cases and Rwanda are also apparent. The youth unemployment factor in these economically floundering African states provided both rationale for and momentum to the killing which their societies suffered. As well as a unique chance to strike back at repression and authority while engaging in some unrestrained looting into the bargain, violence became both an opportunity and an outlet for the jobless, uneducated Rwandan youths who in 1994 signed up for a spree of destruction, killing and mutilation.

In Rwanda, young Hutu men, educationally and economically deprived[15] were easy recruits to the ranks of the *interahamwe* and *impuzamugambi* militias who began to roam the streets of Kigali in April 1994, drunk on beer, often clad in the multicolored *kitenge* tunic and trousers which served as this killer youth cult's uniform. All had one thing in common: a chance had suddenly risen in the midst of a society which had hitherto offered them nothing, to take revenge with impunity if only for a brief time, on the group which had in their eyes been responsible for their deprivation.

The economics of discrimination were very much at the heart of what was otherwise a caste conflict, in Rwanda as in other war-ravaged African countries. However, was the role of the Belgian colonist in its ethnically based patronage and deliberate polarization of Rwandan society the overriding factor which made the outcome in their colony so much more catastrophic than elsewhere?

The nature of Rwandan society as a highly organized, disciplined entity, as a population used to following instructions without challenge, unquestionably facilitated the task of mobilizing the Hutu masses to pick up their machetes and begin the gruesome task which the genocide's ringleaders had set for them.

The tradition of *umuganda*, whereby peasants gave several hours a week of compulsory labor to the service of the regime, was well instilled into peasant life. Whatever tasks were assigned by the authorities that week, the populace unquestioningly carried out. Even the name *interahamwe*, "those who work together," points to the task-oriented, obligatory nature of the genocide's institutions, far removed from the chaotic mayhem of rebellions in West Africa, Somalia or other African insurrections. And so it was that when the Rwandan state ordered the people to "clear the bush" or "cut down the tall trees" in the macabre figurative language of the genocide, the people had no hesitation in going about getting it done.

The special contrasting nature of the part played by authoritarian society in the Rwandan tragedy is summarized by Africanist and historian Gérard Prunier: "In Liberia and Somalia the state has collapsed; in Sudan it totters on the brink.... Here [in Rwanda] we have the exact opposite. The genocide happened not because the state was weak but on the contrary because it was so totalitarian and strong that it had the capacity to make its subjects obey absolutely any order, including one of mass slaughter."[16]

Imperative of Revolution

Such had been the rigidity of the pre-independence Rwandan hierarchy that those favoring a Hutu takeover could not envisage any kind of gradual transition. For the emerging Hutu leadership in 1959 and their colonial backers, the chief obstacle beyond displacing the Tutsis from power was to overcome the ingrained tendency to passivity and subservience. René Lemarchand, an historian and observer of the period, has described the severity of the mental obstacles to assuming power: "One of the most arduous tasks facing the Hutu intelligentsia ... was to break this habit of passive obedience ... the breaking of these cultural norms ... released tremendous psychological insecurities among the Hutu peasantry. If insecurity bred suspicion, both led to aggression."[17]

There was yet another factor in the genocide which allowed so many to be annihilated in such efficient fashion: the constant and pervasive use of the hate radio RTLMC. For weeks if not months before the killing began, the radio station increasingly began to broadcast specifics of what would happen and what to do when it happened, all the while embellishing the demonic portrait of the Tutsis and the threat from the RPF *inyenzi* in the Hutu population's imagination.

By April 6, the night of the downing of the presidential plane, RTLMC was broadcasting lists of names and locations of priority victims for assassination; later, as surviving Tutsis tried to escape, it read out car registration plates of fugitive civilians and announced on the radio when a targeted person or family had been killed, to more efficiently direct the killer squads on to other objectives for elimination around the countryside.

General Dallaire had repeatedly advised his headquarters of the threat from and the role of the RTLMC in propagating the massacres and had asked for the authority to neutralize their broadcasts. His request was denied, although the RPA did briefly manage to silence their transmissions following a mortar hit on the radio station in Kigali.

Elsewhere in the UN system in the region, however, things worked better. In Bujumbura, on the night of April 6, following the plane crash in which the Burundian president had also been killed, Special Envoy Abdallah gathered together a handful of key diplomats and senior UN colleagues and went straight to the national radio station. They broadcast a plea for calm and even denied initially that President Cyprien Ntaryamira had been killed, to buy time and try to defuse the situation. Ultimately, in Burundi, there was no major violence in April of 1994 and relative calm was reestablished in the country after only a day or two of tension.[18]

Given the power of the state over the people and the means to motivate large numbers of killers into eliminating their ethnic cousins, the issue remains of why those in power opted for the objective of a "final solution" to eliminate the Tutsis from the face of Rwanda. Even given a fear of defeat by the RPA and long-harbored Hutu longings for a swift and comprehensive revenge, conceivably the FAR and the Presidential Guard could have defeated the RPA on the battlefield, especially with foreign assistance, while discrediting the latter as the aggressors in breaking the Arusha agreements. They could even have gotten away with engaging in limited internal killings to eliminate the political opposition.

After all, the ordinary Tutsis inside the country had no military means at their disposal and the army which Habyarimana had steadily built up by 1994 totaled some 39,000 men, over double the strength of the invading RPF. But once defeat on the battlefield had been sustained there could be no way back. Even with the most revisionist interpretation of the events of April–July 1994, and (with the possible exception of Paris) with neither sympathy for their predicament nor justification for having orchestrated the genocide, the days of Hutu Power in Rwanda were doomed.

The explanation for the imperative to a final solution can better be found in the almost mystical characterization of the Tutsi threat which had been generated in the minds of the Hutus over the decades since the proclamation of the Bahutu Manifesto.[19] With its enshrinement of the aims of Rwanda's downtrodden Hutu people striving to unburden themselves of what it characterized as the Tutsi scourge, the 1957 document could be compared to a type of African *Mein Kampf*, providing a pseudo-scientific but altogether ideological justification for the need to rise up and eliminate the oppressor race.

Published by a circle of Hutu intellectuals, the Bahutu Manifesto was intended as much for external as internal consumption, as the newly assertive Hutu leadership needed to win over the UN and the Belgians to its wider cause prior to independence to secure support for their assuming power from the monarchy and the Tutsis.

Ominously, one of the recommendations which it contained was that the *ubwoko*— the ethnic designation of every citizen as either Hutu, Tutsi or Twa on their identity card — be maintained through their transition to power. No clearer signal could have been given that the intention of the Manifesto's authors was not to move towards a multi-ethnic, unified society of "Rwandans" but rather that it was the Hutus, as the group who had been historically wronged, who were destined to take power and eliminate the root causes of the decades-old persecution by their racial oppressors.

5

REBUILDING FOREIGN RELATIONS

The triumph of Paul Kagame's rebel army in mid–1994 not only brought sweeping changes to the demographic and political landscape of Rwanda; it also brought about a revolution in the conduct of the country's external affairs. Relations with the UN and other international bodies had been strained by the experience of Rwanda's abandonment during the genocide and differences over the delivery of justice for the guilty. Moreover, financial assistance, even for purely humanitarian reconstruction work inside Rwanda, was also extremely hard to come by in the early years after the establishment of the new transitional government in July 1994.

Throughout more than three decades since independence, first the Kayibanda and then Habyarimana regimes had benefited from well-established client relationships, first with the former colonial power, Belgium, and increasingly after 1990 with France. Paris effectively became the unquestioning defender and protector of the MRND ruling elite, both at home and on the international stage. In addition, as long as the appropriate policies were adhered to, World Bank money flowed, and other donors, such as Germany and particularly Switzerland, would generously make funds available from their taxpayers' wallets for the development of Rwanda. While the World Bank and others began to balk at continuing their assistance in the light of clear evidence of massive diversion of funds towards military expenditures in the early 1990s, for the most part their responses were bureaucratic rather than proactive.

The policy of the west towards increasing tension in Rwanda became focused on the attainment of a power-sharing government and success at the Arusha negotiations. However, the sponsors of the peace process continued towards their aim, all the while in seeming ignorance of the real agenda which was consuming Rwanda from inside. While they talked in Arusha, Rwanda descended into a cauldron of extremist politics and began its preparations for an ethnically based popular coup with premeditated mass murder on its immediate agenda. The international community's policy failed and the end result of the unrestricted rise of extremism in Rwanda was the genocide which lasted from April until June of 1994.

However, by July 1994, with Habyarimana dead and his leadership deposed and disgraced in the eyes of the world, a massive vacuum in Rwandan external relations suddenly existed. This occurred at the very time when the incoming government desperately needed friends and of course financial assistance for recovery and rehabilitation. As the realization dawned on them that a swift and massive destruction of human life had taken place in three short months under their very watch, many UN Security Council members and other traditional western donors preferred to hide their embarrassment. They began to busy themselves with issues in other regions of the world or concentrated their efforts on funneling aid contributions to the millions of Rwandan refugees outside the country's borders in Zaire, Tanzania and Burundi.

Furthermore, through its *Zone Turquoise,* France was now facilitating safe passage away from Rwanda (and from justice) for leading extremist members of the old regime and its successor interim government. President Mitterand and France's Foreign Affairs Ministry at the Quay d'Orsay then actively worked to block the transfer of funds to the new Rwandan government. In international bodies such as the World Bank and European Union, France argued that the aid money earmarked for Rwanda should be released only when the millions of refugees who fled during the genocide had returned to their country.

In some cases, through the use of its military presence inside Rwanda until August 1994, the French authorities were successful in arranging asylum in other French-speaking African countries for leading members of the former government, while the most favored fugitives were accommodated inside France itself.

Among the latter was Agathe Habyarimana, *akazu* empress and arch-supporter of the Hutu hard line, together with her family and close entourage. The former first lady continued to live in Paris with her family for many years, remaining active in anti–RPF exile politics, living in comfort and security at the invitation of the Mitterand administration and its successors. She remained in France long after many others, formerly in positions of leadership in her late husband's regime, had been apprehended or extradited for their part in the planning and execution of the genocide.

The Price of Unpopularity

Rwanda, then, in July 1994 was desperately in need of friends and contributors to sustain its existence and to ensure its recovery as a country of returning exiles and traumatized, devastated survivors. With some in the international community overtly hostile and others preferring to look the other way, who would take up the cause of the diminutive Rwandan state struggling to survive?

Just as France had long been established as the patron of the previous government, it seemed logical to observers and has often since been claimed that Uganda, as the country where the RPF leadership was spawned, would now be the natural supporter of the new government of President Bizimungu and Vice President Kagame. On a closer evaluation, however, Uganda at the time fit uncomfortably at best into the role of sponsor of the new interlacustrine regime, partly because of President Yoweri Museveni's continuing domestic difficulties and partly due to the financial constraints on his own treasury.

Despite the economic and social advances made in recent years, Uganda in the early 1990s was still very much dependent, in its turn, on foreign backers and international institutions for its economic progress and for its leader's survival in power.

If there had been a turning point or at least a harbinger of change in geopolitical realignments in the African Great Lakes region, the critical moment was probably the very beginning of the 1990s, the time when the RPF launched its attack on northern Rwanda. It was then that the wheels were set in motion for a more active political involvement of the major western powers. From that time, on the French side at least, a more proactive military role was embarked upon, with the first deployment of French troops in defensive positions on Rwandan soil in a strategic involvement rather than for the evacuation or protection of their own nationals.

France, with its new role at the heart of European policy-making and a strong and often independent voice in international affairs, committed to supporting militarily a tiny but increasingly repressive regime in the center of Africa. Even if Uganda was the true aggressor in the October 1990 war, which Habyarimana and some in French policy-making circles claimed, few countries other than France in the modern era would have made such a special commitment to overt military action in support for the nasty anti-democratic clique that Rwanda's ruling party had by then become.

October 1990: Behind the Curtains of Diplomacy

Whether strategic, subjective, linguistic-political or a uniquely Gallic combination of all three, France clearly took a decision to raise its involvement in Rwanda's fate from late 1990 onwards. But, other than the fact that the Rwandans who invaded their country in October of that year were English-speaking, and had material support as well as rear bases in Uganda, an English speaking country, did any major Anglo-Saxon power truly take an interest in opposing them at that stage? Was there any substance to the theory of a long-term "Anglo-Saxon plot" to erode French influence in Africa by sponsoring rebel armies such as the RPF against Rwanda? What policies were world leaders pursuing at the official level and what was being said in diplomatic circles at the time of the outbreak of the October 1990 war?

By coincidence, but not unusually in the context of *coups d'état* in Africa, Rwandan president Juvenal Habyarimana was overseas on the eve of the October 1990 invasion. Like Uganda's Yoweri Museveni, he was attending the United Nations' annual meetings in New York, where the ambassadors of France and Belgium as well as the representatives of the U.S. administration of George Bush senior were also in attendance.

On October 2, the day after the invasion, President Bush and U.S. Secretary of State Baker hosted a meeting of African leaders in the Waldorf-Astoria hotel, just as the news was arriving that Rwanda had been invaded from Uganda by a breakaway group of Ugandan army soldiers.

A bilateral discussion between Habyarimana and Museveni was quickly convened, at which the Ugandan leader denied knowledge of the incursion. However, realizing that western intervention was now being provoked, before leaving the United States, Museveni called the Belgian and French ambassadors to urge them to not send troops to Rwanda.

As for the American approach, the Bush administration, with an election only a month away, considered its position as one of relative disinterest. In 1990, it was engaged in negotiations involving Angola, Ethiopia and Sudan, as well as having lesser diplomatic involvement in the conflicts in both Liberia and Mozambique, with no strong interest in adding Rwanda to the list of African trouble spots where it could become committed to taking sides or brokering peace talks.

Despite the Ugandan leader's recommendations, the French in particular accepted Habyarimana's assessment that his country was being invaded by a foreign army and dispatched a strong force in support of

Kigali, ultimately turning the tide of the invasion in the government's favor. But while France took a strong stance on the Rwandan side, there was no evidence of overt U.S. involvement on the side of Uganda or in support of the RPF, despite the fact that Ugandan army officers, such as Kagame, had been on training inside the United States at the exact time of the outbreak of hostilities in 1990. Despite suspicions that have been expressed that he was somehow part of a long-term U.S. strategic plan for central Africa, Kagame was not known to the U.S. authorities as a Rwandan rebel leader until he told them he was preparing to leave for the war, according to his own version of events.

Although Kagame was still in the country at the outbreak of the war, the U.S. was ignorant of the status of the person they had with them under training as a Ugandan officer. "They really didn't understand how connected I was, that's my guess," Kagame said later. "They must have come to know about it when I had left. When I was there and I was openly explaining to the people at the college perhaps the information didn't flow quickly to Washington or to other areas where they would want to know … and by the time perhaps they got to be interested I had already left."[1]

Admittedly, around the time of the October 1990 war, both the United States and the United Kingdom were strategically present in Uganda, in the form of the Defense Intelligence Agency (DIA) and MI6, respectively, as part of their programs of support for the Museveni regime. Training of Ugandan army units, which was inevitably one form which U.S. assistance took, would certainly have extended to the NRA's Rwandan recruits, although explicit planning and assistance in an RPF offensive would be difficult to substantiate.

Indeed, as the conflict dragged on into 1991 and 1992 and the warring parties together with the internal opposition began to get involved in the marathon Arusha negotiation process, the U.S. if anything showed willingness to reconsider its economic aid to Uganda as a consequence of support for the RPF in its cross-border warfare with the Rwandan army.

In a crucial meeting in June of 1992 in Paris between the RPF leadership and the Rwandan government, attended by Ugandan minister of foreign affairs Paul Ssemmogere, U.S. Undersecretary Herman J. Cohen made it clear to the Ugandan side that continuing support for rebel incursions into neighboring countries from bases inside Uganda put the United States government's support for Ugandan economic recovery at risk. Although not yet officially U.S. policy, he specifically told Ssemmogere that humanitarian funds being sent to aid the hundreds of thousands of displaced Rwandans[2] created by the war would count against economic aid to Uganda.[3]

Uganda therefore was not a meaningful backer of the rebel army that attacked Rwanda from its territory in 1990 and finally took over in 1994. President Museveni, a Hima by ethnicity, was an ally and sympathizer but not an overt partner of the RPF, despite assertions by conspiracy theorists to the contrary. Skeptics have pointed to his hurried phone calls to world capitals in October 1990 while at meetings in the United States or the fact that thousands of soldiers of the RPF invasion force assembled in broad daylight in the football stadium at the Ugandan border town of Kabale in September 1990 in preparation for the attack on Rwanda. Such evidence allegedly proves the existence of a joint Tutsi-Hima plot to dominate the central African region by military means.

However, the background, origins and motivations of the Rwandan Tutsis point to a different interpretation of events. Museveni's actions in late 1989 in dispatching Kagame to the United States and depriving Fred Rwigyema of the defense portfolio show that he was wary of their intentions, despite the fact that they had all fought against a common enemy during the early days of the NRA.

Indeed, the RPF had always had its own agenda, which it was determined to pursue with or without Ugandan backing. When the struggle for Rwanda began in earnest in April 1994, Alison des Forges, a veteran observer of Rwandan affairs and Human Rights Watch analyst, commented: "What is going on inside Rwanda is a vigorous, homegrown, autonomous movement,"[4] referring to the committed battalions of the RPF who had just invaded their homeland at the time.

If Uganda was not a true backer of the RPF in its mission to retake Rwanda, neither was the United States, at least in the early days of the rebellion. Washington did not take sides nor show interest in any serious diplomatic involvement in Rwanda prior to 1992, and the United States had no treaty-based background or historical reasons for supporting the incoming transitional regime when it took power in July 1994.

Beginning in 1992, however, with a floundering peace process and mounting insecurity in Rwanda, U.S. Ambassador Bruce Flatten in Kigali recommended an increased negotiating role for the U.S. in the situation, but with a conflict resolution role in mind, rather than in pursuit of any strategic interest or sponsorship of a particular regime. As the protagonists moved towards the opening of the peace conference in Arusha in August of 1992, intransigence on the part of both parties to accommodation of the others' demands became more problematic.

Habyarimana, supported by France, continued to resist the return of the Tutsi refugees while referring to the "Ugandan invasion," and for its part the RPF insisted on the removal of the Rwandan president from power as a precondition for the signing of a peace agreement. Worse still, the polemic about an "Anglo-Saxon" invasion was becoming more frequent in French political circles, irritating Washington and making it harder for a U.S.–French jointly sponsored agreement to be negotiated.

Instead of France putting pressure on the MRND to stop arms purchases and reverse the Kigali regime's support for extremism, President Mitterand unquestioningly allowed his friend the Rwandan president to continue rearming while playing for time at Arusha; on the other hand, the U.S., in its eager sponsorship of an Ugandan private-sector African economic miracle, failed to make Kampala impart the pressure on the RPF which could have averted hostilities. A reduction in tacit Ugandan support and a curtailment of cross-border supply lines could have helped secure a less aggressive stance from the rebels and thereby ease the pressures which the threat of war was bringing to bear on the Kigali leadership.

The Anglo-Saxon Response: Hesitancy or Hypocrisy?

For the United States, there were to be further reasons for hesitation: in the intervening year and a half from Arusha's launch to the start of the genocide, involvement in Somalia had led to debacle and a desire on the part of the Clinton administration for disengagement from world trouble spots in general and Africa in particular. In the summer of 1993 in Mogadishu, in the course of a rescue attempt in the heart of the Somali capital, 18 U.S. soldiers and hundreds of Somalis had been killed. The impact on public opinion and the administration's appetite for further peacekeeping missions was dramatic. Furthermore, the cost for the United States was large and mounting: not only did the U.S. owe some $900 million in arrears to the United Nations, a sum which the Congress was reluctant to authorize, but it was also responsible for one third of ongoing peacekeeping operations in the world, including the costly presence in the former Yugoslavia.

These developments led to the publication of a presidential directive, which, fittingly, was issued in the midst of the genocide in May 1994, but whose spirit had already begun to influence U.S. decision makers in the months before. At the time when the UN was grasping desperately for leadership in formulating its response to the mounting Rwanda crisis, the U.S. was deciding to restrict its future peacekeeping involvements according to strict criteria, including: the pre-existence of a cease-fire and a commitment to a peace process between the parties in conflict; co-involvement of regional or sub-regional organizations; the formulation of a precise mandate; the existence of a clear political goal; and last but not least, that the safety of UN personnel could reasonably be assured.[5]

The impact of this U.S. policy in early 1994 was to impede the UN Security Council from moving to intervene in the genocide and to paralyze the actors on the ground in Rwanda who urgently needed the authority and the resources to prevent the massacres. But the consequences for the Americans' own credibility were perhaps even more harmful in embittering relations with the victims of the genocide. One tragic but farcical result stemmed from the officially enforced reluctance to use the "G" word as a description of what was going on between April and July 1994 in Rwanda.

This policy led the State Department, at the time under Warren Christopher, to issue as late as June of 1994 statements such as, "Although there have been acts of genocide, all the murders cannot be put in that category."[6]

In fact, while the United States had wanted to close the UN mission in Kigali altogether, other non-permanent members of the Security Council, such as the Czech Republic, New Zealand and Nigeria, all wanted to give the Arusha peace process more time to work and pointed to the resources which had been allocated to former Yugoslavia as a standard which should also be followed in the case of Rwanda.

However, the Anglo-Saxons were against giving the Rwandan peace process too much time and money, in contrast to the massive commitments that they had been willing to make in the name of peace for Bosnia. President Clinton was eager to show the U.S. Congress that he was taking a tough stance on new peacekeeping ventures, and the British echoed the American line, evoking the Somalia experience in justification. After the genocide began, UK Ambassador to the UN Sir David Hannay warned that intervention in Rwanda could lead to "a repetition of Somalia and its well-known dire consequences" and the UK envoy also objected to the use of the term "genocide" in late April 1994, reminding the Security Council that peacekeeping was not appropriate in the absence of a cease-fire between the protagonists in the conflict.

What any mildly seasoned observer of modern conflicts in Africa could have discerned was that there was almost no similarity between the conflict in Somalia, with its anarchy and in-fighting between rival warlords, and the genocide in Rwanda. Despite depictions in the media of a Rwandan civil war involving "ancient tribal animosities" and "chaotic fighting between warring factions," which may have been the case in Mogadishu seven months earlier, this was far from an accurate description of what happened in Rwanda in April 1994. A better description of the situation was that a civil war may have been under way, as in Somalia, but "...so was genocide, and genocide does not take place in anarchy or chaos. The genocide in Rwanda was a planned, calculated and organized campaign intended to eliminate a human group, the Tutsi. It was a slaughter at a speed not seen since the Nazi extermination programme against the Jews."[7]

Britain therefore justified a similar non-interventionist stance in the same way as the United States, citing the Somalia experience and the inappropriateness of peacekeeping for the Rwanda situation, even though Britain had neither suffered directly in Somalia as the U.S. had, nor was it in such a situation of political need to demonstrate budgetary prudence as the U.S. administration was at the time. However, the UK's Foreign and Commonwealth Office (FCO) had other reasons which the Americans did not have for wanting to keep out of Rwanda.

British policy in Africa until the early 1990s was mostly concerned with the Commonwealth countries and francophone Rwanda was not a member; indeed, the FCO had little desire for a commitment in a country where France already had such a close involvement and where the regime at the center of the genocide was an established French client state with close ties to President Mitterand. The British ambassador to Rwanda, William Clay, doubled as the High Commissioner to Uganda and only covered Rwanda and Burundi for the FCO on a non-resident basis. In short, there was no particular policy towards Rwanda; it was not perceived as being in Britain's sphere of influence and the FCO had no interest in any deeper involvement than necessary in the little African country's increasingly messy affairs.

Despite this, Britain did have a policy on human rights as well as being a signatory, like the United States, to the 1948 Convention on the Prevention and Punishment of the Crime of Genocide. Furthermore, the British foreign secretary, Douglas Hurd, had established the FCO's first human rights policy department in 1992. Both he and Prime Minister John Major professed themselves in public statements to being committed to using the UK's armed forces in support of this policy, both before and after Rwanda's genocide. In a speech in South Africa in September of 1994, Major referred to "an entirely new effort at preventative diplomacy being long overdue ... to develop a new mechanism ... with our friends in Africa ... to head off conflicts before they become unstoppable."[8]

Despite these legally binding international commitments, human rights policy initiatives and laudable public pronouncements, just a few months before Major's South Africa tour the UK had been almost nowhere to be seen when a clear and massive violation of human rights was taking place at the heart of the African continent.

When Kofi Annan, head of UN Peacekeeping Operations, finally requested soldiers and equipment from a total of 55 member states in May of 1994, the only offers of troops came from African countries, while Britain offered 50 unarmed trucks and the United States offered 14 armored personnel carriers. The U.S. shipment became interminably delayed by U.S. government bureaucracy as well as wrangling over the cost, while the British trucks never arrived in Rwanda at all.

In late 1994, therefore, although the new Rwandan Transitional Government had its active opponents abroad, it had little to rely on in the way of help from powerful allies. With only a mildly supportive but constrained regime in Uganda and a minimal core of humanitarian actors still on the ground, it was time to go in search of international backers using the tools and resources which could produce the best results. The power of the overseas diaspora was important in this effort, but in winning the hearts, minds and monetary muscle of the international community, the leverage to be gained through strength was to prove more valuable than the initial appeals for emergency and humanitarian assistance.

This approach, underlying the imperative of ensuring the security of Rwanda's borders and combined with a skillful and constant evocation of the feelings of genocide guilt on the part of the west, proved a formidable strategy in the RPF's search for powerful allies from among the world community. The public relations successes which soon accompanied Paul Kagame's already established prowess in military matters was to make the difference between survival and submergence for the embryonic government — and it doubtless didn't do any harm among Kigali's new allies that many in the RPF leadership preferred to speak English when they went abroad.

Discovering the CNN Factor — the Hard Way

In July 1994 the new government in Kigali appealed for emergency funds for reconstruction. However, the world was busy watching millions of Rwandan refugees in camps outside the country's borders. The impact of what has become known as the "CNN factor" meant that the lion's share of aid to the region was sent to the refugees, and not the survivors of the genocide. This fact, combined with French determination to keep the new government as vulnerable as possible, meant that for many long months the funds which were urgently needed to relaunch the Rwandan economy were effectively delayed or diverted from reaching those who needed them most.

The European Union approved 300 million ecus[9] in emergency aid for Rwanda in July 1994, but at the insistence of Paris, nearly all of this went to fund the shoals of non-governmental organizations that were setting up shop in and around Kigali. Then in September of 1994, at a meeting convened to resolve the blocking of assistance due to the non-payment of the Habyarimana government's arrears of debt to the IMF, after long negotiations the paltry $6 million required was released by international donors. At least then Rwanda was technically able to borrow again, as according to World Bank and IMF rules, no new loans could be granted when the country was in default on interest payments due from previous credits.

Even in the urgent situation in which the country found itself in 1994, the international institutions could not find a means to allow for the fact that the arrears had been incurred by a government which had orchestrated the genocide. Moreover, it apparently meant nothing to the bankers and diplomats that much of the debt left outstanding by the former Rwandan republic had been used directly or indirectly to purchase arms for its army and their allies in the Hutu Power death squads. Asking the victims of genocide to pay the bills of their persecutors was not unlike the recorded practice of the authorities in Nazi Germany who would require Jews being deported to concentration camps to pay for their own train tickets to perdition.

Within the institutions, genuine efforts were made by some to resolve the injustice of the situation while their own member states played neocolonial political games. Francisco Aguirre-Sacasa, director of the World Bank in 1994, spoke for Rwanda's supporters: "My own impression is that this is a serious government...they are concerned about national reconciliation. Some are even passionate about national reconciliation ..." he said, urging, "we have to help this government get back on its feet."[10]

Things seemed to be improving in January 1995 when a donors' "Round Table" meeting was convened in Geneva and the world's wealthiest nations pledged their support for the reconstruction of Rwanda. A total in excess of $700 million for the "Rwanda Emergency" was pledged at this conference. However, the bureaucratic mechanisms of international aid disbursement and the imperative of showing intent in public versus fulfillment in practice proved to be powerful negative forces in the Rwanda situation as they were elsewhere. One year after the January 1995 donor meeting, no more than $68 million had been disbursed from the funds pledged, of which about one third went to the direct support of the government while almost $20 million was used up in the repayment of loans to UN agencies and the World Bank.

Funding promised from the European Union encountered a similar fate. According to the minister of planning in Kigali, in 1996, out of 284 million ecus pledged by the EU for Rwanda, only 48 million ecus were spent inside the country. In sum, spread across the different beneficiaries of the region, the two million refugees outside the country received around two thirds of the total and the six million survivors received one third. Furthermore, the USAID and the EU, the two main supporters of the Tanzanian, Burundian and Zairian camp structures, revealed that during that period each was spending over $400,000 *per day* on the care and maintenance of the Hutu exile population.[11]

Credibility at Last

Beyond the inefficiencies and hypocrisy of the world of international assistance-giving, the main inhibiting factor in many potential donors' minds related to the durability of the RPF-led Transitional Government in Kigali. The French international spoiler campaign apart, it was not obvious to many that the new authorities would succeed in establishing control and returning the country to a semblance of order; indeed, if the most hawkish French line (and that of the rapidly retraining and rearming FAR in Zaire) were to be believed, a re-invasion by the former government forces might be imminent, entailing a reinstallation of some elements of the former regime — and possibly in the minds of the doubtful donors — a return flight of the RPF to Uganda with their taxpayers' contributions to boot.

Credibility and sustainability therefore had to be established. However, first the diplomatic damage just wrought by the former regime and its supporters had to be reversed, before the new government could hope to make progress. Among the absurd and obstructive situations which persisted at the international level was the continued presence of the Rwandan ambassador to the UN, Jean-Damascène Bizimana, who, as representative of the genocidal interim government, was permitted to maintain his functions throughout the slaughter and thus defend the position of the killers in front of the world forum of leaders. Furthermore, Rwanda at the time held one of the non-permanent seats at the UN Security Council, giving Bizimana the perfect opportunity to argue the case for the "killings by both sides" and the "authorities trying to restore order" interpretations of events. His ability to remain as the mouthpiece of the *géno-*

cidaires even as they fled the country before the invading RPF certainly helped to spread confusion among onlookers and delayed recognition of the new government as it sought to establish itself in the world's eyes.

On July 15, however, the charade finally came to an end as the Clinton administration publicly declared that it no longer recognized the interim government of Rwanda; the following day, thirteen ministers of the crumbling Hutu Power regime fled into the French-held *Zone Turquoise*. When the new Government of National Unity was formed three days later, it was again the United States, followed by Britain, who were the first western governments to recognize its legitimacy.

From that time onwards, the United States took an active and increasing interest in the affairs of the region and in the survival of the Rwandan government. Installing themselves in the buildings of the military academy in Kigali, the U.S. already established a military-intelligence presence in the Rwandan capital as early as July 1994. Reporting to the DIA in Washington, the military attaché at the U.S. embassy was charged with surveillance of the refugee camps and eavesdropping on movements on the Zairian side of the border. Meanwhile, under the guise of a humanitarian contribution, a powerful telecommunications system was installed at the embassy, giving its personnel the "ears" they required to keep informed and help their emerging central African ally if need be.

Stability Before Reconciliation

From the beginning in July 1994, the United States was Rwanda's only strategic ally and its humanitarian friends were only slowly coming back to the table with support for reconstruction. Guilt-ridden about the genocide, confused by the representations of powerful European opponents of the RPF and distracted by the unfolding drama of the three million plus "killers turned victims" in the camps, the urgency of helping to stabilize Rwanda was lost on many who could have helped in the early months of the new government.

Not only could some who held back at first have helped inside Rwanda, but potentially they could have imparted greater influence internationally too. Years later, as governments and human rights organizations berated the RPF and its allies for their exploitation of the Congo and their preference for authority over civil rights in internal society, it bears reflection on how else could the incoming military authorities have acted at the time. Critics were asking for speedy reconciliation in an impoverished war-torn country at the same time as criticizing its aggressive means of financing that reconciliation. As well as displaying more than a hint of hypocrisy, those who waited on the sidelines in 1994–95 may have helped fashion the tactics abroad and the policies at home which many of them later came to deplore.

Although the EU was one such institution which could have helped more when it hesitated, its representative in Kigali in 1994, Achim Krantz, was prescient at the time, writing: "The government of Rwanda must be strong to avoid a new catastrophe inside the country. Once the current government can feel that it is strong and stable it will be able to allow the Hutu population to participate in power. It is only a strong government that can engage in a sincere process of reconciliation."[12]

The government of Rwanda did ultimately become strong, but not through the means that observers such as Achim Krantz would doubtless have hoped for. Nine years later, at the time of the first democratic elections since the genocide, the efforts made by the authorities towards reconciliation have been great, whilst still leaving much to be done and many wounds unhealed. As for allowing the Hutu population to participate in power, the route taken by the RPF for the first election campaign has been to encourage participation but not debate, with real power-sharing for parties outside the RPF becoming more a mirage than a reality.

Much of what was achieved in turning the tide of unpopularity facing the new government of Rwanda which took power in 1994 had to do with building connections with the right friends—and even trying to convert old enemies. Paul Kagame's adversaries in France took the longest to come around to accepting his government's legitimacy and existence, while Paris remained among the last to accept guilt for its role in the preparations, arming and later harboring of the perpetrators of genocide.

In contrast to the persistently chilly relations with France, relations continued to build with the United States, particularly in the military arena. In addition to the 200 American troops who arrived in Kigali for peacekeeping purposes after the end of the genocide, the U.S. established a military training program for Rwandan troops at the end of 1995 and conducted joint exercises inside the country with the RPA. Training was given by detachments of the Green Berets in low-intensity combat, surveillance and other skills appropriate to the conflict emanating from across Rwanda's western border, and later, in September 1997, U.S. special forces from Fort Bragg, North Carolina, arrived in Kigali in a continuation of the military presence.

Certainly in gaining the support and military cooperation of the United States, the performance of Kagame and his army in 1994 helped to sway regional military planners who were anxiously pondering the power vacuum in the Great Lakes sub-region. Interesting too that, after ignoring the country's plight during exile, persecution and genocide, the small central African country should literally appear on the map in Washington after a decisive military victory by an army representing Rwanda's oppressed Tutsis.

It is relevant to remember that a comparable evolution in U.S. international relations took place in the Middle East in the late 1960s, with regard to its policy towards Israel. Washington, although a political defender of Israel since its independence, had had a relatively minor military involvement with the Jewish state until 1967. However, following the spectacular Israeli military victory over the invading Arab forces in 1967, the Pentagon suddenly realized that the U.S. had a potentially powerful proxy in a region where it had enormous political and economic interests.

From that date on, what became an unparalleled military cooperation began between the two countries, with the U.S. taxpayer footing the bill. At the same time the Zionist movement in the United States started to get into top gear in preparation for its mission to alter political opinion in favor of Israel, a highly successful campaign which had a major impact on American foreign policy in later years.[13]

The parallel with Israel has other facets to it beyond that of mutual strategic interests in regions where both the U.S. and its respective proxy had few existing allies. Apart from the greatest bond of all between the Tutsis and the Jews, that of the common experience of genocide and abandonment, the mobilization of the diaspora and the public relations campaign in the west in more recent years have warranted attention. Thus while the Zionists raise funds in the U.S. and constantly remind Americans about the holocaust, so too has the RPF been effective at mustering support in the west through cultivation of sympathy for the genocide of 1994. This reach of political connections overseas in support of the homeland has led to the description of such countries as truly being "virtual states" where their power and resources lie more within international networks rather than inside the confines of international boundaries.[14]

More recently, both the RPA and the Israeli Defense Force have been criticized for brutal tactics in their respective backyards of the Congo and Palestine, but both have deflected criticism through skillful lobbying and reminders of the horrors of their experiences in genocide. Finally, to complete the comparison, years after the end of the genocide the all-conquering RPA finally underwent a name change to reflect its new role in stabilizing Rwanda. Paul Kagame chose a fitting title for his country's lifeblood in uniform: he called it the Rwandan Defense Force.

Closer to the Commonwealth

The United Kingdom's level of involvement and support for Kigali also underwent a dramatic transformation after the genocide ended, both in terms of military commitment as well as for development and humanitarian aid. In August of 1994, Operation Gabriel was launched, with the involvement of 615 British troops. Personnel were dispatched to provide medical assistance, logistics support and infrastructure reconstruction. Although the UK initially also gave a large portion of its financial aid for the sub-region to the inmates of the refugee camps, it steadily and consistently continued to support Rwanda bilaterally too, with combined assistance amounting to about £11 million ($18m) by the end of 1994. By the end of the 1990s, Rwanda was receiving £14.5 million ($24m) per annum from the UK, making it the tenth largest recipient of British bilateral aid in Africa.[15]

Rwanda even applied to join the British Commonwealth, a less absurd concept than it might have been only a few years earlier, as by then English had become one of the country's three official languages, after Kinyarwanda and French. Furthermore, Mozambique had recently been admitted to the British Commonwealth, if further proof of a revolution in the UK's approach to building post-colonial relationships within non–Anglophone states in Africa was needed. Although Rwanda's application was unsuccessful at the time, the UK's support remained firm, even during the years of controversy which led to international criticism and political upheavals in Rwanda itself.

The Enemy in Waiting

Although support for Rwanda's recovery in the second half of 1994 was of vital importance, the former Rwandan government army which had been defeated on the battlefield had not disappeared, it had only gone away. Military resources would soon become the top priority once again and no sooner than he had achieved victory at home, Paul Kagame had to prepare the RPA for the next phase in its battle to protect his fellow citizens from armed attack.

The interim government had continued to control the mass of the Hutu population when it fled into Zaire in July 1994, using the same techniques it had deployed to devastating effect three months earlier in orchestrating genocide. Through the use of radio broadcasts, coercion and propaganda, it effectively commanded a large section of the population to follow it into exile in Rwanda's neighboring countries.

In April 1994, over 400,000 Hutus had already fled into Tanzania, as the early advance of the RPA swept through eastern Rwanda. Now, the interim government and its army had gone to Zaire and it herded a total of around two million people into exile with it. About 1.2 million Hutus went into North Kivu, crossing the border at Goma, and some 600,000 fled into South Kivu, camping in the Bukavu and Uvira areas. A further 140,000 had fled to Burundi by the end of July.[16]

Most dangerous of all, however, was the military force which had crossed into Zaire along with the exodus of refugees. Although about half were disarmed as they crossed the border to Goma, many of the FAR troops and their militia camp followers either brought their weapons with them into the camps which were set up by the United Nations and humanitarian agencies in the Goma area, or they were able to rearm in the weeks and months which followed their flight from Rwanda.

On the 17th of July, 20,000 FAR soldiers arrived in Goma as intact fighting units. Their leaders said that they had run out of ammunition to fight the RPA but they in any case retained much of their hardware. Their equipment included 62 armored cars with either cannon or machine guns mounted, over 250 mortars, 12 howitzers, 35 air defense weapons, 50 anti-tank guns and 6 helicopters, some of which were armed as gunships. Once regrouped with the militias, in September of 1994 it was estimated that the total forces available around Goma from the losing side in the Rwandan civil war numbered between 34,000 and 37,000 fighting men, in varying states of combat readiness.[17]

It was this remainder of an army which then began to prepare an insurgency campaign against Rwandan territory, focusing on attacks on civilians in the northeast and southwest of the country, the regions which were closest to the Zairian refugee camps in which the ex–FAR and militias became based. The nightmare of Rwanda's genocide was not yet over; it had only moved one country to the west. Furthermore, for the hardcore of defeated Hutu leaders and their murderous militia cohorts, the determination to finish off a bloody mission which had begun in April 1994 remained undiminished.

6

REFUGEE RETURN AND THE UNITED NATIONS

Stalemate in Kivu

By 1996 the United Nations was in a state of uneasy paralysis in its management of the Zairian, Tanzanian and to a lesser extent Burundian refugee camps. At the same time the organization was faced with mounting calls from the donor nations funding their operations for action to break the deadlock. A situation which had initially elicited a massive humanitarian response at the time of the 1994 Hutu exodus from Rwanda was by now viewed as a costly farce by its critics as it became increasingly clear that a dangerous stalemate had been reached.

The efforts towards reconciliation with the authorities in Kigali of the refugees in the camps for their eventual repatriation to Rwanda were going nowhere and at the same time the hard-core of the former regime was in firm control of the camps' populations. Particularly in Zaire, the former genocidal militias were effectively holding the refugees hostage, preventing their return and using the camps as bases from which to launch cross-border raids into Rwanda itself.

Antipathy towards the UN by the Tutsi population had always been present after its non-intervention at the time of the genocide, but also, in the months and years which followed, frustration with the international community on the part of the RPF was becoming extreme. More than anything else Rwanda needed funds to rebuild its shattered economy as the retreating Hutu authorities had taken everything they could across the border into Zaire, including vehicles, telephones, computers, typewriters and most important of all, the entire foreign exchange reserves of the central bank in Kigali.

Unable to make payments on the debts incurred by the former gov-

Rwandan refugees set up camps outside Goma following a cholera outbreak in the Zairian city, July 1994. (UN/DPI photograph 186811/J. Isaac 1059L)

ernment, Rwanda was barred from receiving funds from the World Bank and the IMF, according to those organizations' lending rules. European Union assistance was delayed by political opposition and most other donors felt more comfortable giving humanitarian aid to the fugitives in Zaire rather than reconstruction aid to the government in Kigali. In the Goma area of North Kivu cholera broke out in mid–1994 causing an estimated 50,000 deaths, and the sight of this catastrophe on western television screens helped to mobilize humanitarian aid further in favor of the refugees.

Seeing the lion's share of international assistance going to preserving the refugee camps and to feeding and sheltering the former (and potentially future) murderers of Rwandan Tutsis while the victims and their survivors starved at home was extremely frustrating to say the least. The prime minister of the transitional Rwandan administration, Faustin Twagiramungu, expressed his dismay at the situation: "We appreciate what is happening to help the dying in the camps, but beyond that, what? Must we get cholera to be helped?"[1]

Militias' Grip on Camp Populations

The UNHCR was responsible for organizing refugee repatriation once conditions inside Rwanda had stabilized. In the first months following the end of the war, several thousand Hutus returned, taking their chances and coming back to retrieve their property and restart their lives even against the threat of possible reprisals or imprisonment by the new regime.

However, once Hutu Power had had a chance to re-establish its administrative structures and propaganda machine within the new setting of the Zaire refugee camps, very few refugees were allowed to return home, and many of those who tried were found murdered in the camps by the militias. Every week during 1995 and early 1996, the UNHCR organized buses to bring back Hutu refugees from the camps around Goma, Bukavu and elsewhere, and every week for two years the buses left empty or with only a handful of returnees, often mostly Tutsis claiming Rwandan descent, who had been living in the surrounding areas and who were not fugitives from the 1994 conflict.

In summary, the remainder of the FAR's forces and the *interahamwe* militias had regrouped and rearmed within the camps and the Hutu refugees were under their command and control as political and economic hostages in the war against the RPF. Later their role as hostages was to evolve even further, as many were to become human shields in the military struggle which occurred when the RPA-supported Zairian rebels finally stepped in to resolve the impasse by force.

The role of the UN was increasingly seen then, not only by the Kigali authorities but also by outsiders, as one of supporting and indeed financing an army of terrorists on the borders of a sovereign state whilst making scant progress to fulfill its mandate towards protection of refugees and facilitation of their voluntary repatriation.

The RPF-led transitional government consistently took the approach that the refugees must return before the situation could be normalized, and the UN in Kigali to a large extent sympathized with their position. However, in Goma, where the presence of the ex–FAR power structure and its influence was overwhelming, the agencies there tended to side with their own flock and would echo the argument of the Hutu Power leaders, that the refugees "could not be forced" to return and so the status quo, however imperfect, had to be maintained and financed.

In fact, the power of the camp militias over the aid workers went far beyond the level of mere propaganda. The section leaders in the camps were used to controlling the supply of food to the ordinary refugees and thereby sought to inflate the number of residents to maintain an as large as possible surplus under their control. Attempts at intervention by UN or non-governmental organization (NGO) personnel in the verification or distribution stages could result in a beating or worse for any who failed to comply with the militia leaders' orders.

This led to a number of agencies withdrawing their assistance from the camps, among the first of whom were the charities Oxfam and Médecins sans Frontières (MSF). In its press release announcing the decision, Joelle Tanguy, the executive director of MSF (USA), stated the reasons for her organization's pullout: "In Bukavu the situation has deteriorated to such an extent that it is now ethically impossible for us to continue abetting the perpetrators of the Rwanda Genocide ... the members of the former Rwandan authorities, military and militia exert total control over the civilians in the camps of Bukavu, keep them hostages and manipulate humanitarian aid." Her statement went on to cite evidence of militias running a camp policing system, assassinations of camp inmates and military training.

At the root of the problem, according to MSF, was the inability of the UNHCR to register the camp residents and to make food distributions directly to beneficiaries. "In Bukavu," the report read, "food is distributed to the leaders for 350,000 refugees, while MSF estimates the numbers should not exceed 280,000."[2]

However, there were always other agencies ready to take the place of those who were opposed to working with the camp mafias, and since it was clear to all that the UN was staying put, there was no real threat to the militias' stranglehold over the running of the refugee facilities.

Driving around Mugunga, the largest of the North Kivu camps, with over half a million inhabitants in 1995, shops and warehouses controlled by *interahamwe* leaders with food supplies from donor agencies were clearly visible inside for sale to the refugees. Donor supplies were also sold to the local population in the town of Goma, which during this period became a thriving market town not only because of the resale of donor produce but also due to its role as an active arms bazaar. The ex–FAR was being rearmed and reequipped and despite the UN-imposed arms embargo enforced on the region, cargo flights landing late at night into Goma airport were a regular occurrence, suspicious perhaps as the last scheduled flights allowed into the town officially ended before sundown.

In Kigali the transitional government was becoming impatient for action as by late 1995 the buildup of Hutu forces on its border presented an unacceptable threat. At the United Nations in New York and at other international forums there was talk of "separating the refugees" from the armed militias and dispatching some kind of international force to implement such a selection. Unsurprisingly, the complexity of this exercise and the risks involved made any discussions of the specifics of who would organize the task force and how it would operate almost doomed to failure before they started.

Kagame's Ultimatum to Washington

At first there was broad agreement on the need for an international force, but then it became obvious that to do what it would be required to do in Kivu, any UN army would have to be empowered to use force to separate the FAR/*interahamwe* from the genuine refugees. At this point, predictably, those who had earlier declared themselves in favor of resolute action melted away and the situation was relegated to the continuous loop culture of the UN Secretariat's meeting rooms.

In the United States 1996 was an election year and the Clinton administration was seeking a second term in office. While still adamant about maintaining its non-interventionist approach in Africa, the administration was also determined not to be seen as involved in propagating this costly mess which the international community had gotten itself into in

Vice President Kagame (front right) with U.S. Secretary of Defense William Perry, on visit to Washington, DC, 1995. (From the personal collection of President Paul Kagame.)

eastern Zaire. In May of that year Vice President Paul Kagame flew to Washington to discuss the situation and to make the position of the Rwandan government clear. If the international community could not separate the refugees from the hostile army camped on Rwanda's borders, Rwanda would take the necessary action to achieve this itself. Yes, little impoverished Rwanda with its threadbare economy and fledgling government was willing to take on Mobutu's mighty Zaire with all its resources and international friends.

Washington was still used to thinking in terms of dealing with Mobutu as its local power broker in the region, however imperfect he might be. Meanwhile, Paris continued to support the survivors of the former Habyarimana regime, whose army Kagame was proposing to attack in Zaire. All in all, what the RPA was threatening seemed likely to be both diplomatically unacceptable and militarily near impossible.

However, luck and circumstances were on Kagame's side in more ways than one. First, the presence of the Rwandophone Banyarwanda peoples in North and South Kivu would give him an excellent pretext not only for intervention but also for action without the appearance of his own regular RPA's involvement. Secondly, the lingering guilt of the international community, including even France, he gambled, could give him the latitude he would need in effect to conduct a war against his enemies across a recognized international border. Thirdly, as will be seen, the Zairian authorities overplayed their hand in their campaign of ethnic discrimination against the Banyarwanda in late 1996, giving Kagame the perfect opportunity to carry out the military strike he had long been planning to execute.

Meanwhile, at UN meetings in Kigali, lengthy discussions were held and working groups convened to draw up "contingency plans" in the event of a sudden massive return of refugees across the border. This was anticipated partly as a result of an intensification of the cross-border violence — which was happening in both directions, as the RPA would carry out reprisal raids and pre-emptive attacks on known FAR concentrations on the Kivu side of the border — or possibly as a result of some miraculous change in the state of affairs which would release the Hutu peasant masses from the grip of their militia masters.

Burundi Camp Closures

While the UNHCR could neither condone nor participate in any form of "forced repatriation," in mid–1995, this was exactly what happened in Burundi, as the authorities in that country could no longer tolerate the presence of the camps inside the north of their territory for security reasons. The Bujumbura regime therefore moved to forcibly close them down and send the Rwandan Hutu refugees back over the border. Tens of thousands returned in March and April of that year, with very limited violence either during the process or subsequent to the refugees' return, although the RPA made numerous arrests of suspected *génocidaires* among the ranks of those returning, and summary killings and imprisonments resulted. Thousands of others, however, fearing the consequences of an immediate return to Rwanda, fled into Tanzania or South Kivu, to join their fellow refugees and the fugitive killers in the camps around Bukavu and Uvira.

The difference between the Burundian refugee situation and the Zairian one, however, other than being one of scale (there had been an estimated 80,000 refugees in Burundi at the time as opposed to almost two million in Zaire's provinces of North and South Kivu combined), was the nature of the host government and its interests in helping to resolve the issue. While Burundi's government and its army remained Tutsi-dominated and therefore cooperative towards Kigali, Zaire was still ruled by the aging and ailing President Mobutu, whose interests lay more in exploiting the refugee issue to his own ends, if not showing outright support for the anti–Tutsi military movements which were operating in the eastern provinces of his vast chaotic republic.

More importantly, the governors of North and South Kivu, where the refugees were situated, had also been conspiring with the Hutu militants to attack, dispossess, expel and murder groups of their own Banyarwanda populations, ethnic cousins of the Rwandan Tutsi but for centuries settled and living on the Zairian side of the border and therefore technically Zairian citizens. In South Kivu, where many of the Habyarimana administration had managed to flee with the protection of the French *Opération Turquoise* of 1994, Parson Kyemba Walumona, the governor there, had been first tolerating then by September of 1996 orchestrating a persecution campaign against the ethnic Tutsi minority, known as the Banyamulenge (the people from Mulenge, a local mountain range).

Zairian Power Politics

In a vast and disorganized country like Zaire, governors of provinces such as Kivu enjoyed a great deal of autonomy and indeed were regarded as the real power in their immediate domains. Situated thousands of kilometers from the capital, the Kivu provinces are culturally and linguistically very different from Kinshasa (most Kivu residents speaking either Swahili or Kinyarwanda) and they even used a different currency, often the U.S. dollar, rather than the Zaire used by citizens from the west of their country. Combined with the fact that President Mobutu had just been diagnosed with prostate cancer and was preparing to go to France for treatment, circumstances ensured that the power of the Kivu governors was close to absolute.

Enter Laurent-Désiré Kabila and the Alliance of Democratic Forces for the Liberation of Congo-Zaire (ADFL/CZ). Kabila was a Zairian originally from Shaba Province, a veteran rebel and dissident who had fought against Mobutu in regional uprisings against Kinshasa in the 1960s and 1970s.

It had been years since he had been involved in an attempted rebellion but he remained inside the country, still fit for action and prepared to revive his dream of ridding Zaire of Mobutu. The ADFL had been building up its material strength and adding new recruits in the climate of turbulence in Kivu since the Rwandan civil war. As the ethnic cleansing campaign of the authorities progressed in South Kivu, Kabila's force would make convenient allies for the oppressed Banyamulenge and their RPA reinforcements, who were preparing to help defend their ethnic cousins.

Paul Kagame had been introduced to Laurent Kabila in Kampala by Yoweri Museveni. Both were leaders-in-waiting of their respective countries with a belief in the justice of their own rebel cause, but otherwise the two men had little in common in immediate strategic terms. With the October 1996 crisis in South Kivu, all that changed.

Kagame had been watching the situation unfold and seeing the menace that the buildup of hostile forces around Bukavu, South Kivu's provincial capital, represented, he had begun to increase his infiltration of RPA troops across the border in support of the Banyamulenge. At the same time the racist rhetoric from the South Kivu authorities was reaching fever point and on October 8, 1996, Deputy Governor Lwasi Ngabo Lwabanji set a one-week deadline for all the Tutsi Zairians of South Kivu to "leave the province."

In the context of any reasonable government or society, to set a deadline for the departure of a people who were its own citizens would be thought of as ludicrous and unacceptable. It could amount to nothing less than ethnic cleansing and was backed up with threats which had clear genocidal implications, especially in the light of the recent history and experiences of the region.

For both Kabila and Kagame, this was the signal that they had been waiting for. The Banyamulenge counterattacked and with the ADFL and its Rwandan supporters, proceeded to rout the Zairian army and the Hutu extremists in the space of a few days. Fleeing in all directions, the Zairian forces and their FAR/*interahamwe* allies were driven out of South Kivu in disarray. The lightning success of Laurent Kabila's new movement was to become internationally famous and the Bukavu action would mark the beginning of a campaign that took his forces all across Zaire's thousands of kilometers of territory, and ultimately into government in Kinshasa itself.

Rebels Sweep Through Kivu

With the South Kivu refugee camps disbanded and the towns of Bukavu and Uvira in the hands of Kabila, the ADFL forces then marched around the western shore of Lake Kivu and entered North Kivu, attacking the Zairians there. The town of Goma fell on November 2 and the rebel forces prepared to confront the ex–FAR and its militias, estimated at around 40,000 men, regrouped and rearmed two and a half years after their flight from Rwanda and holding some one and a half million refugees as human shields in the five camps of North Kivu.

Meanwhile, at the official level, Kagame and the RPA were only observing from across the border and any accusation of RPA regular troops' involvement was met with flat denials from Kigali. It would not be until seven months later, after the change of regime in Kinshasa, that the RPF would formally admit that its own troops had been active all along in the campaign inside Zaire.

Unofficially the Kigali authorities were delighted with the outcome of events as a major security threat had been removed from its southwestern border and thousands of refugees were also finding their way back into Rwanda, freed from the grip of the Hutu Power camp militias.

External observers, especially those western donor countries who had by now become painfully aware of the state of paralysis (if not the preparations for a second genocide) that their contributions had been encouraging in the name of humanitarian aid, were prepared to quietly turn a blind eye to what was going on. Even France, long the protector and defender of the old Rwandan regime and its military apparatus, was not in a position to make an aggressive move in such a cloudy and controversial situation. Furthermore, the rebels' progress was rapid, which contributed to their ultimate success, as those on the outside who might have opposed the movement had little time to organize and react.

As Kabila's rebel forces swept into Goma and began to attack the outlying camps at Katale and Kahindo, many thousands of refugees did cross the border back into Rwanda. However, the FAR militias, retreating westwards, managed to herd the bulk of their captive refugee hordes before them, towards Mugunga, the largest of the camps, situated about ten miles west of Goma. Incredibly, the UNHCR also assisted some of the refugees to move towards Mugunga at this point, rather than taking this golden opportunity to let them return to Rwanda freed of the shackles of the militias. The UN and humanitarian agencies feared catastrophe but as in the past with their hollow calls for an "intervention force," the initiative for action was by now well out of their hands and once again most were reduced to the status of observers, reacting to events on the ground which were for the most part beyond their control.

What occurred in the coming weeks in and around Mugunga stunned the world and baffled the aid community whose massive, seemingly immovable flock that they had tended for over two years was now faced with attack by a rebel army and its foreign supporters. Kabila's ADFL, its Zairian Tutsi allies and the RPA were well aware of the likely tactics of their adversaries: to place themselves among and between the refugees and the attacking rebels, thus once more creating a human shield, using the real refugees as hostages.

At this point there was finally an outcry from the UN and the NGO community as well as the international media, who by now had descended upon Goma, as they did in 1994, to record the "humanitarian catastrophe" that was certain to occur, many said, if access to these people would not be allowed and soon. Elements in the media began to dream up numbers of persons who by now must surely be starving: figures of thousands, even tens of thousands of persons were created and found their way into press articles and the broadcast media in the west. In reality, having been among the best fed and best cared for Africans in the region for over two years, most of the refugees were well able to survive without new supplies for a number of weeks.

Suddenly, however, the standoff came to an end and the situation was transformed again as quickly as it had arisen. Attacking from the rear of Mugunga, rebel forces broke through the camp's defenses and sent the ex–FAR and their allies into full flight, westwards towards the interior of Zaire, taking a major portion of their refugee shields with them.

Massive Return to Rwanda

The bulk of the refugees, over half a million people, were by now no longer trapped as their kidnappers had fled, and in the space of around 48 hours, the vast majority of them simply took their belongings and walked back to Rwanda, in silence and often with trepidation, but in reasonable conditions of security and humanity. Some of the humanitarian observers who had been predicting massive starvation and suffering among their trapped and traumatized former caseload were astonished to see them clogging the road back over the border into Rwanda, walking quietly of their own accord and in reasonable health, towards their homeland and an uncertain future.

Without assistance, other than the provision of some trucks and buses which waited at the other side of the border for the injured and infirm, an estimated 550,000 refugees did for themselves in a few days what the UN had been unable to do for them in over two years: repatriated, for the most part safely and humanely, reaching their home communities the way they had left them in 1994, carrying their own belongings and on foot.

Some weeks later the Tanzanian government began a concerted effort to close its camps too and return the masses of Rwandan Hutus in the northwest of their country back to their homeland. Although many tried to flee at first, in December 1996 some 400,000 refugees were forced to return by the Tanzanian authorities, herded at gunpoint by the army westwards along the roads towards and across the Rwandan border. The Tanzanian leadership, unlike Zaire's Mobutu, had no games to play with the international community and no tactical incentive to have a militarized camp community and its refugee populace within its borders any longer.

In this way, in a matter of days of decisive action, they too were ridding their country of the festering sore which their neighbor's fugitive population and its accompanying security and political and environmental complications had by now become.

Thus a tumultuous chapter in the story of Rwanda's post-genocide era came to an end. It was also the end of an era for the UN and the myriad agencies that had, it seems, been the perpetual guardians and sustainers of the Hutu government in exile, the *interahamwe* and its captive population. Having abstained from involvement at the time of the genocide and having failed to effect the repatriation of the vast majority of the more than three million returning refugees, what role could the UN now play in Rwanda's reconstruction and what confidence would the new government in Kigali be willing to place in them?

UNAMIR: A Tenuous Presence

While the UNHCR and the other assistance agencies of the UN together with literally hundreds of NGOs remained inside the country, UNAMIR had finally departed in April of 1996. Until that time, its mandate

A crowded boatload of returning Rwandan refugees crossing Lake Kivu, December 1996 (UN/UNHCR/L. Taylor).

to remain had been renewed on a quarterly basis, each time in response to increasingly mixed signals from the transitional government of President Pasteur Bizimungu and Vice President Paul Kagame. Finally it became clear that the host country would rather have them leave than stay, and indeed at the time of their leaving Kagame went as far as to make a statement that he thought their presence had served no purpose.

A few months later the Kigali authorities also gave expulsion orders to over 50 NGOs, whose presence the government deemed no longer desirable or helpful in its reconstruction efforts. Although the local landlord community may have been disappointed to no longer be able to rent its properties at premium prices to the banished international organizations, it was clear that there were scores of smaller agencies that had raised funds through what could be labeled the "CNN window" of the genocide.

Conducting fund-raising campaigns on the back of the cable TV footage at the time of the events of 1994 in Rwanda and particularly in Goma, many had been able to set up their outposts in Kigali in the second half of that year. Paying some expatriate salaries and costs and employing hundreds of grateful Rwandan personnel in a shattered local economy, they were often nevertheless carrying out uncoordinated and ad hoc assistance work, sometimes omitting to consult with the appropriate government

Massive return to Rwanda from Tanzania across Rusumo Bridge, December 1996 (UN/UNHCR/R. Chalasani).

ministries which were struggling to get up and running again and to manage the affairs of their own country. By 1996 the government saw many of these NGOs as being merely in self-preservation mode, rather than having anything constructive to add in the way of expertise or specialist resources.

Despite the Rwandan leadership's mood of active indifference to the presence of the international community, UNAMIR managed to give itself a send-off in Kigali's Amahoro Stadium, including congratulatory speeches from its own UN ambassador and selected members of the diplomatic corps with a polite presence from members of the Rwandan cabinet. Outside the stadium, however, groups of citizens stood by with a variety of banners proclaiming not only "Goodbye UNAMIR" but also "Go Home UNAMIR," reaffirming from the grassroots level the very mixed feelings of the population towards their departing international guests.

Some months later at a fund-raising forum in Geneva,[3] UN ambassador to Rwanda Shaharyar Khan gave a speech to his UN colleagues and donor country representatives including words of praise for UNAMIR's role in Rwanda in 1994. He congratulated the force for its conduct during the difficult circumstances of the genocide and went on to commend the UN Secretariat for having *reinforced* its presence in response to the country's peacekeeping needs.

With the passage of such a brief time since the withdrawal of the bulk of the UN force in the face of the genocide (although UNAMIR did later rebuild its strength to 5,500 men in August of 1994, over a month after the end of the fighting), it is clear that senior UN officials had a quite different view of their organization's role and record in Rwanda during the genocide than that of most Rwandans.

This ability of the UN's representatives to self-delude — or at least to gloss over the harsh facts, perhaps in the hope that history might somehow change, reflecting a more UN-flattering version of events— seemed to continue for quite some time after the end of the genocide. Furthermore, it reached to the highest levels of the organization. UN Secretary-General Kofi Annan, who was head of the Department of Peacekeeping Operations (DPKO) in 1994 and directly responsible for the UNAMIR operation in Rwanda at the time, finally decided to pay a visit to Rwanda for 36 hours, in May of 1998.

The secretary-general's hosts were full of anticipation at the prospect of the UN's figurehead finally coming to set the record straight by making a formal apology to the Rwandan people. After a runway-side VIP welcome at the airport from the heads of the other UN agencies present in the country, Annan was driven straight to a specially convened session

The Rwandan Parliament Building, Kigali.

of the parliament, in a building whose exterior still showed the pockmarks of artillery shells and whose interior displayed the devastation of the fighting of three years earlier. What more could be needed to remind the secretary-general that he had not come to Kigali for diplomatic small talk and an exchange of pleasantries in a serene African capital city?

Diplomacy and Denial

The parliament was first addressed by the minister of foreign affairs, whose speech set the scene for a revisiting of the record of 1994 and a facing of the truth once and for all before the survivors of one of the UN's greatest failures. Secretary-General Annan was then invited to reply. To the stunned assembly of Rwandan parliamentarians, his oration contained no expression of remorse, but rather a template UN address on the challenges and achievements of the UN in Rwanda past and present. Further invited by direct follow-up questions from the deputies in the chamber to explain the role and actions of his own unit (the DPKO) during April and May of 1994, the unmoved Ghanaian head of the UN merely retorted that he didn't feel that the forum was appropriate for "engaging in polemics."

The session concluded in a formal but uneventful stalemate as the assembled members of the parliament were numbed in their incredulity that this opportunity to rebuild relations with their country's decision makers with a frank statement and formal apology had been blatantly passed over. Not only that, but indeed the standard UN façade of non-culpability, hitherto reserved mostly for western consumption, was now being served up as acceptable in an address before the very people who could bear firsthand testament to a different reality.

Early that evening a reception had been scheduled for the secretary-general at the invitation of the president and vice president of Rwanda in the refined atmosphere of Kigali's Jali Club. Assembled in advance for the reception line to meet Mr. Annan, the entire Kigali diplomatic corps, parliamentarians and ministerial heads of cabinet, their wives and chiefs of the main aid agencies and NGOs awaited the arrival of the guest of honor. The official car arrived at the main entrance to the mansion, and the head of the UN stepped out with his entourage, sporting an understated diplomat's smile. As the assembled guests parted to allow his passage, he strode towards the reception dais expecting to be greeted by his hosts, the head of the Rwandan state and his vice president.

The unsuspecting Annan, a UN career bureaucrat who had risen through the ranks of the organization, was horrified as he quickly realized that the end of the reception line was distinctly lacking a head of state and a deputy head of state to greet him. Indeed, upon surveying the other assembled VIPs, he ascertained that both the president and vice president of Rwanda had refused to attend their own event. His Rwandan hosts had boycotted the welcome reception in response to the secretary-general's address to the parliament earlier that day where he had failed to apologize for the UN's role in Rwanda during the suffering of the genocide.

Annan's attendance at that particular function was surely one of his briefest official appearances ever. Following a formal handshake with the Papal Nuncio and one or two other dignitaries, the UN's top diplomat left his own welcome reception in under ten minutes. Needless to say, the remainder of his stay in the country was tense and after only one night spent in the capital, the figurehead of the United Nations was once more on his way out of the country, doubtless relieved to return to his usual program of considerably less controversial engagements.

As a postscript to this diplomatic incident, a formal apology was finally issued over a year later by Annan, recognizing the failure of the UN body during the 1994 genocide. Prior to that, in December of 1997, Madeleine Albright, United States ambassador to the UN, had apologized on behalf of Washington before an assembly of the OAU in Addis Ababa for her country's stubborn refusal to recognize the reality of genocide until

Paul Kagame (left) with United Nations Secretary-General Kofi Annan. (Courtesy the Rwandan Presidency, Kigali, Rwanda.)

it was too late to act, preferring to avoid at all costs the "G" word which would have legally committed the United States to action.[4]

On March 25, 1998, President Clinton stopped at Kigali airport during a tour of African nations, met and talked with survivors of the genocide and made a formal apology to the Rwandan nation for the international community's failure "to recognize the events of 1994 for what they were, as acts of genocide."

Justice and Recovery

Meanwhile, back in Zaire in early 1997, the fate of the remaining refugees who were being pursued along with their FAR/*interahamwe* masters into the interior of the country was much harder to ascertain, but it rapidly became clear that many thousands, if not tens of thousands, had perished as they and the fleeing pro–Mobutu forces dispersed into the forests and retreated towards Kisangani, the capital of Zaire's Eastern Province.

The UN continued to pay lip service to interventionist measures, but

Paul Kagame with President Bill Clinton on his visit to Kigali, March 1998.
(Courtesy the Rwandan Presidency, Kigali, Rwanda)

once the rebels' military triumph had become fully apparent, the attention shifted to calls for an "inquiry" into the fate of the refugees, presumed killed by the ADFL/RPA forces or starved to death as a result of their flight into eastern Zaire's remoter regions. Although the world media attention had now all but disappeared (no refugee camps under attack, therefore no refugees to film and write about), the relationship between Kagame's forces and the UN was entering a new phase of controversy.

In the earlier stages when they had been unable to prevent genocide, then unable to separate killers from refugees, the UN decision makers' focus was on highlighting the obstacles to their taking action. Now that the necessary actions had been carried out by someone else, their focus switched to demanding to know what had happened. The UN policy consisted of dispatching monitors to the middle of Zaire to "observe" the conflict and to report on the occurrence of human rights violations, whilst at the same time of course calling for an end to hostilities and attacks on civilians.

Not surprisingly, Vice President Kagame had little patience for the UN officials in Kinshasa and New York who were issuing these demands.

Almost three years had passed since the genocide and no official report into the UN's role during the slaughter of one million Rwandans had yet been produced by the United Nations.[5] Now, however, with the perpetrators of the genocide fleeing with their hapless human shields into the interior of Zaire, an indignant UN human rights community was demanding information on the welfare of the protagonists in the action.

The rhetoric continued as the fighting progressed, and even after the fall of Kinshasa and Laurent Kabila's ascent to power in the newly renamed Democratic Republic of the Congo, Kagame insisted that Kigali would cooperate in such an inquiry only if a simultaneous independent report into the events surrounding the genocide was also produced.

In this way, relations between Rwanda's new transitional government and the international community were off to a contentious start. Things were not to improve as time went on, either, as the government sought to focus on the dual priorities of recovery and justice in the immediate post-genocide years, the latter of which was to bring it into almost continual disagreement and controversy with those at the UN who continued to disapprove of their policy.

At a mass rally in July of 1998, to mark the fourth anniversary of the ending of the genocide, Kagame addressed 35,000 people assembled in Kigali's Amahoro Stadium. "People shed blood on the road to liberation," he said. "But now there must be other ways of finding peace and developing the country other than sacrificing lives."

However, with a majority Hutu population and continuing insecurity in the northwest of the country, despite the breakup of the Goma refugee camps, measures to restore confidence for the population were necessary to prevent further mass unrest and a return to wholesale ethnic bloodshed. One important step taken by Vice President Kagame was the reintegration of 4,000 former Hutu soldiers and officers into the Rwandan army, to boost confidence among the ethnic majority and dispel the sentiment that the country was somehow "under occupation" by a foreign army, as many of its critics continued to allege.

Accusations of this nature had been leveled at the transitional government since the end of the genocide when it took power. Always at risk of being seen as an ethnically biased minority party by Hutus, the RPF had placed Pasteur Bizimungu, of mixed parentage but officially a Hutu, in the position of president, with Kagame as vice president and commander in chief of the armed forces. Bizimungu had joined the ranks of the RPF in the October 1990 war, after his brother, a colonel in the army, was murdered by the Habyarimana government.

Kagame nevertheless was the true power behind the presidency, and the army remained the dominant force in the maintenance of civil order and administration of justice as well as ensuring the security of the country's borders. The main reason for the predominance of the RPA in these roles, especially in the early post-war months, was the simple fact that it was the only entity which had any resources at its disposal. This was particularly so following the flight of the FAR and their policy of scorched-earth looting of their own ministries upon departure in July of 1994. With no police force, no judges and civilian government ministries with hardly a vehicle or a telephone at their disposal, the RPA was forced to fulfill numerous functions normally not within the jurisdiction of military authorities.

Beyond logistics and basic resources, however, the political arm of the RPA, Kagame's Tutsi-dominated Rwandan Patriotic Front, remained supreme in its control of government. Although a majority of ministers were Hutu by ethnicity, in the same way as the presidency was held by a Hutu, Pasteur Bizimungu, these cabinet posts were in many cases largely symbolic. In almost all posts which were held by a Hutu minister of state, the deputy minister or the all-important cabinet director of the same ministry would be a handpicked member of the RPF to keep a tight rein on things and exercise true control.

Insecurity in a Reborn Rwanda

The confidence-building measures taken by the authorities may have been laudable from a government which was inviting back a people whose extreme elements had only a few years before almost succeeded in exterminating the entire Tutsi population. They were not, however, successful in ending the insecurity and distrust felt by each of the communities towards the other. Inevitably, among the millions who had returned to Rwanda in 1996, there were many ex–FAR and *interahamwe* extremists who had mingled in with the population and were able to regroup inside Rwanda and terrorize the local population, carrying out regular attacks against Tutsi civilians.

In the southwest, in the region of Cyangugu, and in the northwest near the Zairian border, 1997 saw an almost constant series of attacks on villages, ambushes of vehicles and massacres in schools, houses and places of work by Hutu militias. In some weeks five or ten people would be murdered, but in other weeks the death toll would be in the hundreds. The day before Madeleine Albright's visit to Kigali in 1997, following her apology at the OAU, about 300 Tutsis were murdered with machetes in Ruhengeri by ex–FAR soldiers and Hutu militias.

In fact the genocide had never really ended, and although more localized and on a lesser scale, the *génocidaires* were still able to continue in their mission to rid Rwanda of its Tutsi minority.

The attackers were as brutal and blatantly racist as ever. Buses would be stopped at roadblocks, emptied of their passengers at gunpoint, then Hutus separated from Tutsis. The Tutsis would be shot or hacked to death. In one incident a group of schoolchildren were confronted in their classroom and the militias demanded that they separate by ethnicity. Refusing to do so, they told the armed men that they were Rwandan, an incredible act of bravery especially on the part of the young Hutu pupils. The *interahamwe* nevertheless slaughtered them indiscriminately despite this show of courage and defiance.[6]

In at least two other incidents, international aid workers were attacked and killed, which effectively meant a withdrawal of the assistance community for many months, further allowing the infiltrating Hutu forces to tighten their grip on the local villagers on whom they relied for cover and sustenance.

Operating with supply lines back in Zaire, the ex–FAR and *interahamwe* were able to mount sustained attacks in the northwest with forces of as many as a thousand men, in some cases even managing to take on the RPA for days on end in set-piece battles before melting back into the civilian population, who were their ultimate cover. The RPA, frustrated at the continued ability of their enemy to mount attacks and then disappear, increasingly resorted to revenge against civilians, not all of whom were necessarily involved in the stream of terrorist attacks.

Reprisals by the RPA were often combined with score settling by individual soldiers, who on seeing known killers, or killers of friends and relatives from 1994, would take the law into their own hands and abduct the accused, or simply kill them on the spot. Ordinary civilians would denounce alleged killers in public, often gathering around suspects in the street or in marketplaces and pointing and crying, "Hutu killer!" which was often enough to have the targets either taken away or intimidated into fleeing their homes.

In this way the genocide rumbled on and neither the Hutu nor the Tutsi community was able to feel secure within their own country's borders. Many of the Hutus had come back either because they were forced to at gunpoint, or because they had nowhere else to go. Their grudging acceptance of this new insecure existence was mixed with a deep distrust of the oppressors, as they saw it, who now ruled their country and who, many believed, were about to try to massacre them at any moment.

Many of the ordinary Hutus who returned to Rwanda had by this time been completely brainwashed by their militia masters, arguably since the early 1990s when the Hutu Power campaign went into full swing, but particularly during the months immediately before the genocide and the years in the camps outside the country. Most of those returning at first would not recognize that there had been a genocide, or if there had been one, they would claim that the Hutus were its victims. On the other side the Tutsi population was totally obsessed with the experience of the genocide and the collective guilt of the Hutu race, and any pro–Hutu action or expression of support was immediately suspect.

Distrust was almost total and the concept of "reconciliation" was really only a word to be recited by RPF ministers and ambassadors at international meetings while at home it meant almost nothing. In 1996, Minister of Justice Gerald Gahima instigated a policy of offering sentence reductions for those who came forward to confess to crimes of genocide. However, there were almost no takers for this initiative; there was neither cooperation nor trust on the part of the *génocidaires* and their accomplices.

The propagation of two totally different versions of the events of 1994 and their aftermath would persist not only internally but especially vigorously when encounters with any influential foreigners occurred, either inside or outside the country. The RPA and Tutsi sympathizers would play the guilt card to its utmost to garner support from their friends and allies overseas, whilst downplaying stories of reprisals and atrocities by the army. Meanwhile, their Hutu counterparts would deny the full extent of the genocide and seek to disseminate a version of events that there had been a civil war and mass killings on both sides and that the illegitimate rebel army was only temporarily in control of the country until the rightful "democratic" majority government in exile should be restored to power.

Thus the two communities restarted their existence together in a climate of distrust, denial and insecurity, starved of the resources necessary for the rebuilding of an economy to provide a future for its population, which over time could be the sole hope for any kind of enduring peace for Rwanda.

7

HOT PURSUIT IN THE CONGO

The lightning military campaign prosecuted in the Kivus by the ADFL and its Rwandan allies in late 1996 resolved a major issue for Rwanda's security in the short term: deprived of their secure bases inside western-funded refugee camps within miles of their enemy's frontier, the *interahamwe* and former Rwandan army elements could no longer attack civilian targets at will and retreat back across the border afterwards to the security of Zaire.

However, as in the wholesale retreat of 1994 through the *Zone Turquoise*, in late 1996 the FAR and Hutu extremists bent on an armed return to Rwanda fell back, dispersed into the forests and fled westwards. Once again taking much of the civilian population with them, the routed Hutu forces were driven first towards the provincial capital of Kisangani then on towards the capital Kinshasa and in some cases over the border into Congo-Brazzaville and beyond.

Laurent Kabila and his allies drove rapidly through the countryside, scattering a demoralized and disorganized Zairian army before them; indeed, for much of the ensuing conflict the underpaid and undisciplined forces of the ailing President Mobutu put up only a token struggle against the rebel invaders.

However, unlike in 1994, this time there was neither a sympathetic and protective foreign intervention force to act as a rear guard for the vanquished *génocidaires* and their camp followers, nor a friendly foreign regime just across the border to provide asylum and to act as a rallying point for a massive western effort to shelter and care for the fleeing multitudes.

The French were by now out of the picture in the military sense, although many of the leaders of the Habyarimana regime, their advisers and their families had resettled in France or in pro–French African states. The international donors, particularly the United States, were in no mood to sponsor a rerun of the embarrassing and costly farce of 1994–96 in eastern Zaire, and so the scattering Hutu populace as well as the hapless local Zairian civilians who fell in the path of Kabila's advancing forces were left without protection or refuge as the fighting continued.

In addition, from the communications and access point of view eastern Zaire was not Rwanda. With near-impassible roads, few airports and lack of communications infrastructure, the western media found it much more challenging to record and relate the humanitarian disaster which was to overtake Zaire in the coming months and years. The ADFL and its allies did little to facilitate access for those few journalists who were willing to brave the trail of the advancing rebel army as it swept westwards. Therefore, unlike in July–August of 1994, there was no compelling television footage of cholera-stricken refugees in makeshift camps, "fleeing from genocide," and in consequence the world looked away as catastrophe overtook the retreating Rwandan Hutus and the Zairian civilian population.

An estimated 200,000 fugitive Rwandans were stranded in the aftermath of the camp dispersals in 1996; for most their fate will remain unknown, as will the fate of those caught up in the path of Laurent Kabila's advancing army. Only years later would estimates be made of how many perished during the war in Zaire, and few then would have imagined that over the coming five years the death toll in what was to become the Democratic Republic of Congo would far surpass the number of victims of Rwanda's holocaust of 1994.

Throughout the Zaire rebellion of 1996 until the fall of Kinshasa in May of 1997, the official position of the Rwandan army was one of nonparticipation, albeit from a highly sympathetic standpoint. Clearly the military objectives of Paul Kagame in 1996 meshed closely with those of Laurent Kabila and indeed, for the early stages of the campaign at least, the defense of Rwanda was almost synonymous with the defeat of Mobutu and regime change in Zaire.

Clandestine Support for Rebellion

Naturally, Kigali had been supportive of the oppressed Banyamulenge in South Kivu as they prepared their revolt against the persecution of the Bukavu Zairian authorities. The Tutsi-dominated RPA were eager to ensure the success and survival of their ethnic cousins to the west as they joined forces with Laurent Kabila, and so it could hardly come as any surprise that both arms and irregular Rwandan troops had been infiltrating

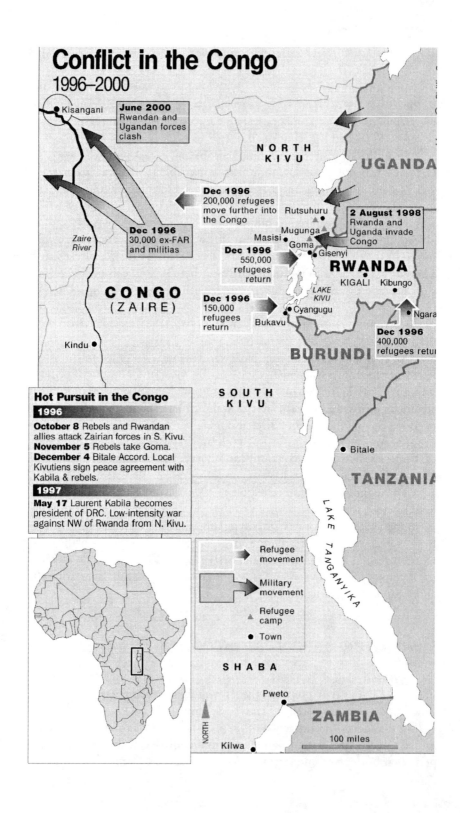

Conflict in the Congo
1996–2000

Kisangani

June 2000
Rwandan and Ugandan forces clash

NORTH KIVU

UGANDA

Dec 1996
200,000 refugees move further into the Congo

Rutshuru

Dec 1996
30,000 ex-FAR and militias

Zaire River

Masisi • Mugunga
Goma
Gisenyi

2 August 1998
Rwanda and Uganda invade Congo

Dec 1996
550,000 refugees return

RWANDA

KIGALI • Kibungo •

CONGO
(ZAIRE)

Dec 1996
150,000 refugees return

LAKE KIVU

Cyangugu

Bukavu •

Ngara

Dec 1996
400,000 refugees retur

Kindu •

BURUNDI

SOUTH KIVU

Hot Pursuit in the Congo

1996

October 8 Rebels and Rwandan allies attack Zairian forces in S. Kivu.
November 5 Rebels take Goma.
December 4 Bitale Accord. Local Kivutiens sign peace agreement with Kabila & rebels.

1997

May 17 Laurent Kabila becomes president of DRC. Low-intensity war against NW of Rwanda from N. Kivu.

• Bitale

TANZANIA

L A K E

T A N G A N Y I K A

Refugee movement

Military movement

Refugee camp

• Town

SHABA

↑ NORTH

Pweto •

ZAMBIA

Kilwa •

100 miles

across the border to join the ranks of the ADFL as it prepared to launch its rebellion in late 1996.

However, according to all official statements, the RPA was not involved in Zaire; indeed, Kagame denied the involvement of regular Rwandan forces in the struggle almost until the time of Kabila's arrival in Kinshasa on May 17, 1997. Only then, once the sick and deposed President Mobuto had departed from Zaire for treatment in Morocco and Laurent-Désiré Kabila had been sworn in as the new president of the renamed Democratic Republic of Congo, did the true extent of Rwanda's involvement become clear.

However, the outside world was not excessively concerned and the sympathy expressed for the new regime in Kigali in the wake of the 1994 genocide was matched by a media acquiescence in the overnight success of the previously unknown Congolese rebel leader. After all, in five short months, Kabila had succeeded in overthrowing the tyrannical regime of Mobutu Sese Seko, a feat that many in the west had long dreamed of achieving.

In this vast and mysterious country at the heart of Africa, whose president and former cold-war ally of the west had become both strategically irrelevant as well as a potential embarrassment to a newly re-elected Clinton administration, it seemed as if a mighty current of fresh air had miraculously blown through its expansive territories. The success of the rebel army and its Rwandan allies offered a glimmer of hope for its downtrodden people to make a new start and share in the world-renowned mineral riches of their own state.

With headlines such as "The Fall of Mobutu" to ponder, at first it mattered little to the outside world that Rwanda had been involved to a much more serious extent from the very start of the war. Indeed, the simultaneous intervention in Zaire by Ugandan forces under Yoweri Museveni also went largely uncriticized, if unreported, in the confusion and awe that was wrought by the ADFL's dramatic success in reaching Kinshasa in under half a year's fighting. Moreover, as if to add final confirmation of the end of an era, news reached the world on September 5, 1997, that President Mobutu Sese Seko, exiled after nearly 35 years in power as leader of one of Africa's wealthiest nations, had died of his illness in Rabat, Morocco.

Staggering success on the battlefield and tumultuous regime change in Zaire, now Congo, had overwhelmingly positive repercussions for Rwanda's internal security and the ability of Paul Kagame's RPA to police the country's frontiers. However, the determination of the hard-line remnants of the Hutu Power extremists was enduring and despite their rout and dispersal, within a year they had regrouped in North Kivu and reestablished contact with their collaborators inside northwest Rwanda. Many of the ex–FAR and *interahamwe* remnants had succeeded in infiltrating the ranks of the refugees who had returned from the camps in 1996 undetected and were now in position to link up with extremists on the other side of the border to resume their war of ethnic hatred against the Tutsi population.

Reversal of Allegiances

Just as Major Kagame's fledgling RPA had regrouped in the Virunga mountains after its defeat in 1990, so now were the *interahamwe* redeploying around Rwanda's northwestern fringes, conducting coordinated hit-and-run attacks against the civilian population and selected government targets.

There was soon to be frustration and disappointment with regional allies too: President Laurent Kabila quickly proved to be a fickle and inexperienced statesman who succeeded in making more enemies on the international stage than friends. Among those with whom he was to fall out was the leadership of his key former ally Rwanda, as the new regime in Kinshasa sought to free itself from the shackles of its former military alliance and reestablish control over the outlying provinces of the freshly conquered territories.

While the populations of Tutsi ethnicity in North and South Kivu welcomed the ADFL's ascendancy, not all of the Congolese population were as thrilled with their new masters, particularly as the hand of Kigali became increasingly dominant in the commercial as well as military and administrative life of the conquered regions of the former Zaire. The indigenous Zairians of the region accepted the new order more grudgingly than willingly. Suffice to say that all ethnic differences aside, many had stood to benefit materially from the expulsions of the Banyamulenge in South Kivu as well as the Masisi and other Tutsi Rwandophone minorities in the north. There is no doubt that the farms, cattle and houses of the victims turned rebels would have fallen directly into the hands of the local Zairians of the province had things turned out otherwise.

Accepting reality, however, the Kivutiens signed a peace agreement with the ADFL on December 4, 1997, at Bitale in South Kivu. Not only did this mark the end of hostilities in the region, but it also marked the beginning of an economic and commercial dominance by Rwanda in the Kivus, matched by an equally exploitative occupation by Uganda in the northeast.

Flashbacks to Berlin

For those with a sense of historical perspective, there were echoes of an earlier aspiration for territorial and economic expansion by an over-populated Rwanda looking to expand its borders and support itself through access to its western neighbor's resources. In 1881, a mere four years before the Berlin Conference at which Rwanda's (and much of the rest of Africa's) colonial borders were drawn, the Rwandan king Kigeli Rwabugiri IV was slain on the battlefield leading his army in a failed conquest of South Kivu.

Since that time, the dream of Rwandan expansionism and the night-mare of Kivutian autonomy was an armed return from the east; over a cen-tury after Berlin this scenario was becoming a reality, a reality that was strongly resented by the indigenous populations. As its presence consoli-dated, examples of de facto colonization by Rwanda in administrative life became increasingly evident: the *franc rwandais* increasingly became a currency of everyday commerce and cars were issued with registrations valid only for Rwanda and Kivu, but not for the rest of the Congo.

The local population resisted, however, showing its distrust and resentment in sometimes alarmingly poignant fashion: reportedly when the World Health Organization and UNICEF were trying to carry out vac-cinations of children in the region using needles brought from the Rwan-dan side of the border, suspicious Congolese mothers would refuse, preferring to wait for the unreliable delivery of supplies from Kinshasa instead; and when school diplomas were issued, graduating students rejected those issued locally, distrusting the validity of any document not issued from the capital.[1]

The Second War in the Congo, 1998

In this way the stage was set for a renewed clash between former allies, and when Laurent Kabila visited Bukavu in January 1998 he quickly real-ized that he was far from being master of all the domain that had been the former Zaire. However, at this time he still resisted active involvement in rearming Rwanda's enemies inside his country, despite later accusations from Kigali that this was the case.

However, what was undeniable was what was happening in 1998 to the ethnic Tutsi populations of the Masisi region in North Kivu, no more than fifty kilometers to the north of Goma. Here, local Hutu groups were stepping up their campaign of armed expulsions, begun the year before, in collaboration with Rwandan Hutu extremist groups based in the Goma refugee camps. The result was a steady flow of Masisi refugees to Rwanda, in what amounted to a clear campaign of ethnic cleansing.

By mid–1998, it became clear to Kagame that Laurent Kabila was indeed siding with anti–Rwandan groups inside the eastern part of his country, arming and supporting the *interahamwe* whilst still paying lip service to his continuing alliance with Kigali. On July 28, the change of allegiances was formalized when Kabila required the Rwandans in the DRC to leave the country and Kigali duly pulled its troops out of the country in seeming compliance with the expulsion *diktat*. However, the Rwandan vice president was by now sure of his former ally's motives and had been preparing, in conjunction with longtime ally Yoweri Museveni in Uganda, for a move of this sort; on August 2, both countries turned the tables on Kabila and a new invasion was launched into the DRC, once again catching its enemy off guard and sweeping with lightning force across the country.

Kagame's justification for relaunching hostilities against the DRC was as clear as it was calculating:

> ...In 1998 the Congolese government and allies made statements to the effect that they would take the war to Rwanda and we took this threat very seriously.... They moved their troops to as close as Kindu and we were not going to wait for them to move closer than that. We swiftly moved in to deny them bases from where they could launch air attacks on Rwanda supported by helicopter gunships belonging to their allies. We had to take all that territory on foot, to deny them the capacity to launch air attacks on us. That is why and how we got so deep inside the Congo."[2]

Thus the leader of Rwanda's armed forces explained his motivations in security and military terms some three years after the conflict began. In essence, an asymmetrical response to a threat from better-armed potential aggressors necessitated, in Kagame's view, the capture of over one third of the DRC to protect Rwanda's borders.

This interpretation falls short of the full reality, however, of what happened in the Congo from 1998 to 2001, as the struggle became one of geopolitics more than self-defense and the Congolese people were to be overtaken by a humanitarian tragedy of dramatic proportions.

The Congolese war of 1998 was different in several key ways from the conflict which preceded it two years earlier: not only had the Congo's main actor behind the 1996 rebellion changed sides, but also the intervening two years had given President Laurent Kabila time to consolidate alliances with his comrades in arms from the earlier days of anti-colonial African opposition. The increasingly embattled Kabila could still count on President Dos Santos of Angola, Zimbabwe's Robert Mugabe and even President Sam Nujoma of far-off Namibia to support him in the war against the east African aggressors.

Within weeks, a full-blown regional war was raging in the Congo, with at least six countries involved through provision of equipment and firepower and to a lesser extent with contributions of troops to back the Kinshasa regime in the conflict.

A further difference was the degree to which the 1998 war was more about economics than politics this time around. Rwanda's Zairian incursion of 1996 had largely been condoned by the world community out of sympathy for the victims of the 1994 genocide and the need to protect its frontiers from attack. In 1998, however, while Kagame still used this justification as vehemently as before, it became clear over time that both the invaders from the east as well as Kabila's allies and defenders from southern Africa were as much motivated by the spoils of war as they were by a desire to achieve military victory.

The third and most tragic difference between the second conflict in the Congo and its predecessor was the scale of the humanitarian catastrophe which accompanied it and the tardy and meager humanitarian response with which it was met. Indeed, the interest displayed by the international community in coming to the aid of the displaced and vulnerable populations who became scattered around Congo's countryside as a result of the 1998 fighting was close to non-existent. Following battles for strategic locations, many were driven out of their towns and villages by the invaders and left to perish in the forests and hills of central and eastern Congo.

On August 31, 1998, the United Nations called for a cease-fire and the withdrawal of foreign troops, but its presence could do little to alleviate the plight of the victims of the war. However, the RPA and its allies had by now become skillful masters of public relations and the art of disinformation. Everything possible was done to deny journalists access to the fighting zones, while visible evidence of alleged massacres of civilians and looting of homes or businesses was nowhere to be found after each town or village had been emptied of its inhabitants.

It was not until July of 2001, when the war was in its third year, that a UN Security Council report on the conflict would begin to reveal the extent of the casualties and wholesale looting of the DRC's mineral and agricultural resources. While numbers varied and different agencies would disagree with the UN and each others' methodology and results[3] it is by now clear that in the four years of war in the Democratic Republic of the

Congo which began in 1996, probably well over three million people died from attack, disease, or malnutrition as a direct or indirect result of the hostilities.

A fourth and final difference between the first and second Congo wars was the change in allegiances and composition of many of the ordinary fighting men in the armed forces, particularly on the Rwandan side. While both sides used mercenaries in one form or another, by 1999 the RPA had recruited tens of thousands of Hutus into its ranks and even managed to successfully "recycle" some extremist elements from the period of the genocide, sending them to re-education camps inside Rwanda and later using them in the front lines in the DRC. Here they often came across their former comrades in arms from the mid–1990s, some of whom had been recruited by Kabila, given around $150 each and retrained, with a promise of an eventual passage back to their homeland if all went well.

The decision by Kabila to recruit these ex–FAR and *interahamwe* fighters into the ranks of his army to oppose his former RPA allies was probably the one single action which ultimately sealed his fate and that of his country, plunging the Congo into its most destructive and brutal war thus far.

Further denials about the level of involvement from Kigali and Kampala were issued as the conflict once again escalated and the capital Kinshasa came under siege for the second time in two years. An anti–Kabila faction backed by Rwanda almost seized power in Kinshasa, but only with the resistance of the *Kinois* and the backing they received from Angolan troops was the assault on the capital repulsed.

In November of 1998, President Kabila went to Brussels in a belated diplomatic mission to generate support for the defense of his country. In contrast to the continuing sympathy which the regime in Kigali had by now managed to cultivate, however, Kabila found himself received as a quasi-pariah, almost snubbed by the Belgians and certainly not accorded the level of courtesy and protocol that even a visiting African head of state could normally have expected.

Indeed, through a combination of poor diplomacy and the negative publicity given to his actions in the region, Laurent Kabila was now not only branded as being responsible for the deaths of many refugee Hutus and fleeing civilians from his own country, but he was also seen as the key perpetrator of the Masisi massacres and the force behind the retraining of the *interahamwe* in their determined attempts to regroup and launch attacks against Rwandan territory.

Thus President Kabila's standing was further reduced and his ability to rally western support for his cause diminished. For the next two years, despite military support from his southern allies, albeit support given at a price, the *mzee* would never regain control of vast tracts of the DRC's territory, and indeed, he would continue to be forced to relinquish land to both allies and rebel groups as well as the proxies of foreign powers to the east. Despite the subsequent peace agreements which officially brought an end to outside military involvement, the rebel-in-waiting who had swept to power on a wave of popular support in 1997 became embattled and encircled, exercising effective power in only half the territory of his republic and disliked or distrusted through much of the rest.

The Lusaka Accords — False Promise of Peace

In July of 1999 the parties to the second Congo war were invited to a peace summit in Lusaka, energized by the shuttle diplomacy of the EU's Aldo Ajello and brokered by Ketumile Masire, former president of Botswana. Flawed in many ways from the outset, the Lusaka negotiations were destined to further weaken Kabila, recognizing the power of the rebel factions in the east and in many ways setting the stage for an even more rapacious assault on the humanity and resources of the DRC than anything that it had been subjected to thus far.

The mediation effort, based in Botswana's capital Gaborone, was too distant and too easy for the protagonists of the conflict to ignore; the advisors selected to guide the process were chosen from neutral but far-off countries and had insufficient background or expertise in the DRC's particular problems; and the western backers of the talks were more intent on a short-term diplomatic solution at any cost, rather than a lasting peace that could take account of the long-term issues underlying the confrontation — particularly, with the 2000 U.S. election campaign already in full swing in the autumn of 1999. Furthermore, Kabila and Masire were soon to fall out, further aggravating the process, while the ultimate signatories of the accords, some 50 in total, mostly preferred to participate as individuals, not committing their respective factions and movements by name to the cease-fire agreement which they were signing.

Kabila thus signed, reportedly on the suggestion of President Mugabe, who argued that the deal, no matter how unjust, would give the Congolese president time to regain control and work towards his ultimate goal of reunifying the Congo. Moreover, Kabila knew that despite the conquest of his country and the epidemic infiltration of the corridors of power in Kinshasa, he was still popular in the east of the DRC, his base for the decades in the wilderness prior to 1996; from there he hoped to expose the true intentions of the foreign-backed factions and opponents of his regime and thereby regain support from outside the country when military and political conditions were more favorable.

The western powers were eager to see the signature of the accords and the implementation of a cease-fire, deployment of a UN observer mission and the disarmament of the "negative forces," as the ex–Rwandan army and *interahamwe* had by now become known in the parlance of the international diplomatic circuit. However, there was ultimately little in the agreements for the Congolese people, despite provision in the Lusaka Accords for the launch of a national dialogue intended to lead to elections in approximately two years' time. The UN mission which the accords spawned, known as MONUC (United Nations Observer Mission in the Congo), was a predictably under-equipped, under-manned and under-mandated force, with the familiar implications for the effectiveness of such a UN mission in a region where cease-fire breaches were the rule and observance the exception.

Almost from the moment of signature, therefore, the Lusaka Peace Agreement proved unsatisfactory. In addition to the multiplicity of actors, each with their own interests at stake, the core bilateral issue between Kabila's DRC forces and Kagame's RPA remained: Rwanda had signed on condition that the ex–FAR and *interahamwe* be disarmed and sent home; this, however, was an increasingly difficult requirement for the DRC to satisfy, not least because by this stage the "negative forces" from Rwanda had been to a large extent integrated into the Congolese army.

When asked about the disarmament process and the whereabouts of those hostile elements whom Rwanda sought to eliminate, Kagame explained: "They are located wherever the DRC government is located. They are in the northwest of the country, they are in the central part where fighting has been taking place recently. They are there in DRC government units...."[4]

In this way, the RPA continued its engagement in the DRC after the signature of the Lusaka Accords, the other outside forces remained and the UN deployed an observer mission that was largely without function as the war intensified and the crisis deepened in the ensuing two years.

Kisangani: End of an Alliance

By mid–2000, with the war still raging well inside the borders of the DRC, the increasing complexity of the struggle and the true motivations of the invading forces were becoming apparent. While Zimbabwe was repaid handsomely for its support for Kinshasa with the right to extract copper, diamonds and other mineral resources from Shaba and Kasai

Provinces, both Rwanda and Uganda were enjoying the spoils of war as they established or took over gold and diamond mining operations in the areas which they occupied.

In Kisangani, capital of the DRC's eastern province, Rwanda and Uganda, former allies of the first Congo war, ultimately clashed for control of the city. Following earlier fighting between Ugandan forces and the RPA, a UN-negotiated agreement for the demilitarization of the city had been signed in early June. However, the strategic and commercial importance of the regional capital to the rival invaders was irresistible and days later fighting broke out in earnest with the civilian and UN observers, composed of Uruguayans, Canadians, Pakistanis, Bangladeshis and Nepalese, caught in the middle.

The RPA finally prevailed in Kisangani, leaving a coalition of the RPA and its local allies to take control of the city and the key that it held to regional wealth and logistics. UN observers recording the cease-fire violations could only take refuge in a nearby church as shells fell all around their offices. At first they would call in the leaders of the warring sides to have them acknowledge the violations and sign the appropriate documentation; often the commanders would go right back to the attack after each visit, in at least one case reportedly giving orders to restart an attack by mobile phone whilst inside the UN observer mission's office.[5]

Shortly after their victory, the RPA withdrew from the city and ceded effective control to the Rassemblement Congolais pour la Démocracie (RCD), its main ally in the fighting. The RCD, which was to become Rwanda's main proxy army in the occupied territories, was composed of an unlikely collection of bedfellows, from former Mobutuists bent on regaining center stage, to sidelined leaders from the early Kabila administration, many of whom were Tutsis, to disgruntled army officers who most of all wanted to end the war on the winning side.

The new movement was headed by an even less likely figure, a former university professor of politics from Dar es Salaam, named Wamba dia Wamba. Exiled from Zaire in the early 1960s but a respected dissident political analyst and writer during the Mobutu years, Wamba made an astonishing comeback: after initially being called to Kinshasa in 1996 by the new rebel leader, he began by proposing the establishment of a research institute for Kabila, to be attached to the presidency. However, like so many who could have been helpful allies for Kabila in the days of his ascendancy to power, Wamba dia Wamba was ignored by the new president and he soon became disaffected from the cause. He returned to Dar, feeling powerless to help bring order to the confusion which reigned in Kinshasa.

After the failure of the Rwandan-backed rebels to take Kinshasa in

1999, the revenge killings orchestrated by Kabila began in earnest. It was at this time that Professor Wamba decided to stage his comeback, first flying to Goma and assuming the leadership of the new anti–Kabila movement. In this way another influential figure from Congolese civil society — a seasoned player whom he could ill afford to lose to the opposite side — ended up in military opposition to the troubled regime of President Kabila. The RCD later split into two factions, one under Wamba dia Wamba and primarily owing allegiance to Kampala, while the other, RCD-Goma, became the Rwandan proxy in the region.

Debacle in Pweto Hastens Kabila's End

By late 2000, things were going as badly on the battlefield for Laurent-Désiré Kabila as they were on the diplomatic front. With North and South Kivu occupied by the RCD-Goma and other pro–Rwandan forces, the president decided to stage a counter attack to retake his home city of Pweto in eastern Shaba Province, strategically located at the gateway to a mineral-rich region and some 400 kilometers north of Lubumbashi. Having rallied his forces and borrowed expensive new firepower from Robert Mugabe's army, Kabila threw everything into the assault to retake Pweto.

The attack proved disastrous, however, with many of his generals giving up the moment fighting began, troops deserting and much of the valuable materiel falling intact into enemy hands. Mugabe was furious at the outcome and from this moment on yet another of Kabila's powerful allies in the region would begin to give up on his long-time friend and ally, joining the ranks of those seeking a radical and urgent change of leadership in Kinshasa.

The non-implementation of the Lusaka Accords was frustrating the international community as fighting continued unabated and a humanitarian disaster of incalculable proportions was certainly unfolding, despite the UN monitoring presence. In November 2000, assembled in Kigali at a key donors' "Round Table" meeting, delegates called on Kagame to withdraw his forces from the DRC, this time with a greater urgency and unison than in previous years.

The winds of change were blowing hard and some three years of near-unabated conquest and wholesale dismemberment of half of the Congo's territory was coming to an end. On January 16, 2001, Laurent Kabila was assassinated in Kinshasa, and was succeeded three days later by his son, Joseph. Remarkably the turmoil and return to confusion that many had anticipated from the violent changeover did not materialize. On the contrary, the young Joseph Kabila quickly proved his ability to deal with the regional and international power brokers who mattered with considerably more diplomacy and skill than his late father had.

With the *laissez-faire* attitude towards a Rwandan military presence fast coming to an end, it was time for President Kagame to negotiate rather than ignore the international community, as he now risked losing the support of key backers such as the U.S. and the UK, who had for the most part turned a blind eye to the RPA's adventure in the DRC thus far. Kagame pledged to withdraw from Pweto on condition that a UN force move in, still claiming the threat from the "negative forces" harbored in the Congo, whom he maintained were preparing to move closer to threaten Rwanda at the first opportunity.

Adding further to the momentum behind international calls for a withdrawal from the DRC, in July of 2001 an interim report of the UN Security Council's panel on the exploitation of the Congo's resources by foreign powers was released. It revealed the extent to which the Ugandan and Rwandan armies had engaged in the plunder of the DRC's natural resources, including coffee, timber, diamonds, gold and the highly prized coltan, or "grey gold"—the columbite-tantalite used most notably in the assembly of the late generation of mobile phones. The report, which France had originally urged the Security Council to conduct, was not universally acknowledged as authoritative, with some critics pointing out that the forces of Kinshasa's allies such as Zimbabwe and Angola had also been engaged in the illegal exploitation of minerals whilst in the country and the report had ignored this.[6]

UN Investigation Reveals Extent of Ravages

Despite these criticisms the evidence that the UN Security Council produced could scarcely be ignored and a further report by the panel, although published as late as October 2002, was even more damning and much harder to refute. The study revealed, for example, the extraction by Ugandan forces of much of the timber and cattle wealth of the Eastern and Equator Provinces, with the region's entire coffee stocks being transported across the border for resale in Uganda during 1998–99.

In South Kivu, Rwandan forces were reportedly responsible for the mining and removal of an estimated 1,000 to 1,500 tons of coltan, while in Kibila, for example, an entire sugar refinery was dismantled and taken across the border to Rwanda. There were also reports of banks in major towns being methodically surrounded by Rwandan troops while their local allies raided the premises and removed hundreds of thousands of dollars.

Despite the late publication of these details and predictable denials from Kigali and Kampala, the extensive research that had led to this mass of evidence against the RPA and its allies could now no longer be ignored. The UN report revealed the existence of "elite networks" of military-commercial operations, related to the Rwandan, Ugandan and Congolese governments, in alliance with local groups who acted as proxies for their backers' exploitation of mineral and farm resources.

The report also detailed the activities of international businesses, many based in Europe or outside the region, who were the main beneficiaries of the illegal exploitation of the DRC's wealth during the period under study. This was particularly the case in parts of the government-controlled area of the country where the Zimbabwean military-political interests were dominant. In the northeast of the country, where Uganda was the preeminent force, the report identified individual businessmen, albeit with military connections, as the key culprits, rather than an overt operation coordinated from the government in Kampala itself.

However, in the case of the Rwandan presence in Kivu, the analysis uncovered a more complex and penetrating strategy beyond the short-term removal of minerals and goods to the other side of the border. The findings pointed to a Rwandan government objective of repopulating the region with Rwandans, in addition to using its military might to extract and exploit the wealth of the occupied lands. In this way, Kigali was in fact realizing the long-term goal of the conquering Rwandan monarch Kigeli Rwabugiri, who in the late nineteenth century had sought to extend to the west the lands available to support the population of his overcrowded Rwandan kingdom.

Evidence was presented by the UN panel that President Kagame's oft-repeated justification for being in the DRC, namely the tracking down, disarmament and repatriation of the *interahamwe* and ex–FAR, was rapidly becoming a fiction. In fact, the authors of the UN report learned that in at least some so-called conflict areas, the "negative forces" were being left largely unmolested, provided they in turn left the RPA mining brigades to carry out their work unhindered. One *interahamwe* fighter interviewed in Bukavu in early 2002 for the report described the situation in his area as follows: "We haven't fought much with the RPA in the last two years. We think they are tired of this war, like we are. In any case, they aren't here in the Congo to chase us, like they pretend. I have seen the gold and coltan mining they do here…. The RPA come and shoot in the air and raid the villagers' houses but they don't attack us any more. If you are lucky, you might have a big brother in the RPA, he might be able to get you some food and ammunition."[7]

Although these are the words of only one interviewee, his testimony points to the changed nature of the military conflict and highlights the contrast between public pronouncements from Kigali and the reality on the ground. Firstly, the reference to the "big brother in the RPA" demonstrates that a young Hutu fighter who had fled to Zaire in 1994 would be more likely to come across a fellow Hutu on the battlefield in 2002, rather than his traditional Tutsi racial adversary. Secondly, it supports the thesis that the main priority of the occupying forces had become that of economic exploitation rather than hot pursuit of the enemy; and thirdly, as mentioned, it suggests the emerging co-existence and even interdependence of Rwandan Hutus and Tutsis in the Kivus, recalling the way of life of those Rwandans who left their homeland and inhabited the region some two centuries earlier.

Collapsing Public Infrastructure and Humanitarian Catastrophe

The humanitarian tragedy caused by the collapse of the public sector in the process of the systematic extraction of resources was also exposed in the UN report: quite apart from the civilian victims of violence, the majority of the casualties in the region resulted from disease and malnutrition during the occupation, a situation which in turn was exacerbated by the collapse of basic public utilities and services. While always drained by corruption under Mobutu, there had still been some semblance of public finances to provide hospitals, schools and water for the populations in the eastern provinces of Zaire. Now, with economic anarchy reigning across the region, the tax base had disappeared and basic maintenance and public services could no longer be supported. The impact on public health was devastating.

According to the UN panel of experts, water production in North and South Kasai was functioning at no more than 20 percent of their previous capacity, while a cited Médecins sans Frontières study of infants in the city of Kilwa (population 350,000) in southern Katanga found a death rate for under 5-year-olds of 3.2 percent per 10,000 *per day*. This translates into a staggering death toll of almost 12 percent per annum of children under five.

On the Rwandan side of the border, the picture was very different. Starting from scratch in 1994 after the former regime's scorched-earth retreat into Zaire and initially starved of resources by the international community during the early post-genocide years, the new Rwanda was suddenly enjoying a remarkable boost to its finances, largely from new military-economic adventures in the DRC. Or at least a new prosperity was finally reaching those associated with the upper echelons of the military, if not the Rwandan population as a whole.

The "Congo Desk" of the Rwandan government, the unit charged with managing operations in the DRC, was taking in revenues of some five times the official RPA budget of $80 million in 1999, according to a source contacted for the UN report. If true this would imply that either Rwanda's DRC activities were enormously profitable, to the tune of around $320 million per annum after paying for the military, or that the RPA's budget was many times greater than the official level, or a combination of both.

The director of Rwanda's information agency, Joseph Bideri, denied the existence of the Congo Desk as an explicitly military-commercial coordinating unit. "There is a political liaison unit for relations with the Congolese government," he said. "Not for mining or commercial operations."[8] He was also at pains to mention that Rwanda, Burundi and the former Zaire had long ago established a customs-free zone in a tripartite intergovernmental agreement, to liberalize movement of goods and services between their respective countries. Under the treaty establishing the Economic Community of the Great Lakes Countries (known by its French acronym, the CEPGL), the export of minerals and goods which was being criticized was perfectly normal and legal, Bideri argued. The CEPGL had, however, lapsed some time before as a result of the regional conflicts. Furthermore, it is unlikely that the community's founding fathers had envisaged the heads of their region's import-export operations to be mostly men in uniform, as the UN panel's report asserted.

Perspectives on the Casualties and Spoils of War

If the existence of massive exploitation of the Congo's resources since the Rwandan invasion of 1998 has now been established, can there be any justification for those actions? How much of the economic ravages of the Congo were carried out by and for the benefit of the Rwandan, Ugandan and Zimbabwean states and how much was managed by businessmen and companies based outside Africa? As the international community struggled to regain the initiative in its effort to deliver humanitarian relief in a devastated country, to what extent could the invading forces be blamed for the human wreckage of the past five years in the DRC? Did the three million deaths in the Congo during this period amount to genocide and if so, how were they different from the massacres carried out in the Congo during the centuries of European rule?

The answers to these questions could facilitate a better understanding of the context of Congo's conflicts for policy-makers and ordinary citizens in the advanced countries, as well as for those who would judge the main actors behind the turmoil or the perpetrators of the crimes committed. What were Kagame's views then and now on some of these issues? His own words begin to explain part of the answer. Regarding the killings as well as the economic exploitation he said: "…These deaths have been going on for long, in Congo and other countries and with various causes, some of which are diseases, hunger, epidemics and many others. The genocide in the Congo dates as far back as the times of King Leopold, who is alleged at one time to have decimated close to ten million Congolese.… They will find that the rich countries that are making these allegations are the ones looting the resources of the Congo."[9]

There can be little doubt that during the rule of King Leopold II, easily ten million Congolese could have died as the Belgians and other European business interests ravaged the country for timber, minerals and especially rubber, following the advent of the motorcar in the industrialized world.[10] During those years the Belgian monarchy waged an active campaign against humanitarian and media interests who sought to expose the devastation caused in King Leopold's colony. The RPA has also been widely criticized for covering up its activities and for concealing the disastrous impact of the war that it waged on the Congolese people. It may, however, be some time yet before the full impact on these civilian victims of the wars of the late 1990s in the DRC can be fully measured, if ever.

To add historical perspective, it may be instructive to look back at some of the better-known cases of civilian casualties of wars in the economically advanced world over the past century. For example, the genocide of the Jews of the 1940s in Europe and the effects of the atomic attacks of 1945 on the Japanese population are now extensively documented; but how much of an outcry was there in the west at the end of the Second World War as nearly six million Germans died of starvation or malnutrition in their own country, largely as a deliberate policy of the occupying American and British forces—and was their fate as victims of war not as widely denied, then buried by the victorious allies bent on remolding Europe according to their own political and economic vision?

Documents declassified since 1988 show that 5.7 million German civilians died but were not reported as dead in occupied Germany between October 1946 and September 1950, that is, seventeen months to five years after their armies had surrendered. Over one million Germans did not return from prisoner of war camps and over two million people expelled from their homes in the East died during this period. In all well over nine million and possibly over twelve million died, mostly from starvation, over a period of years and under the eyes of the occupying powers. Apologists in more recent times have pointed to either the brutality of the Stalinist occupation of Germany following the war or to a world food shortage which existed at the end of the conflict in mitigation of the now undeniable facts of the policy of famine. However, world food production had almost totally recovered (to 97 percent of its wartime level) by 1946, and there was a deliberate policy of preventing food from reaching civilians in the British- and American-occupied zones of Germany, which resulted in many more deaths of Germans than had been killed in the war itself.[11]

A comparison with the official account of the economic exploitation of defeated Germany and the facts which subsequently emerged also forms a benchmark for judging the actions of the victors of the Congo wars of the 1990s. In disclosing the assets (known as "removals") which had been taken from Germany by way of reparations, General George C. Marshall stated at the end of the war that some $10 million had been taken in total by the United States' occupying forces. More recent evidence has revealed that the value of the assets and resources removed at the time by the United States were closer to $5 billion, and that a similar amount of removals were carried out by the British. Adjusting these amounts for economic growth and inflation, in year 2000 terms these amounts would approximate to $200 billion in German resources removed by the two allied powers following the end of World War II.[12]

The 2002 Peace Accords

By early 2002, the regional and international momentum for an end to the situation in the DRC was growing, and with a more pragmatic president in Kinshasa and allies who were tiring of war, an agreement was signed in Sun City, Pretoria, on July 30 of that year between Rwanda and its supporters on the one side and forces loyal to Kabila on the other. Brokered by South Africa, the Pretoria Accord provided for the complete withdrawal of Rwandan forces from DRC territory in exchange for an international commitment to the disarmament of the *interahamwe* and ex–FAR. The following week, with Angolan mediation, a similar accord providing for the departure of Ugandan troops and its replacement in the Eastern Province by a UN peacekeeping force was signed in Luanda.

Although Kigali's formal withdrawal from the occupied regions was indeed effected under the terms of the agreement and South African and other international forces quickly moved in to supervise the disarmament process, the implementation of the Luanda Accord proved much less attainable in the short term. Fighting raged on in Ituri, for example, for

President Kagame (left) with President Thabo Mbeki of South Africa at the Pretoria Peace Accords, South Africa, 2002. At right is the president of the Democratic Republic of the Congo, Joseph Kabila. (Courtesy the Rwandan Presidency, Kigali, Rwanda.)

many months after the signature of the agreement, with Ugandan regular forces becoming the de facto peacekeepers between different warring factions, most notably around the gold-rich area of Bunia near the Ugandan border.

The withdrawals of foreign forces by no means marked the end of the regional conflict, however, and the local allies of the previous invading armies merely exchanged their uniforms for civilian clothes. The RCD had by now split into various factions, each continuing to battle for control against its rivals and each representing to a greater or lesser extent their former foreign backers: the RCD-Goma continued to control the Kivus, reporting to Rwanda-based commanders; northern Shaba and parts of eastern Kasai Provinces were under the control of the RCD-ML (Mouvement de Libération), which also still held sway in the northeastern corner of the country. In the government-controlled area, an alliance was struck between Kinshasa and another rebel group, the Mouvement de Libération Congolais (MLC), whose base was in the northwestern Equator Province,

Paul Kagame (left) signing the Pretoria peace agreement, with Joseph Kabila, president of the DRC, December 2002.(Courtesy the Rwandan Presidency, Kigali, Rwanda.)

while on the ex–FAR side, other groups representing the will of the militant Hutus continuing to support an armed return to Rwanda also began to reemerge.

Thus the Hutu Power fighters who evaded disarmament became members of ALIR I and ALIR II (Alliance pour la Libération de Rwanda) backed by indigenous Congolese elements and the Zimbabwean forces, respectively, while other anti–Kigali elements continued to regroup elsewhere in the region. Some found refuge and support in Tanzania, in Burundi and even in Uganda, where a latent anti–Rwandan movement continued, condoned by Museveni, perhaps as part of a new strategy to place a check on any future territorial ambitions of his comrade turned rival, Paul Kagame.

Extracting the Most from an Agreement

After the official withdrawal of foreign forces from the Congo, there were further allegations that the economic activities of the "elite networks" had been going on almost uninterrupted. The UN panel of experts continued its work and in October 2003 produced new findings against the Rwandan, Ugandan and Kinshasa-based structures. According to the Security Council's experts, the same networks were in effect still operating, reporting to their former military commanders in many cases, but now they acted through their respective local proxy groups inside the Congo. "…The Rwandan Defense Forces (RDF) still play an important but highly discreet role in the [RCD-Goma's] operations …" claimed the report, which also referred to a letter from Kivu governor Serufuli to the RDF chief of staff, supporting Rwanda's proposed "deployment of your elements" throughout the entire province and the imposition of "our policy" in additional territories of his province.

The UN panel found the Rwanda-linked network to have the objective of "permanent, autonomous control over territory in the eastern DRC" and cited ongoing training operations, reporting lines and other evidence of continuing effective control leading back to Kigali.[13] Whatever the interpretation, the Rwandan government at least did not ignore the UN's report this time around. Among their allegations the panel named two specific instances of illegal exploitation by Rwandan entities. Shortly after the report's release, Foreign Minister Charles Murigande announced that he would set up a commission of inquiry to look into the accusations and report back to the UN. It seems almost as if things in the region had come full circle: the UN was getting better and better at intelligence gathering, which had long been a strong suit of the RPF. Meanwhile, the Rwandans had learned the value of the international community's favored ploy of calling for an inquiry whenever potentially embarrassing information emerged.

8

TRANSITION AND CONTROVERSY

Nurturing an Overseas Opposition

By 1999 security inside Rwanda had improved significantly following the successful military campaign against the ex–FAR and *interahamwe* remnants in the Democratic Republic of the Congo, and cross-border raids as well as internal terrorist attacks against civilians had diminished. At home, however, problems of a different nature were growing, and Vice President Kagame and the RPF leadership entered a new crisis phase in their attempts to govern the country, a phase which was to be marked by political scandal, corruption allegations, human rights abuses at home, high-level resignations and legal problems both nationally and internationally.

From the late 1990s until the eve of the presidential elections on August 25, 2003, there was to develop an active and flourishing Rwandan opposition to the ruling government in Kigali, but one which was scarcely represented by the candidates who ultimately participated in the final campaign against incumbent Paul Kagame. Indeed, much of the unarmed opposition became entrenched in neighboring capitals, particularly Kampala and Kinshasa, while many active opponents of the regime remained in Europe and North America, continuing to conduct their campaigns against Kagame through media, legal and diplomatic means. Furthermore, despite the Pretoria Accord and the efforts of South Africa and others in demobilizing the "negative forces" in the Congo, an armed opposition still remained inside the DRC's borders, with a combined strength estimated in late 2002 at between 10,000 and 15,000 men.

In addition to controversies arising from the RPA's activities in the DRC, new evidence was also emerging regarding old issues dating from the period of the genocide and civil war, much of which was potentially damaging to the RPF leadership and to Kagame in particular. Influential opponents of the regime representing a variety of positions and alternative aspirations for the future of Rwanda had by now formed or reformed themselves in exile under a series of alliances and umbrella organizational titles. In addition to the former Hutu leadership, much of which had been saved by the French *Opération Turquoise* intervention in June–August 1994, there were new Hutu alliances, such as ALIR, still favoring an armed return, while moderate Hutus advocating unarmed resistance were also regrouping.

The newest and for Kagame perhaps the most problematic section of the organized opposition came from Tutsi political groups abroad, some representing survivors' organizations who felt they had been passed over in their extreme needs during the post-war reconstruction of the country, while others were defectors from the RPF ranks who had gone into exile. The RPF defectors, mostly moderates who opposed the trend towards erosion of representation for Hutu interests, were being steadily purged from office as the hard-core of the RPF closed ranks in the pursuit of the party line. Also dissenting, mostly but not exclusively on the Tutsi side, were the supporters of a restoration of the monarchy, headed by Kigeli V. The *mwami* and many of his close supporters remained exiled in the United States and continued to believe that the true future of Rwanda ultimately lay in a return to power of the royal family who had run Rwanda until the late 1950s.

These dispersed and disparate groups of opponents attempted to continue their opposition to Kagame, using political, media and business connections abroad, supporting their alternative viewpoints and trying to expose damaging elements in his performance or associating the vice president with known RPF atrocities in the past. Now that the army of the former regime had been routed by the RPA in two countries in the space of five years, the name of the game was to continue the struggle through non-military means.

Tarnishing the RPF's Image

Throughout its early history, both on and off the battlefield, the Rwandan Patriotic Front had gained a reputation for discipline, tight organization, superior strategy and strong ideology. Much of this had been due to the vision, leadership and training imparted by officers such as Fred Rwigyema up to October 1990 and particularly by Paul Kagame from 1990 onwards. The momentum of military success and the movement's image in the eyes of the international community, the diaspora and potential allies was key to the RPF's survival. But by now the public relations campaign waged by Kagame on the international stage was becoming as successful as his military offensives.

Although western supporters were reticent at first, the RPF steadily gained the confidence and tacit backing not only of the UN, but notably also of the United States and Britain and several other major European countries with the exception of France, the latter continuing its stance of muted hostility towards Kigali. Kagame was also able to consolidate alliances in his own region, although relations with the Congo's Joseph Kabila continued to be hostile and the rupture in Rwanda's long military alliance with Uganda's Museveni, although stabilizing after 2002, was never fully repaired.

However, cracks were beginning to appear in the party at home and a key vulnerability of the RPF, namely its increasingly tenuous claim to being a non–ethnically based movement, began to worsen, threatening the unity, image and effectiveness of the party. The 1993 Arusha Accords, from which much of Rwanda's interim constitution was derived, provided for the establishment of a multi-party system, with a cabinet composed of a

President Kagame (center) in December 2000, with (left to right): Bishop Rubwejana, speaker of the National Assembly Joseph Sebarenzi, former president Pasteur Bizimungu and Prime Minister Pierre-Célestin Rwigyema. (From the personal collection of President Paul Kagame.)

balanced membership from all the major parties. Initially, the transitional administration had adhered to the letter of Arusha, allocating the required number of posts to members of the main democratic Hutu parties, although it is debatable whether the spirit of multi-ethnic government was the true aim of the rebel movement which first took power in July of 1994.

From its beginnings, the RPF had skillfully managed to draw on the support of moderate Hutus opposed to the former Kigali regime. The first president of the transitional government, Pasteur Bizimungu, the new regime's second prime minister, Pierre-Célestin Rwigyema, and Interior Minister Seth Sendashonga were all prominent Hutus and each gave a semblance of multi-ethnicity to the regime, while Speaker of the National Assembly Joseph Sebarenzi was a vocal representative of the Tutsi survivors' community. However, by the middle of 2001, Rwigyema was in exile, Bizimungu was under house arrest, Sendashonga had been assassinated in Nairobi and Sebarenzi had fled to the United States. Also banished or otherwise eliminated from the scene were many of their key advisors and members of the media who sought to publish details of the background to their precipitate departures.

The façade of multi-ethnicity crumbled quickly and Kagame increasingly found himself forced into the stance which he had long sought to avoid: that of an embattled military dictator, maintaining power by force and internal repression, representing the interests of only a minority of the total population which he purported to govern. At the same time, the reputation of the RPF for clean financial management of overseas assistance and adherence to international agreements and embargos also disintegrated, among scandals involving the diversion of, for example, World Bank funds.

Around this time in the Democratic Republic of the Congo, allegations were beginning to surface of looting and illegal export of minerals, timber and other resources by Rwandan elements involved in the military conflict, which sparked international controversy and led to UN Security Council investigations into the actions of the RPA and its allies. Kagame initially denied many of the allegations of direct government involvement in the exploitation of the Congo's resources and gave detailed public justification for his country's controversial invasion of the DRC. News of atrocities committed against civilians by the RPA and its allies, although scantily documented due to the difficulty of access to the areas of conflict, also led to concern and criticism of the Rwandan presence. As international attention heightened, the volume of evidence reaching the west both from internal and external sources increasingly confirmed a breakdown of the structure and discipline of the RPA for which it had formerly been admired.

More controversial, however, is the issue of whether the purge of non–Tutsi, non–RPF members of the government which occurred, together with a crackdown on the Hutu population internally, was all part of the Kagame strategy from the outset, signaling that multi-ethnicity had by the late 1990s served its purpose but was not an essential element in long-term RPF strategy. By then, perhaps, with secure borders at home and strong allies abroad, he could arguably afford to dispense with his former colleagues and move on to the task of creating a mono-ethnic military regime.

Combating Revisionism

The rising tide of controversy and the passing of the sympathy factor attached to the immediate post-genocide years not only spawned a greater willingness on the part of outside human rights agencies and investigators to criticize President Kagame's current actions, but it also led them to probe more deeply into past accusations of wartime RPF atrocities which had up till then been largely overlooked.

While many of these investigations and subsequent revelations by their authors, accurate or otherwise, may well have been motivated by an objective desire for revealing the truth and redressing the balance in the overall account of Rwanda's wartime atrocities, others had a more political motivation and indeed an interest in seeing a certain version of recent events gaining a greater acceptance among the international community.

In particular, the "revisionist" tide among the Hutu opposition in exile is a dangerous source of distortion, a tendency which has sought at every opportunity, for example, to exaggerate the deliberate killings by the RPA of Hutu civilians during and after the genocide while minimizing the numbers of deaths of Tutsis during the same period. The aim has been to obscure their own guilt by rewriting history and at the same time to undermine the legitimacy of the current regime. For example, some Hutu opposition revisionists have sought to make reference to a counter-genocide or "double genocide" in 1994, minimizing Tutsi deaths to below 500,000 and estimating civilian massacres by the RPF to be in the hundreds of thousands, so as to almost equate the degree and thereby the nature of the casualties suffered by both sides.

Bearing all of this in mind, it is nevertheless true that in the years after the RPA's victory, new evidence of massacres perpetrated by the rebels during and after the war came to light, much of which tarnished seriously the reputation of the rebel army for discipline in dealing with its vanquished

Hutu enemy and its population. The Kibeho massacre of 1995 shocked many in the diplomatic world who for the first time saw clear evidence of the RPA going after Hutu civilians in hot pursuit following the forced closure of southern Rwanda's last major displaced persons' camp. Other reports of massacres of civilians in the RPA-controlled zone in northern Rwanda in the early weeks of the war resurfaced, and accusations were made that Hutus who were massacred in April 1994 may later have had their bodies thrown into the same graves as Tutsi genocide victims, either to try to cover up their deaths or perhaps to increase the estimates of Tutsi genocide victims.

Perhaps most damning of all was evidence of massacres by RPA soldiers which took place between July and September of 1994, which were the subject of a report prepared by a UNHCR team working on refugee repatriation in northwestern Rwanda at that time. Later named the Gersony Report after its principal author, evidence of alleged systematic killings of Hutu civilians by the RPF, totaling between 25,000 and 40,000 victims in all, was produced and then quickly became the subject of another UN coverup. The UNHCR representative in Kigali, the Tanzanian Roman Urasa, went as far as to write to the UN human rights representative in April 1996, saying that the report "didn't exist, but had only been given verbally in September 1994."[1] Ultimately, a failed UN attempt to protect the RPF in the climate of post-war reconstruction later served only to diminish the credibility of the government that it sought to protect.

As these various reports and other evidence of RPA atrocities emerged at regular intervals in the post-genocide years, Kagame as commander in chief and minister of defense bore direct responsibility for dealing with the perpetrators and restoring discipline within his armed forces. Following Kibeho, the Gersony Report and other evidence pointing to RPA excesses, senior commanders in the field were ultimately tried and imprisoned, although typically officers were convicted for lesser offenses and not for the most heinous crimes of organizing systematic massacres. The commanding officer at Kibeho, Colonel Fred Ibingira, was finally disciplined by the authorities, but not until 1996, over a year after the excesses which occurred under his authority.

In other instances, such as the spate of killings which occurred around Byumba in the northern zone at the beginning of the war, where the international community was initially not present and was subsequently barred from visiting, Kagame admitted that his forces committed atrocities. However, he also sought to stress the relatively low number of victims in the context of the huge slaughter which was ensuing in the rest of the country at around this time.

In the final analysis, the aim has been to selectively admit failures, but at all costs to avoid any possible tarring with the same genocidal brush as the *interahamwe* and the ex–FAR, by pointing, rather, to random breaches of discipline in the field rather than any kind of systematic intent to eliminate civilian populations. With the possible exception of Gersony, for the most part the RPA has to date been absolved of the counter-genocide charge. However, the emergence of such new evidence several years after the end of the war and failed attempts to conceal human rights abuses by the RPA have continued to harm its credibility as a force for confidence-building in a country clawing its way towards democracy in the early years of the twenty-first century.

End of the Multi-ethnic Experiment

The resignation of President Pasteur Bizimungu in March 2000 was the confirmation that the multi-ethnic façade of reconstruction in Rwanda was now at an end. However, the writing had been on the wall for many years, indeed, it seems since the beginnings of Bizimungu's involvement with the rebels. Rwanda's first RPF president joined the movement in 1990 when the former regime executed his brother, then a colonel in the national army. Bizimungu denounced the Habyarimana leadership and moved to Uganda to join the RPF just as it was launching its offensive in October of that year.

Rising through the RPF ranks, upon victory Pasteur Bizimungu was appointed president, but significantly, even at his inauguration ceremony in July 1994, Paul Kagame, as incoming vice president and minister of defense, was the only minister who did not swear allegiance to the new president as he took the oath of office.[2]

In the following year, the first prime minister of the transitional government of 1994, Faustin Twagiramungu, a member of the MDR (who had also held the premiership in the pre-genocide Arusha-mandated cabinet), fled to Belgium, claiming direct threats against him from Kagame. Twagiramungu then began his own opposition movement in exile, campaigning against the Kigali administration. (The former prime minister was to return to Kigali in June of 2003 to contest the presidential elections, being the only exiled opposition leader to return to participate in the campaign.) Thus by 1995 high-level dissent among leading Hutu moderates had already been established, giving a credible voice to the RPF's opposition abroad.

In July of 1999, the five-year transitional government came to an end and a new interim constitution provided for a four-year Government of National Unity (with Bizimungu remaining as president), culminating in elections, which were to be held in 2003. In the following month the first major RPF public defection occurred, as Jean-Pierre Mugabe, formerly an intelligence officer in the RPA and later a journalist and editor of the *Tribune du Peuple*, fled to the United States. Shortly afterwards he accused Kagame and the RPF of large-scale corruption and responsibility for provoking the civil war and genocide, and his accusations were published in a U.S.-based political journal in April 2000.[3]

With clear evidence of development funds having been diverted to the personal and political projects of ministers, Kagame began a crackdown on a series of cabinet colleagues accused of involvement. High-level resignations followed, beginning in October 1999, and a number of convictions were handed down, although mostly for minor offences. Most significantly, however, at the end of the corruption-cleansing purge, not a single RPF resignation had occurred, nor had any prosecutions of RPF ministers or officials been carried out.[4]

Most prominent among the non–RPF resignations was that of the prime minister, Pierre-Célestin Rwigyema, who stepped down on February 28, 2000, claiming that he was the victim of an official smear campaign and that he had been targeted by parliamentary colleagues. Around the same time, Joseph Sebarenzi, former speaker of the National Assembly and a leading member of the Liberal Party, was forced out following what he claimed were fabricated allegations of misconduct. Sebarenzi, formerly a member of the RPF while he was speaker, had been tipped to win the Liberal Party leadership and would have then been in a strong position to run for president as Bizimungu's successor. Sebarenzi fled to Uganda in early 2000 and later moved to the United States; in the first week of March 2000, Assiel Kabera, one of his supporters and a Bizimungu advisor in the parliament, was shot dead by assassins outside his home in Kigali.

On March 20, 2000, President Bizimungu began to speak out against the deliberate targeting of parliamentarians by elements in his own party and in particular the victimization of former prime minister Rwigyema, a fellow Hutu. In response, RPF parliamentarians accused the president of involvement in tax avoidance, irregularities in construction deals and the blocking of a law aimed at censure of members of the assembly. Within a week, Bizimungu too had resigned and shortly afterwards he also fled to the United States.

Assuming the Presidency

Less than a month after this, Paul Kagame was elected president of Rwanda by parliamentary approval, receiving 81 out of 86 votes cast. His only "opponent" in the election was Charles Murigande, secretary-general of the RPF. This action confirmed what most had already taken as the reality of the situation: first, an increasingly sidelined figurehead Hutu president had been ousted on quickly assembled charges when he finally spoke out on a major issue involving hard-line members of his own RPF party. Second, the real power behind the scenes, Paul Kagame, until now the vice president, had been formally placed into the position he already held de facto in what amounted to an internal vote with only token opposition.

The deposed president did not disappear from Rwanda's political scene for long, however. In exile, he raised a strong voice of criticism against the Kigali regime, alleging that its current actions were destined to carry the country once more down the path of ethnic warfare. In June of 2001, after returning to Rwanda, Pasteur Bizimungu founded a new political party, the PDR (Democratic Renewal Party), also known as *Ubuyanja*, or "rebirth"[5] party, together with Charles Ntakirutinka, a former minister of transportation.

Although the 1991 constitution as modified by the 1993 Arusha Accords had clearly provided for the foundation of new parties, the launch of *Ubuyanja* was declared illegal and Bizimungu was arrested for having formed a party in violation of the country's electoral laws. He was later released, but was subjected to continuous harassment. On August 8 he was assaulted in the Remera neighborhood of the capital and on August 17, RPA soldiers drove him and Charles Ntakirutinka to secret locations while their homes were searched for PDR documentation. Other core party members were subjected to similar harassment or imprisonment during the following months.

Purging Divisionism

A core transitional government doctrine upon assuming power was that the politics of ethnicity should never be allowed to return to Rwanda, as this had been the root cause of the forces which ultimately unleashed the 1994 genocide. Later, this doctrine was reinforced and the introduction of individuals or parties advocating "divisionism" became grounds for banning or expulsion. An early example of this was the banning of the

MRND, the party of the late President Habyarimana, as a party with a clearly ethnic agenda. Although the party had split into moderate and extremist wings and members of the former had been prominent critics of the genocide, any reincarnation of the party was banned from the Rwandan scene. A further key condition of any political party's participation was the exclusion of any denial of the genocide and a statement supporting such a revisionist view of Rwanda's recent past would be grounds for banning the party.

In an interview shortly after the PDR's banning, Pasteur Bizimungu said:

> We are convinced that if the current state of affairs continues, the Hutus will prepare for war and in 15 or 20 years they will have driven out the Tutsis with all the foreseeable consequences that this would entail. Mechanisms need to be set up so that each community can genuinely participate in the government, until we have forged a national identity that transcends Hutu-Tutsi divisions.... If the situation does not change, the only possible outcome is violence. The war of 1990 is not over.[6]

Ironically, although his public words warned of the risks of a return to division, the same "divisionist" label had been applied to the PDR as grounds for its exclusion from Rwandan politics.

On April 7, 2002, on the occasion of a speech marking the eighth anniversary of the genocide, President Kagame sent a clear message to the supporters of the former president and those inside the country who would follow in his footsteps. He said that "They hold high political offices in this country, they are still advocating division among Rwandans and spend their time looking for support at the embassies. The day our patience runs out, these means will no longer be of any use to them." His words could hardly have been more directly aimed at the activities of Bizimungu and his supporters.

Finally, on April 19, 2002, Bizimungu and Ntakirutinka were imprisoned in Rwanda and a score of supporters and sympathizers were also arrested. The charge against them was "continuing the activities of a political party which has been banned." They remained in detention up to the time of the elections of 2003, despite international outcry and demands for their release by donor representatives and human rights organizations.

Until that time, the banning of political parties under Rwandan law had been reserved for extreme cases such as that of Habyarimana's MRND, for explicitly being responsible for inciting and conducting genocidal actions. The MRND, whose Arusha-designated seats were reallocated when the new government came to power in 1994, disappeared, although other parties such as the MDR, which also had an extremist wing until April 1994, was allowed to continue in existence for the time being. The banning in 2002 of the PDR marked a distinctly more expedient and less liberal interpretation of the laws governing the legitimacy of political parties in Rwanda.

Unwelcome Flashbacks

While humiliated on their home territory, Kagame's opponents based abroad were able to do more damage to the RPF's reputation and his prestige as leader, partly by refusing to let issues centering on the most controversial date in the country's recent history be forgotten. The April 6, 1994, plane crash in Kigali which killed Presidents Habyarimana of Rwanda and Cyprien Ntaryamira of Burundi and which triggered the three-month genocide of a million Rwandans was still shrouded in mystery. Since 1994, in the outpouring of sympathy for the genocide victims and due to the state of chaos which reigned in Kigali in 1994 for much of the year, no hard evidence leading to identification of the perpetrators of the missile attack had been publicly available. Many had been willing to assume that the evil architects of the genocide must also have been responsible for the event which triggered their actions in 1994. Since the *génocidaires* had by now been exposed, and defeated, the matter could be laid to rest as a tragic but unsolved mystery from a violent, confused and turbulent time, but an incident as well forgotten in the interests of Rwanda's future recovery and reconciliation.

This stance would certainly describe the official position of the Kagame regime in 2001 as well as that of the United States and other pro–Kigali western governments, together with the upper echelons of the United Nations Secretariat. For the UN, the last thing the organization needed was the re-ignition of a controversy refocusing world attention on the Rwanda of April 1994, which together with Mogadishu in 1993, Srebreniza in 1995, Monrovia in 1996, East Timor in 1999 and Democratic Republic of Congo in 2001–2, ranked among the darkest hours in recent times for the conduct of the international body on the world stage.

However, others in opposition to Kagame — his Hutu adversaries in exile and their media and political allies— were not willing to take such a passive approach to the details of recent history. Furthermore, although the crash site where Habyarimana's Mystère Falcon 50 jet had been brought down had been quickly sealed off by the Presidential Guard on that night in April 1994, and officially few details about the evidence of what happened to the presidential plane were available, this had not stopped an inquiring UN official, working on a different mission in Rwanda in 1997 relating to the progress of the International Criminal Tribunal for Rwanda (ICTR), from piecing together other evidence which he had come across during the course of his assignment.[7]

The report disappeared in the secretary-general's office and its findings were never revealed, until Steven Edwards, a journalist writing in the Canadian *National Post* on April 11, 2000, referred to a leaked version of its findings which strongly implicated then Major-General Kagame in the planning and execution of the April 6 attacks. Less than two weeks later, the Paul Mugabe article implicating Kagame and others was released, and around the same time, two Montreal lawyers defending a Hutu ICTR genocide detainee petitioned the UN for release of the report as material evidence in the motivations of their client's actions in Rwanda in 1994.

Furthermore, in 1998, the relatives of the two French pilots killed in the April 1994 crash initiated an investigation which was carried out by the French anti-terrorist judge Jean-Louis Bruguière. The intent was to identify the true perpetrators of the crime with a view to seeking financial restitution, although the case was replete with potential political ramifications.

In late 2001, a Paris-based Cameroonian journalist named Charles Onana, in collaboration with exiled Rwandan journalist Deo Mushayidi, published a book titled *Les Secrets du Génocide Rwandais* containing allegations of Kagame's complicity in the downing of the presidential plane in April 1994. Kagame and the Rwandan state both sued the author, mostly for symbolic damages, but after a number of false starts, the case was finally thrown out on a technicality in April 2002. While Onana trumpeted the decision as a victory for the truth, the court in fact ruled that Kagame's lawyers had failed to meet a three-month filing deadline for such cases, indicating that the defamation case had not been brought in timely fashion under French law and therefore could not be tried.

Evolution of the Armed Opposition

While the attempts of those seeking to pursue change through internal democratic opposition during the transition were largely frustrated, the remainder of the armed Hutu opposition inside the DRC was both striving to reinvent itself and struggling for survival while never renouncing its declared goal of a return to power in Rwanda by force.

The Rassemblement Démocratique des Refugiés, the RDR, which was originally formed in the Goma refugee camps in 1994, had been decimated by the campaigns of the ADFL from 1996 onwards and owed its existence to whatever support Kinshasa could continue to offer. However, the RDR lacked international credibility as did its sister movement the ALIR. Although ALIR was able to carry out attacks into northwest Rwanda until 1998, it had no backing from outside its own immediate power base and efforts to find supporters overseas diminished sharply after the signing of the Pretoria Accords.

A Blood Pact in Exile

If the attempts of the armed opposition to gain credibility were faltering at best, the moderate opponents of President Kagame in exile suffered from their own frustrations, and various groups struggled throughout the closing years of the transition to forge alliances which would allow them to gain some traction in moving a credible anti–Kigali agenda forward. On the Hutu side, notable developments were the creation by Seth Sendashonga, former interior minister, of the Force Démocratique pour la Résistance (FDR), which was to merge in 1998 with the RDR in an attempt to broaden its appeal while at the same time lending much needed non-violent democratic credentials to the refugee movement from the camps.

On the Tutsi side, the frustrations of the survivors of the genocide began to emerge during the reconstruction of the late 1990s. Initially focused on a deep grudge held regarding what was felt as the scant resources going towards those who had suffered the most, their argument also had its foundations in the nature of the diaspora itself and the role and character of each of the main returning groups. In as much as the ruling faction in Kigali since 1994 came largely from the Ugandan diaspora where the RPF had its origins, those from the Burundian and Congolese Tutsi returnee communities soon began to feel their own particular frustrations after the initial period of "pulling together" to rebuild the country after the genocide.

Therefore, on the one hand the genocide survivors felt that their needs were being overlooked, as the group who had suffered the most while the Ugandan-exiled Tutsis simply walked in and took over, not only politically but materially as well; on the other side the non–Ugandan diaspora felt marginalized in the new order of things, under which top government and military posts, for example, were frequently allocated to the "Left-

Hand drivers," as the dominant group from Ugandan exile were nick-named. The returnees from Burundi, Tanzania and Zaire increasingly felt that they had to settle for a type of second-class status in Rwanda's transition society.

The political expression of these Tutsi dissident voices took the form of a movement known as *Ibuka*, which became an umbrella organization for survivors' groups. Among the more prominent members of this group was Assiel Kabera, the Bizimungu advisor who met an untimely end in Kigali in March of 2000.

Outside Rwanda, two opposition political movements with strong Tutsi participation, principally francophone, were founded in 2001: the Alliance for National Reintegration (ARENA) was founded in the United States and NATION, a pro-monarchist movement, was launched in February of that year in Belgium. ARENA brought together many of the leading figures from the post–1994 political class in Rwanda, including former president of the parliament Joseph Sebarenzi and former prime minister Pierre-Célestin Rwigyema. Its spokesperson, Alexandre Kimenyi, formerly a senior member of the RPF who had left for the United States, claimed that the party was open to all Rwandans, not only those with monarchist sympathies. NATION is a more overtly monarchist group, seeing the best future for Rwanda as a return for King Kigeli, currently in exile in the United States, to lead the establishment of a parliamentary monarchy, with real powers for the monarch particularly in the selection process for key political appointments.

A major flaw in the credibility of the opposition groups claiming monarchist affiliation, however, was the low profile of the king himself. Although his supporters could at times be quite vociferous, Kigeli rarely issued statements or attempted to challenge the status quo inside his homeland. The secretary-general of the Rwandan Red Cross, Alphonse Kalinganire, didn't see much likelihood of a monarchy-based challenge for these reasons. Kalinganire, a recent returnee to Rwanda himself, having been exiled in various countries since 1973, said: "He [Kigeli] doesn't say himself what should be done, it would be better if he told Rwandans what he wants for the country, not leaving it to his supporters."[8]

Therefore, while the Tutsi opposition groups were able to gather considerable support and command respect from elements of the diaspora outside the country, like the moderate Hutu opposition, their ability to influence events inside Rwanda remained limited. While the Forces Démocratiques de Libération du Rwanda (FDLR) and the RDR had guns, they lacked credibility, being chronically tainted with the brush of the 1994 genocide; but what the unarmed Hutu and Tutsi opposition gained in respectability and democratic credentials they at the same time lost through having no military threat behind them. In the context of 1990s African Great Lakes politics no political movement without a military force to back it up could expect to make much headway through the channels to power in the region.

An attempt at a resolution of this dilemma for the diverse and divided elements of the opposition, Hutu and Tutsi, armed and unarmed, exiled outside the region or based on Rwanda's frontiers, was the establishment of an unholy and unlikely alliance to form a common front against the RPF which became known as *Igihango* or the "Pact Sealed in Blood." Thus former sworn enemies from the Hutu-Tutsi divide came together with the facilitation of a defector from the ranks of the RPF, Valens Kajeguhawa. Formerly a prominent businessman and supporter of the new Kigali regime, he piloted the launch of *Igihango,* which was officially known as the Alliance for Democracy and National Reconciliation (ADRN). The ADRN brought together the leaderships of the Hutu FDLR armed movement on the one side and the mostly Tutsi democratic ARENA and NATION alliances on the other, in a coalition that was both political and military in its ambitions.

The prospects of such a pact retaining cohesion given the past history of enmity between its component members seem in doubt. The creation of the alliance recalls the words of an ancient Rwandan fable in which a childhood lover and his sweetheart are about to be separated but vow to remain loyal whatever befalls them. The boy and girl, just before parting, each utter in turn the Kinyarwandan words: *"Uramuka urongowe n'undi, igihango kikakwica"*— "If you marry with another, this blood pact will kill you."[9]

Although in the fable the boy and girl are reunited and eventually marry and live happily ever after, in the context of the modern Rwandan diaspora the childhood threat would probably better predict the future course of the opposition's *Igihango* than the prospect of the happy ending in the Rwandan fairy story.

Authority versus Democracy in the Post-Genocide Transition

Clearly there was no shortage of opposition to the RPF-dominated Rwandan government, and the constituencies opposed to Paul Kagame became broader and more organized as Rwanda's process of political transition unfolded. The underpinnings, methods and day-to-day consequences of the RPF political strategy clearly alienated many important groups and individuals who could have played a part in the country's reconstruction. But how appropriate has the approach of Rwanda's rulers been since 1994 and to what extent has the dissent encountered been a necessary cost of the survival of the country, its internal security and the recovery and reconciliation of the majority of its population who chose to return or remain in the years after the genocide?

The origins of the RPF, in molding its strategy and political philosophy, are a good starting point for an examination of the record. Born out of its association with the successful rebellion of Yoweri Museveni's National Resistance Army in Uganda, the ideology of the RPF since taking power has many parallels with the Ugandan model. Initially a guerrilla movement striving to overthrow an overtly racist and tyrannical regime, once in power Museveni explicitly avoided any early attempt to hold democratic elections, preferring to create his famous "No-Party State" with the NRM at its helm.

In so doing, since the late 1980s Uganda succeeded in building an economy if not a society which has been held up as a model of successful development, with a strategy of pro-western free market economics and privatization that has pleased the World Bank and IMF as well as winning adulation from political leaders in the United States and Europe. A persistent civil war against the Lord's Resistance Army in the northern part of the country and the criticisms that accompanied Uganda's role in its military/economic exploitation of the eastern part of the DRC have been serious difficulties for the NRM. However, consistently high economic growth rates and a successful containment of HIV/AIDS, among other achievements, have won Museveni's style and philosophy more admirers than detractors internationally over the years.

Paul Kagame sought to emulate much of Uganda's success if not the underlying philosophy of Museveni's National Resistance Movement in his administration of post-genocide Rwanda. Clearly, given the country's demographics and the experience of the closing years of the Habyarimana regime, an early return to pluralism was out of the question. What the RPF stressed in its approach was the need for *consensual* government, already enshrined in the Arusha Accords, but with priority to be given to political education and awareness-raising among the general population as first steps towards building a new constitution.

The stress given to these building blocks was judged appropriate at this stage for Rwanda's divided and largely illiterate society, in its search for a way forward out of ethnic division and recovering from the trauma of the genocide. Critics have pointed to Rwanda's absence of protection for civil rights, freedom of speech and the media, or the ability to form new political parties and engage in debate about the government's policies, but in the government's view, for the time being and in its fragile state, Rwandan democracy was unprepared for such freedoms which observers elsewhere might consider fundamental.

The experiment with multi-party government in Rwanda which occurred from 1990–1994 could in other circumstances have served as a precedent for rebuilding democracy in transition Rwanda, but in the light of the tragic consequences of that period, any political division along ethnic lines was explicitly excluded by the new administration. In Kagame's own words:

> ...If you try to organize elections, to authorize parties to grow like mushrooms and allow competition, you create an even bigger problem for yourself than you already have: dividing people who are already divided.
>
> What does the multi-party system mean in our African societies? That I will use every tactic to distinguish myself from my neighbor with the aim of winning more votes than he wins.... We will never have democracy: people will prey on each other. One party would emerge to defend the perpetrators of genocide, while another would emerge to say that the perpetrators should be tried. We would end up with a great war...[10]

In this way the vice president of the new transitional government of Rwanda both warned of potential dangers and summarized his party's philosophy which would guide the political reconstruction which lay ahead for his country. In the process of launching the new Constitutional Commission, an action already provided for in the 1993 Arusha agreements, Kagame stressed cohesion, political education and accountability as prerequisites for the restoration of political rights. The crucial emphasis at the core of the process, which culminated in a popular vote to approve the new document in May of 2003, was the priority which the economic and social rights of Rwandans were to have even though this may have come initially at the cost of some of their civil rights.

The commission was established in late 2000 and encompassed distinct phases, ranging from awareness-raising and consultation with grassroots voters, to data collation and analysis, to drafting and finalization of the document, to the referendum in 2003 at which Rwandans ultimately gave their seal of approval to the whole process.

Despite the lack of civil rights which would be cause for outrage in many advanced western democracies, the suitability of the approach for the extreme circumstances of the times as well as the temperament and condition of the Rwandan people was undeniable. Furthermore, President Kagame made one major concession to his political opponents in 2002 by confirming that the forthcoming presidential and legislative elections would be conducted by universal suffrage — against the advice of some of his closest advisors, particularly in the military, who preferred a form of indirect elections using pre-screened candidates who could be relied upon to support the incumbent regime.

In making this concession Kagame took a gamble, as he would need to win over a substantial proportion of the Hutu majority in order to remain in power. (Opponents of universal suffrage could point to the precedent from the 1993 elections in Burundi when Pierre Buyoya, a Tutsi who took power in a coup but then later went to the polls in the belief that his policies would be favored by both Hutus and Tutsis, lost the elections to the opposition candidate, Melchior Ndadaye.)

As the transition proceeded, the increasingly authoritarian element in the RPF's policies drew criticism both at home and abroad, resulting in both political and media opponents being either muzzled, expelled or otherwise eliminated from the political scene as described earlier in this chapter. It is clear that political opponents from the Hutu majority would always clamor for democracy, not only because it is such an obvious rallying point of support for western sympathizers, but also as it was the birth of democracy, or more accurately, majority rule, which brought them to power in the early 1960s after decades of minority dominance.

Is Rwanda Exceptional?

The decision to prioritize security, social cohesion and political awareness over free expression and broad civil rights has numerous parallels in societies which have been thought of as successful and moderate in other respects and at other times in their history. The early progress of the emerging Asian economies such as Malaysia, Taiwan and South Korea in the aftermath of World War II was partly achieved through decades of authoritarian rule, which was accepted by much of the population as a necessary sacrifice and only gave way to democracy some time after their economic and social miracles had been achieved.

More economically advanced nations have also shown their willingness to suspend civil rights not as much for reconstruction but instead for security reasons — as evidenced most notably in recent times by the continued assertion of the George W. Bush administration since September 2001 that the United States was engaged in a "war on terror." This declaration and its almost daily repetition across channels of national communication proved more than sufficient for Americans to accept a steady curtailment of civil rights through restrictions on the media, detentions without trial, global military interventions and the passage of new laws to underpin many of these actions. Few of the measures implemented between late 2001 and 2003 would have been acceptable to the majority of Americans in the preceding half-century of economic prosperity and evolving liberal institutions which were a model for much of the democratizing world. However, during that period, they quickly became acceptable to a population fed a regular diet of media hysteria and color-coded warnings on television of potential terrorist attacks.

Without prejudice to either the example of the Asian Tigers, where economic development was prioritized, nor the experience of post–September 11, 2001, in the United States, where security against terrorism took center stage, it would be difficult to deny that Rwanda in the decade since the genocide has been constantly challenged by overwhelming difficulties in both its economic reconstruction and its national security. In this context, recourse to authoritarianism and suspension of civil rights can be put in perspective against the familiar non–African examples from other recent situations where similar policies have been pursued.

Beyond the economic and security challenges, Rwanda in transition has also been trying to undertake the impossible in reconciling its populations: with a devastated economy in the 1990s and a near-constant security threat from across its border, the government had to work to resettle and reconcile Tutsis with Hutus, the survivor community with returning refugees, victims with the accused, rapists with widows, soldiers with trauma victims and returning diasporas with the dispossessed.

All this the government stated since the outset in July 1994 that it would try to achieve. Since the very first days of the Tanzanian and Zairian camps, Paul Kagame said that the refugees would have to return, that justice would not only have to be done but also be seen to be done and that the perpetrators of the genocide would have to be disarmed either inside or outside Rwanda's borders. The RPF shrank from none of these tasks, although it meant committing over 100,000 of its own citizens to prison, many of whom the authorities knew could never be tried. It also meant risking renewed social fracture and antagonizing international human rights groups by executing the ringleaders of the genocide in the name of their victims. Finally, it also entailed provoking international criticism by invading the territory of Rwanda's neighbor, where those who would continue the genocide found a safe haven from justice for a time.

To draw another parallel from the developed world, imagine the task that would have faced post-war Germany if the surviving European Jewish and German populations had been required to rebuild their lives in the same shattered economy, sharing the same territory and moving back into neighborhoods together to reclaim their properties and start afresh. Would it have been possible for Jewish genocide survivors to face former Nazis on a daily basis only months after the end of the holocaust? How much more complex would the reconstruction of Germany have been if the onus of reconciliation had been added to the other massive challenges which post-war Germany had to face?

It is this type of question that outsiders might ponder before judging the restrictions and the imperfections of Rwanda in the decade since the genocide. Even considering this comparison, with accepting its validity should go part of an improved understanding of the Rwandan experience and adding context in advance of criticism for the foreign observer of contemporary politics in the African Great Lakes.

9

FROM GENOCIDE TO *GACACA*: DELIVERING JUSTICE IN RWANDA

A Foundation for Healing

By late August 1994, the militias and leading *génocidaires* had left Rwanda; the former government had fled with the country's skilled manpower and economic resources, taking more than three million of the Hutu population with it; the French forces deployed under *Opération Turquoise* had flown back to their bases in nearby African states and beyond; and the killing, for the meantime, was over. What was left of the country was nothing more than an empty ruin full of corpses, a shipwreck of a state peopled by traumatized, destitute survivors washed up against a landscape of unimaginable terror.

A newly constituted UNAMIR, fully discredited in the eyes of the population, was filtering back to set up again inside a militarily secure Rwanda, and the Tutsi diaspora was steadily making its way across the country's borders to what was in practice a foreign land for many of the returnees. But neither the UN, with its absence of moral authority, nor the newcomers from Uganda with no experience of government could contribute what was now urgently needed to put together the society and infrastructure that had completely imploded over the past four months.

Only the victorious rebel army had the means to operate in the country, not only to provide security and order, but also to succor the survivors and attend to the administration of the basic functions of government and reconstruction.

Although material impoverishment was acute and outside aid for the newly formed Rwandan government was slow in coming, of equal urgency for those who were left was a need for healing before reconciliation, for retribution before forgiveness and for punishment of the guilty before allowing back inside Rwanda a Hutu refugee community much of which, in their eyes, had blood still fresh on its hands.

In short, although Rwanda could only get back on its feet again with injections of outside money, little of lasting worth could be achieved without justice. But how to administer justice in a country with no judges, no courts, no formal legal code, only an embryonic police force and a central prison system designed for 12,000 inmates faced with a caseload of potential criminals that could easily number in the hundreds of thousands?

Resisting Impunity

The traumatized population was baying for retribution and in this environment revenge killings were commonplace; the country could easily slip back into anarchy without the establishment of judicial order and the swift arrest, if not trial and punishment of the thousands of genocide suspects still walking freely through Rwanda's streets and fields.

In scenes that were commonplace in the months following the RPA's victory, ordinary peasants would alert the notorious RPA *abakada,* the vigilante soldiers who effectively meted out justice on Rwanda's hillsides during those times, identifying neighbors who they accused of involvement in the genocide. The military also had their own targets of *génocidaires* for elimination, some of whom they recognized as having killed family members or their own neighbors. In this way, through their operations, Hutus would routinely disappear or be taken away, either imprisoned or killed in a system of rough-and-ready justice with no basis other than local denunciation by survivors or selection by *abakada* who had effectively taken the law into their own hands.

The RPF's policy on taking power excluded a return to mob rule or uncontrolled vigilante killings, however, and Kagame soon ordered the arrest and often the imprisonment of RPF soldiers caught carrying out unauthorized revenge murders in the country. More importantly, the new government set about implementing its goals of ending the cycle of ethnic hatred, exposing the architects of the genocide and outlawing the ideologies and institutions that had made it possible. Furthermore, it was committed to punishing the killers and above all reconciling and reconstructing the country on the basis of justice, a goal shared by those few in the international community who already supported Rwanda's cause.

However, the new RPF administration was then without the means and the majority in the international community was still without the motivation to create a justice system for Rwanda equal to its huge needs and to the unique circumstances of the mass crimes that had just been committed.

It was even quietly suggested to the new regime by some that, facing the insurmountable task of trying and sentencing what was reliably estimated as fully a tenth of the Hutu population as potential *génocidaires*, it would be better to just let bygones be bygones, try to move ahead and look to the future and let time heal the wounds of the Rwandan people's sufferings.

This sentiment was unacceptable to the RPF leadership and Kagame found it nothing short of an insult. Some two years later he said: "Some people even think we should not be affected. They think we are like animals, when you've lost some family you can be consoled, given some bread and tea — and forget about it ... sometimes I think that this is contempt for us. ...These Europeans used to come, giving us sodas, telling us 'you should not do this, you do this' and I said 'Don't you have feelings? These feelings have affected people'"[1]

Legal Bases for Action

Since independence, Rwanda had had no legal profession or bar for the formation of lawyers and judges and only a rudimentary court system. The codified law was largely unpublished and very out of date, and not available in local Kinyarwandan language. Therefore the law was often administered arbitrarily, by the executive rather than judicial authority and according to the policy and preferences of the country's rulers who were often liable to corruption.

Even in the absence of a formally trained legal profession, those with experience in the administration of justice at any level had mostly fled the country: 90 percent of police and detectives had left or had been killed; almost two thirds of the 719 accredited magistrates were gone; the tribunal buildings had been looted, reference materials, files and case records had been destroyed[2]; so Rwanda was faced with the task of starting from zero to establish the process through which those responsible for the genocide could be tried.

If Rwanda had no formal national legal framework for apprehending and prosecuting the guilty, however, the international community already did. In fact a law had been on the international statute books for 46 years before Rwanda's genocide occurred. On December 9, 1948, the UN General Assembly adopted resolution 260A(III), the Convention on the Prevention and Punishment of the Crime of Genocide. Among its more pertinent clauses, the signatories to the convention confirmed that genocide "...is a crime under international law which they undertake to prevent and to punish." The document further listed a series of acts which defined the crime as "...acts committed with intent to destroy, in whole or in part, a national, ethnical, racial or religious group." Having failed in one of the undertakings of its own convention, the prevention of a genocide in Rwanda, there still existed the obligation to carry out the punishment of the perpetrators, conspirators, accomplices, and inciters of the crime.

As early as May 1994, with the genocide fully under way, Kagame had already called on the international community to establish a tribunal to arrest the killers and punish the guilty. Rwanda in May 1994 was in a state of terror and the international community was in a state of paralysis; but when the killing came to an end two months later, it seemed that the paralysis of the outside world had yet to run its course.

Although the UN Security Council had an enormous amount of evidence to the effect that a genocide had occurred by mid–1994, in the famous spirit of the organization, before acting it was able to find time in early July to establish one more commission of experts to examine and analyze "information concerning serious violations of international law, including genocide."

The commission duly produced an interim report in October 1994 and found that there had been "mass extermination perpetrated by Hutu elements against the Tutsi group" and that these acts had been "concerted, planned and methodical" in nature and "constitute genocide." Details of massacres in villages, streets, on hillsides and farms, inside churches, schools and hospitals were produced. The documented evidence was overwhelming. Finally, on November 8, 1994, with its resolution 955 the Security Council voted to establish the International Criminal Tribunal for Rwanda (ICTR) with the South African Richard Goldstone, veteran of the similar tribunal set up in the mid–1990s for the former Yugoslavia, later nominated as its chief.

The court was desperately slow in starting its proceedings and was fundamentally flawed in its conception; furthermore, the inefficiency and expense of its operation were soon to become an embarrassing farce which added fresh insult to the Rwandan people as well as ultimately working counter to the judicial needs of their fragile society. Many critics have described its main purpose as to assuage the guilt of the west for its inaction during the genocide rather than to provide a worthy legal forum for the trial and sentencing of the *génocidaires.*

One such critic was Charles Murigande, at the time chairman of

Rwanda's Presidential Commission on Accountability for the Genocide. He summed it up thus: "The tribunal was created essentially to appease the conscience of the international community, which has failed to live up to its conventions on genocide. It wants to look as if it is doing something, which is often worse than doing nothing at all."[3]

After every kind of bureaucratic delay in the preparation of its buildings, personnel and administration, the first trial of the ICTR began in early 1997 in Arusha, Tanzania. While Rwanda was crying out for the resources it needed to build prisons, train judges and establish a civilian police force, the international tribunal was granted an annual budget of $180 million.

The International Tribunal: An Expensive Embarrassment

With these funds at its disposal its investigators were able to apprehend only a handful of those on its already minimal wanted list. Its cumbersome preparations, tardy deployment of investigators and excruciatingly lengthy proceedings were often overtly exploited and wantonly subverted by the suspects themselves to further delay their potential conviction.

Such was its performance that for many years only a few of the indicted suspects on the ICTR's list had been apprehended, with some of the most notorious of the genocide's architects remaining at large in the west and other African countries as the pantomime in Arusha continued. In the case of one of the genocide's military masterminds, Colonel Théoneste Bagosora, who was apprehended in Cameroon in March 1996, the UN actually opposed Rwanda's extradition request to have him stand trial at home and was ultimately successful in bringing him to the tribunal in Tanzania. Bagosora's trial began in April of 2002 and was still under way there in September of 2003.

The region's old guard of rulers initially obstructed the process too: Zaire's Mobutu and Kenya's dynastic Daniel arap Moi were more in the mold of, if not loyal to the memory of, the deceased Habyarimana and his extremist successors. The pursuit of the criminals in Zaire was complex, muddied by the continuing war and the numerous factions struggling for power and resources within its borders; in Kenya, however, Vice President Kagame took matters into his own hands on the occasion of a state visit to Nairobi in July 1997, making an issue of the fugitive killers who were still being harbored in the aging ruler's republic.

At that time Kagame spoke of "a feeling of betrayal, even by our African brothers." As a thinly veiled warning to his neighbors' rulers he went on: "What happened here can happen elsewhere — it can happen in these other countries — and then I am sure they will run to us. ...Things have happened and they can happen again."[4]

Within days of Kagame's state visit a total of nine suspects on the ICTR's wanted list were handed over by the Kenyan authorities, including the former prime minister of the April 1994 "interim government," Jean Kambanda; Hassan Ngeze, editor of the Hutu Power *Kangura* magazine; and the Belgian broadcaster for RTLMC, Georges Ruggiu. Kambanda was sentenced to life imprisonment and Ruggiu received 12 years, while Ngeze's trial was still continuing over six years after his apprehension in Kenya.

Another contentious issue between Kagame and the ICTR focused on the starting and ending dates of crimes committed which could be within the jurisdiction of the court. Arusha was given jurisdiction over offences occurring between January 1 and December 31, 1994, although the genocide had ended in early July. The implication was that abuses committed under (and therefore probably by) the new regime could equally be brought before the ICTR as could offences which occurred during the genocide. This clearly changed the scope and the nature of the tribunal into something much wider than a court for the trial of genocide and, the RPF leadership would argue, made it more open to political manipulation.

While the issue did not surface in a serious way for several years, by 2002 the insistence of the then chief prosecutor, the Swiss-born Carla del Ponte, on investigating alleged abuses by the RPF led to a clash with President Kagame. Ms. del Ponte, speaking about the showdown with Kagame and quoted in the September 13, 2003, issue of *The Guardian*, afterwards, said that the Rwandan president had said to her that his job was to investigate the army and her job was to investigate the genocide. "This work of yours is creating political problems for me ... you are going to destabilize the country this way," the chief prosecutor reported him as saying to her. She said he had screamed at her "as if he was giving me an order" but that she had refused to back down.

The compromise solution that Kigali had suggested was to split the two trials, not to confuse the genocide trials with the pursuit of alleged atrocities by the RPA. Carla del Ponte, who was also presiding over the trial of Slobodan Milosovic in The Hague, remained adamant that the issues should remain combined in a single trial.

President Kagame had made it clear to the secretary-general of the UN, Kofi Annan, that he felt the country's stability was being threatened

by the court's stance. It was decided that a replacement for the chief prosecutor would be required in order to defuse the issue and Ms. del Ponte
was forced out from her position. Referring to Kagame's intransigence on
the issue, del Ponte commented: "…if I had given in, if I had accepted his
orders, I would still be there."

Although its functioning improved markedly in the later years of its
operation, with many of the most senior military and civilian planners and
executors of the genocide being detained, by mid–2003 the ICTR had managed to complete a total of only 15 trials, with a further 20 under way and
30 in detention awaiting trial.[5] The average cost of trying each suspect
before the ICTR up to that time was an estimated $50 million.

A limited amount of international support had already been offered,
with Belgium sending 300 junior personnel funded by international NGOs
to help with compilation of criminal dossiers in late 1994. The Netherlands
provided support for training judges and the United Kingdom later provided support for the civilian police force. Around the same time the UN
and European Union deployed teams of young human rights monitors,
many of whom were going for their first time to Africa, let alone on a mission to monitor the effects and repercussions on human rights of a genocide.

These teams were unpopular with the RPF not so much for their inex-
perience but more for the fact that their brief was more to observe what
was *currently* happening — more likely to be violations of Hutu civilians'
rights by the RPA in the climate of the times— than to help investigate the
mass of undocumented suspects from the genocide of a few months earlier. Worse still, from all of the work that the observers ultimately carried
out, none of the dossiers compiled was shared with the manpower-starved
Rwandan judicial authorities.

Capital Punishment:
Controversy and Catharsis

Meanwhile, in the reality of resource-strapped Rwanda, the first genocide trials had begun in December 1996. Not all the accused had legal representation, and trials were slow although not by the standards of the
ICTR. Judges still had limited legal training but time was working against
Rwanda's reconciliation and the authorities felt that they had to move forward. Admittedly with imperfect procedures and limited facilities, some
important sentences were handed down and the trials of the first suspected
capital offenders of the genocide were completed during 1997.

While the intentions of the international tribunal were laudable, it would be impossible to underestimate the importance for the survivors and genocide victim community of seeing swift and appropriate justice for the known mass murderers and organizers of the genocide. In order to alleviate grief, to restore faith in the current authorities' commitment to justice and security more generally, punishment had to be administered and had to be seen to be administered before Rwanda as a country could move on, with the hope of one day once more becoming a more normally functioning society.

African Justice for African Healing

This meant that the convicted killers had to receive justice in front of their own communities, not in a neighboring country, and that they should be given the sentences that contemporary Rwandan society demanded — meaning the death penalty for the most serious offences. To an African widow whose husband has been murdered or a father who has seen his family hacked to death with his own eyes, it is not enough to know that the organizers of the genocide are sitting with no fear for their lives in a comfortable modern prison cell in Senegal or Sweden. Only capital punishment would reassure a Rwandan living with such a legacy that justice had been delivered satisfactorily.

The timetable and modus operandi of the ICTR and the needs of Rwandan society were therefore very much at odds with one another, and once again, when the Ministry of Justice in Kigali decided on controversial actions, it was often met with a chorus of criticism from the community of international observers and human rights agencies.

On April 24, 1998, a total of 22 people were killed in public executions throughout Rwanda, all for the part which they played in the genocide. Included in those taken before a firing squad in Kigali was the notorious Froduald Karamira, an arch-propagandist of the Hutu Power movement. He had been arrested in Ethiopia and extradited to Rwanda, the first such international extradition of a Rwandan genocide suspect to take place. He was tried in January 1997, and after only three days in the courtroom was sentenced to death. Sneering at the prosecution as his sentence was read out, he had challenged the legitimacy of the court and defied his captors to carry out the sentence, say that he would gladly die if it would do any good for the people of Rwanda.

A year and three months later, Karamira and three other convicts, including one woman, were taken to a public hill in the center of Kigali dressed in pink Rwandan prisoners' uniforms, then tied, blindfolded and bound to stakes, where they waited for some 15 minutes for the firing squad to do its work. At the moment of the executions, the crowd roared with approval, testament to the intense need of the people to see the necessary justice done, in public and above all in front of survivors and families of the genocide victims.

Various international bodies including the UN High Commission for Human Rights (UNHCHR) had protested and demanded clemency for the accused, indeed clamoring for a stay of executions right up until the final moment. The rhetoric of the UN had often been an irritant to the RPF-led government, but this time the meddling in Rwanda's internal affairs, as they saw it, was too much. After some bitter exchanges following the April executions, the authorities gave the representative of the UNHCHR in Kigali just three days to leave the country.

Although the executions were widely criticized at the time by international human rights agencies, the psychological healing offered by those sentences to the ordinary survivors of the genocide was palpable as evidenced by the cheer of approval that the executions of Karamira and others were met with in 1998. For this reason, many otherwise moderate leaders in Rwanda's new administration argued strongly for the ICTR trials to take place on Rwandan soil and for the death penalty to be allowed.

As Kagame himself said, paraphrasing certain patronizing Europeans who wanted to transplant a sentencing regime suitable for another continent onto a society with totally different needs and expectations, "do it like this, don't do it like that" is an insult to Rwandans and it does not work. A court operating hundreds of miles away in another country, with a snail's pace of proceedings, rapidly became irrelevant to the mass of Rwandan people looking for visible evidence of justice being done before moving on to the task of rebuilding their lives.

The case of Colonel Bagosora highlights another key flaw which the absence of the death penalty at Arusha created for the ICTR. Without question, as one of the main figures behind the genocide Bagosora would have received a capital sentence in Rwanda, in the same way as Karamira and several other of the ringleaders apprehended by Kigali. But in his case, the international community visibly denied the catharsis which his eradication could have afforded — even to the extent of successfully contesting his extradition to Rwanda. For most Rwandans, the lighter the sentences for the biggest offenders and the less visible their punishment, the longer it will take to move on and put the trauma of the genocide behind them.

Following his election as president in 2003, Kagame reflected on the international court's performance: "It should have come long ago that the international community dealt with the question of justice ... Rwanda is capable of dealing with these justice questions itself.... For all the time it has been there and the resources it has consumed, the ICTR could have done more," he said. Defenders of the court's location pointed to the chaos of Rwanda following the genocide and the impossibility of setting it up properly in a devastated country. Kagame only partially accepted this explanation, however. "I find that it was very important to bring the court here to operate in Rwanda…. At the beginning I understood, as maybe at the beginning there was not the infrastructure, but after five, six, seven years, they should have brought it here."[6]

Prisoner Politics

In all between 1996 and 2000, Rwandan justice had tried around 6,000 genocide suspects and the trials of 2,500 more suspects were by then under way. However, with a rapidly growing detainee population, at the pace at which trials were being managed, the process could theoretically last for decades longer, frustrating both the letter of the law as well as the purpose of justice in satisfying the needs of the victims.

Starting in late 1994, the prison population grew rapidly as rudimentary civil order returned to the country and arrests of suspects began to replace revenge killings by vigilante civilians' groups and the RPA. In November 1994 the prison population was estimated at 10,000; but by the middle of the following year it had grown to over 40,000 and in November 1996 there were 86,000 detainees.[7] Former minister of justice Gerald Gahima estimated by 1998 there were no fewer than 130,000 suspects in detention awaiting trial.[8]

Kigali Central Prison, designed for 5,000 inmates, had over six times that number by 1997. The countryside was full of detainees, many held in makeshift *cachots,* basically rural huts where small numbers of suspects were locked up in minimal conditions of space and sanitation. In all, by early 1998, there were an estimated 120,000 people awaiting trial on charges relating to the 1994 genocide.

Clearly the number of arrests would rapidly outpace the ability of the Rwandan judicial system to cope initially, while it struggled to muster the resources to put in place the necessary personnel and facilities to try and sentence the accused. In 1996, $30 million was received and put to work in training judicial police, compiling dossiers of the accused, expanding the prison system, establishing a supreme court and recruiting magistrates and procurators. All this should have relieved the pressure on the system as time went by and as stability gradually returned to the country. However, the rapid growth and persistent high numbers of detainees drew increasing attention from a political standpoint throughout the late 1990s, leading to the identification of another agenda in play than the problem of the legal resources of the state.

Criticisms have been leveled that the authorities deliberately dragged their feet in trying suspects in order to keep the detainee population high, indeed to maintain the overcrowded prisons and bulging communal lock-ups as a reminder to the world, as a kind of permanent exhibit of the unhealed wounds of Rwandan society. Furthermore, the ability of the army to detain suspects effectively knowing that no trials would occur due to the backlog also proved useful to the maintenance of security in the country, particularly after late 1996 when the insurgency in the northwest became a serious menace to the regime.

Against the "internal control" argument, however, is the equally strong argument in favor of the survivors' feelings and memories of the victims. If large numbers of lesser offenders were tried, with some being found guilty and others doubtless released while the genocide's leaders were still at large outside the country's borders, there would remain the risk of a kind of watered-down justice having been done, a substitute for the real thing which the Rwandan people still demanded. Kagame himself spoke of both the government's responsibility to the victims and the need to heal Rwandan society.

In other words, trying a large number of small culprits to appease the relatives of their victims would help in one sense, but if the cost was to allow international pressure to be taken off the need for arrest and detention of the genocide's masterminds, then it would be a wasted effort. The world would become weary of the search, point to the substantial numbers already tried and utter "enough is enough" and "time to move on" and other sentiments to that effect.

In a different time and place, in the Nuremberg trials of Nazi war criminals in the late 1940s, many of the most notorious suspects were tried and executed or imprisoned. But as time wore on and the new pressures of fighting the cold war against communism became the priority, as many as possible of Germany's top people were needed for that new effort; in many cases those awaiting trial were quietly released back to civilian life — although others still at large, particularly those responsible for the holocaust against the Jews, would be pursued relentlessly for decades across the globe by Jewish survivors' organizations and self-styled "Nazi-hunters" such as Ephraim Zuroff[9] of the Wiesenthal Center in Tel Aviv, Israel.

In this vein, Rwanda's new leaders could rightfully point to the need to maintain the relentless struggle for justice, not to let up the international search for the *génocidaires* even if it meant keeping a showcase mass of other detainees in prison in the meantime as a reminder to those who would otherwise have preferred to quietly forget.

In the climate of accusations of go-slow in the Rwandan post-genocide system, criticism also arose over Kigali's refusal to accept foreign judges who were offered as a form of "humanitarian aid" to the struggling regime. The government stood firm, however, rejecting the notion of any judge from a francophone African country presiding over Rwandan genocide trials. Although the use of additional trained judges from overseas could in theory lend not only impartiality but also much-needed professional expertise to the massive task before the Rwandans, the leadership in Kigali had strong grounds to be suspicious of the offer.

Not only was there proof that many of the indicted criminals thus far apprehended had fled to countries like Zaire, Cameroon, Mali, Togo, Benin, Burkina Faso, Côte d'Ivoire and indeed to France itself — but had it not been the mother country of *francophonie* which had — through her intervention in the southwest of Rwanda in June–August 1994 — helped many on the wanted list to escape to those states in the first place? Quite apart from France's role in hampering the work of the ICTR, the offer of foreign judges from the same francophone African countries which had harbored the very criminals that they would then be asked to try was unlikely to be seen as anything other than another attempt at subverting rather than expediting the post-genocide judicial process.

Alternative Medicine for Open Wounds

Even as the new judicial personnel were put in place, however, difficulties of a different nature came quickly to the surface, complications which even the arbiters of justice at Nuremberg had never had to face. At least in the trials which followed World War II, the accused were Germans and the judges were from the allies. But in post-genocide Rwanda, despite the background and career of many of its members, the RPF was not a foreign occupying power and many of the judges themselves were from the Hutu community.

In the context of the reconciliation which the Government of National Unity was trying to foster, this put judges from both sides of the ethnic divide into near-impossible positions: the Tutsis could always be accused of partisanship in finding accused genocide suspects guilty, while the Hutu judges, if harsh, could face a backlash from their own community, or if lenient might risk being removed from office and accused of condoning crimes against Tutsis and siding with the *génocidaires.*

In 1995 an experiment was tried with the establishment of a Triage

Commission—a body whose aim was the release of selected prisoners for whom there was insufficient evidence to bring them to trial for crimes of genocide. Under this scheme, many were let go, among them former provincial civil servants and other public office holders. At that still tense moment in Rwandan society, however, the urge for quick justice of any kind was strong, and not all of those released could return to civilian life in security.

One extreme case was that of Placide Koloni, a former deputy governor who was released by the Triage Commission in late July 1995. A few days after his release, he and his family died following an explosion which occurred late one night at their Kigali home.

In the early post-genocide phase it was not only high-profile prisoners but also many ordinary detainees who made the grim calculation that they might be better off inside prison for the time being rather than being released, with or without trial. While numerous reports of torture and abuse of prisoners were voiced from the informal countryside *cachots*, in the central prison system, overcrowded as it was, the inmates were for the most part left unmolested.

Indeed, such was the system that the guards did not enter into prison cells and the detainees very rarely attempted escape. Some of the reasons for this mutual distancing and respect for order had less disinterested origins, however. On the part of the guards, there was the public relations aspect, as Kigali Central Prison and other major centers of internment were almost compulsory stops for visiting foreign journalists as well as Red Cross staff and human rights observers. Inmates were frequently given an opportunity to voice their complaints, and so it was in the interests of the authorities to make sure that there were as few grounds for scandal as possible.

On the part of the prisoners, especially in the days preceding the Congo uprising and invasion, many took the stance of protesting their innocence, denying that the genocide had been a deliberate massacre of Tutsis by Hutus and in general continued to follow what was the "party line" in the Hutu Power–controlled refugee camps. Not infrequently, prisoners would say that they expected to be out soon since "the others," i.e., their former partners in killing, now in the camps—or even operating as guerrillas from villages inside northwest Rwanda—would soon return and liberate them from detention.

"If you tell the truth you can be forgiven, or your punishment reduced" (Poster campaign in Kigali)

Clearly this kind of stubborn solidarity made the concept of pardon for the many, based on their ultimate confessions and testimony against the few, all the more difficult for the Rwandan judiciary. Nevertheless, this was one objective which the authorities began to work towards as part of their strategy of clearing the backlog of minor offenders.

The continuing prisoner problem and the accompanying mood of constant fear of internment by ordinary Hutus worked counter to other key policies of the government, including the campaign to secure the refugees' return from the camps. Quite apart from the vice-like grip which the *interahamwe* militias and ex–FAR remnants were able to maintain over the captive Hutu masses in the Tanzanian and Zairian camps—mostly through threats of violence — there was also a propaganda war being waged to deter those brave few who were tired of life in exile and wanted to try their luck in the new recovering Rwanda. Although in the context of a crowded, foreign-based refugee camp it was not hard to control and manipulate information, any instances of real human rights violations or stories of arrest or murder by the authorities which the militias could point to would aid their cause.

To counter this and mindful of the ever-watchful international eyes fixed upon their embryonic justice system, it was important to rebuild confidence with the ordinary Hutu civilians at home, many of whom could inevitably be in communication with families and ex-neighbors on the other side of the border. Evidence of atrocities or flagrant violations of human rights, which could then be used as propaganda by the former government in exile to deter returnees, could be highly damaging to Kigali's aims.

A second issue stemming from Hutu insecurity was the mounting criticism of the RPF approach from Hutu MDR coalition partners such as Prime Minister Faustin Twagiramungu and dissident RPF Minister of the Interior Seth Sendashonga. As evidenced by their resignations in 1995, the mood of fear in the country threatened the cohesion and continuity of the coalition government itself. Lastly, but closely related to the other factors, the government's broader long-term strategy for repairing and reconciling the disparate elements of Rwandan society could only be put at risk by the absence of a working justice system and a solution to the festering detainee problem.

Therefore, despite its initial insistence on the need for internment and trial of every murderer, the RPF was forced to find another way of delivering justice for society as a whole rather than striving for the impossible aim of administering individual sentences to every guilty party.

The importance of long-term reconciliation would have to take precedence over short-term retribution for the victims and for this a strategy was developed to allow the many who "followed" the genocide's leaders, or were forced to kill because they had no choice, to be pardoned and let go, if they would confess and ask forgiveness.

In 1996 the government passed a law[10] in which it devised a ranking of criminals by category from the masterminds and planners of the genocide, for whom the death penalty was the only option considered; to the lieutenants, the operators of the roadblocks and willful local instigators of killing, for whom prison sentences awaited; to the unwilling or coerced killers who were caught up in the wave of violence sweeping across the countryside and who were forced to become accomplices in the harvest of death.

This last category, which perhaps accounted for the majority of those in prison, was the key to an expedited handling of the huge prison population and was at the heart of the amnesty initiative which ultimately became the preferred solution of the RPF. Gerald Gahima, at the time deputy minister of justice, described the new approach as "getting as many ordinary people off the hook as possible" and further qualified the strategy, imperfect as it was, as the lesser of two evils: "...that's not justice is it. It's not the justice the law provides for.... It's only the best justice we can try for under the circumstances."[11]

The new law also established the principle of reduced sentences for those who confessed as well as attempting to strike a balance between individual accountability for crimes under the law and the needs of society for reconciliation and stability and without further dividing communities already split by the genocide.

The people whom the law was willing to pardon were people like Noel Kayanda, who was in his village of Nyagukombe, east of Kigali, in April 1994 when one day a truckload of soldiers drew up with a woman and a girl and told Noel to kill them. After the soldiers shot his brother, who had refused to kill the people, Noel took a machete and cut down the two Tutsis whom the soldiers had brought. He then fled to Zaire where his wife died of starvation in the jungles, after which he came back to Rwanda and was imprisoned.

In 2003, however, Noel Kayanda was set free after confessing and asking forgiveness. He got a job making bricks and was accepted back into his village, even by the Tutsi survivors who remember what he did. Speaking of his crime, Noel explained: "I had no choice. So I killed the girl then I killed the woman ... I did not know them." Then, Noel pointed to a banana grove nearby and added: "That's my land. It was stolen from me when I was in prison. By a Tutsi. I've offered to share it with him but he says no."[12]

Although Kayanda's story of confession and forgiveness may offer a beacon of hope for the resolution of Rwanda's genocide detainee problem, the final comments he made by the banana grove highlight another unresolved issue in the reconciliation of Rwandan society: managing the return and reallocation of property after genocide between the various communities that now inhabit the crowded, psychologically crippled corner of territory that is contemporary Rwanda.

Gacaca—*Justice of the Forefathers*

In unison with the new policy of confession, forgiveness and reconciliation for the lowest category of killers, Rwanda turned to an ancient remedy for its societal ills—a system of trial and judgment without defense lawyers or state prosecutors, but only with local citizens as witnesses and lay judges to pronounce decisions of innocence or guilt. The accused stand in the open among the villagers or neighbors of their former communities; any and all are asked to speak up, either in favor of or against the one on trial. This system, which was used in traditional Rwandan society to resolve property disputes or matters of theft and damage at the local level, is known as *gacaca* (pronounced "Gah-**cha**-cha").

Since 2002 Rwanda's leaders rehabilitated and extended this ancient means of administering justice, by extending it to the hearing and resolution of crimes committed in the 1994 genocide. There are obvious drawbacks to a system which relies on untrained and inexperienced lay judges. While human rights groups initially expressed concern about bias against the accused who have no legal representation, others have criticized a system where certain communities may be inclined to acquit one of their own for reasons of ethnic solidarity.

The key to the success of *gacaca* lies not as much in its ability to deliver formal sentences, but more as a cost-effective means to provide a hearing of the facts, an airing of the truth and a mechanism for healing in the affected communities. The admitted weaknesses of the system against the huge savings in money, desperately needed for social programs together with the opportunity to resolve the otherwise intractable problem of formally trying every genocide suspect, were seen by the RPF as a trade-off with more benefits than risks.

The importance of timing in introducing *gacaca* was paramount: the incoming government had considered its use as early as 1995 but rejected the idea then as the population, it was felt, would never accept its methods and place their faith in its pronouncements. However, by 2002 the time seemed right to try, eight years after the genocide, when people were preparing for elections and beginning to scent the first comforting whiff of economic recovery in the air.

The initial pilot program of *gacaca* trials led to a fuller implementation of the system in 2003 with the selection of 250,000 local judges who would pronounce sentences in their communities, combined with an awareness campaign to explain the system to the people who would soon participate in it at grassroots level. Under *gacaca*, the maximum sentence that can be given is 15 years, of which half can be substituted with military service.

In the 12 months from October 2002 when the process began, 25 percent of all detainees were released under *gacaca* law, either as low-category offenders or because of the impossibility of sufficient evidence being brought against them.

The revival of the *gacaca* system, as bold as it was unconventional, was taken up with surprising readiness by the ordinary people on Rwanda's hillsides. Indeed, as government planners began to seek out the senior citizens with knowledge of its functioning, known as *bashingantahe* or "wise men" of the towns and villages of the country's prefectures, they found that in many instances, a form of *gacaca* was already in use.

Natural as it was for ordinary people to understand, the system is particularly suited to Rwandan society and potentially an ideal solution for dealing with the very special case of intercommunity, ethnically based offences, of which genocide is of course the extreme example. Its suitability

Roadside poster promoting participation in *gacaca*.

stems from two sources: firstly in the simplicity and openness of its functioning and the "after-trial participation" of both the convicted and the witnesses, in the vitally necessary process of healing and reconciliation which follows judgment; but secondly, it also could be combined with the other core element of traditional Rwandan justice, involving the provision of economic reparations to the victim's families.

In traditional Rwandan society, everything pivoted around the economics of the hillside: the number of cows owned or the piece of land worked by each peasant and his family gave life and status and, it could even determine a kind of "economic ethnicity." Therefore, when a victim's house was burned and his cows were stolen and particularly if his sons and daughters, the workforce on which the family livelihood depended, had been killed, the expectation was that compensation would be proffered to right the material loss, whether or not the emotional and human loss could so easily be made good.

So it was found that by 2002, returning *génocidaires* and accomplices in some instances had already been through a form of *gacaca* and were rebuilding the houses or working the land for the families of their former victims, according to the traditional way.

The other part of *gacaca*, where both criminal and witness, offender and victim are supposed to work together in a process of reconciliation and healing, may be less easy to achieve in the context of the massive trauma of genocide. In a stark departure from western-style justice, those who testify against an accused are also supposed to be responsible for guaranteeing his repayment to the community and ultimately his reconciliation within it.

However, the burden of post-genocide justice may ultimately strain a system which was able to function well in cases of theft of property or minor injury, but may still not work in the context of mass murder. Like Noel Kayanda, who confessed and was forgiven by many in his village, offering to share his former land with the ethnic opposite who took it from him while he was in prison was not enough. Forgiveness and healing does not always extend to letting the guilty recover what once was theirs. *Gacaca* may help to heal Rwandan society and empty its prisons, but for many the memories will not go away and the resentment will remain for a long time to come.

Justice for Rwanda

For a nation recovering from a preventable catastrophe, not only are there questions of individual justice to address but there is also the issue of social justice for a country whose people have been wronged. For Rwanda's leaders, the priorities which the international community set in providing recovery assistance to Rwanda in the years following the genocide fell far short of properly compensating for what had happened in 1994. In the field of justice, too, there was waste where there could have been hope.

Gerald Gahima, the chief prosecutor of Rwanda, posed the question to a symposium of international observers in September 2003, asking why it is that "...international donors give less to the Rwandan court system, about $2 million per year, when they still give over $100 million a year to the ICTR ... instead of choosing to provide retroviral drugs for HIV rape victims costing around $50 per month."[13]

10

CONSULTING THE PEOPLE

The transitional administration in Rwanda extended its term in 1999 for an additional four years to allow further time for stability to take hold but also to work through the process of developing a new constitution for the country. The culmination of the constitutional consultation was to be a popular referendum to approve its terms, followed shortly thereafter by presidential then legislative elections, all of which had to be completed by the end of 2003, signaling the official end to transition in Rwanda.

Since 1994, there had been no unified constitution in force. Some of the earlier provisions of the Arusha documents, such as the commitment to multi-party democracy, had been retained, but there were also elements of existing Rwandan law and new declarations from the RPF's victory statement in July 1994 which formed the basis for certain sections of the interim constitution. One such provision was the commitment made by the RPF on assuming power to ending government based on ethnic definitions, such as the imposition of quotas for education and employment according to the racial origin of the applicant.

For the most part, Rwanda had no experience of government by constitution, however. The previous administration had largely exercised power in arbitrary fashion, with little reference to any underlying principles of law, whether civil, criminal or constitutional. Under Juvenal Habyarimana, things were done mostly according to the will of the president and so the concept of constitutional democracy which was above and beyond the modification of the executive branch was largely a new one for the Rwandan population.

Involvement and Awareness

The first phase in launching the constitutional consultation process was a grassroots information campaign, intended to run from July 2001 to July 2002, for which a "training" booklet was published and distributed throughout the country. This was combined with political awareness sessions in the districts, which were conducted right down to the level of the commune by Commune Development Committees. Information on models of different international constitutional arrangements were assembled by the Constitutional Commission then presented to the ordinary people for discussion, comment and feedback.

Questionnaires were devised to facilitate the process, although with such a high proportion of illiterate citizens, other arrangements had to be made to involve the wider population. Local commissioners held discussion groups in which their role was to "facilitate," to elicit reactions and proposals from ordinary citizens, rather than leading the groups towards any particular conclusion. A wide range of topics was put forward for discussion, including subjects such as types of regime, individual rights and responsibilities, nationality, sources of conflict and their means of resolution, justice and law enforcement, political arrangements and provision for special representation of youth and women.

The results were then inserted into a database and analyzed before being drafted and resubmitted to the local groups for validation. Commission chairman Tito Rutaremara illustrated the techniques which were adopted: "We needed above all participation and involvement with the issues, even by those who could not read the training book.... We set up free telephone numbers to receive responses and suggestions. Many people discussed the proposals in their local bars and called in from there to add their comments. Even ideas which were already good were debated at local level to ensure the involvement and acceptance of the population."[1]

Then a special system of weighting inputs on specific issues according to the qualifications of the respondent was devised. Ordinary individuals' replies received a weighting of one. However, if the topic was, for example, health and a doctor responded, that input was given a double weighting. Group responses received three points and groups of specialists in their field received four and so on. In this way an attempt was made to obtain a filtered but authoritative sample of ideas from the populace, while taking account of the knowledge and human resources available in the community.

In the final analysis, however, did the whole process really make a difference to the content, as opposed to awareness of the constitution which was finally drafted and later submitted in referendum for popular approval? Rutaremara said that in some cases it definitely did. "We asked people to tell us what they thought were at the origins of the country's problems. They said, for example, 'different interests combating for power' and 'the arbitrary means of taking decisions affecting society.' They told us that we, the leaders of the country, have to put ourselves together and find solutions through consensus. So when we came to draft the constitution we addressed these points in certain specific provisions."

In the Constitutional Chapter on Fundamental Principles, Article 9 reads:

> The State of Rwanda commits itself to conform to the following fundamental principles:...
> 2. eradication of ethnic, regional and other divisions and promotion of national unity;
> 3. equitable sharing of power;
> 4. building a state based on the rule of law, a pluralistic democratic government ... ensuring that women are granted at least thirty percent of posts in decision making organs....
> 6. constant quest for solutions through dialogue and consensus.[2]

The enshrinement of consensual government is confirmed as is the maintenance of power-sharing, a long-standing principle since the days of the Arusha agreements. The revolutionary inclusion of a minimum quota for women in the legislature was an idea which the RPF had long adhered to but which it forced into the constitutional debate — bringing its inclusion into the fundamental principles of the document by initiating discussion and gauging the reactions of ordinary people. "Although not used to the idea [of serious representation for women] at first, especially in rural areas," Rutaremara said, "through a process of sensitization and after debating locally, women soon grasped it and the concept gained acceptance then finally inclusion in the constitution."

In its efforts to consult the widest group of Rwandans possible in the drafting of the constitution, members of the overseas diaspora, including opposition groups, were invited to comment and participate, although few made the trip to Rwanda to join the process. According to Commission president Rutaremara, no formal inputs were received from groups such as *Igihango* and others claiming to represent Rwandans in exile. "We even met with Alexandre Kimenyi [the leader of U.S.-based group ARENA] in San Francisco, at the time of the state visit in March 2003, inviting him to participate, but he didn't come," said Rutaremara. Kimenyi's *Igihango* followers continued to comment and criticize, but the group made no formal submission of inputs to the Constitutional Commission.

The early part of 2003 saw the winding up of the constitutional consultation process, with the final processing of the preceding year's series of questionnaires and popular interview sessions, which were then analyzed and incorporated into a new draft document. Experts on constitutional law from the United States, Belgium and South Africa were brought in to appraise the preliminary work and assist in refining the final document.

The third phase of the consultation, the validation of popular inputs, was undertaken to ensure full acceptance of the findings of the initial discussion and drafting exercise. Once validated and approved by the Transitional National Assembly, the date for popular approval of the constitution by referendum was fixed for May 26, 2003.

With the financial support and monitoring of international bodies such as the European Union, the referendum was duly carried out and the new constitution received a massive seal of approval from the population. Some 95 percent of the electorate voted in favor of its adoption, paving the way for democratic balloting for both the presidency and the national assembly later that year.

The constitution provided for the election of a president who could serve for a maximum of two seven-year terms. In Kagame's case, since he had already been in power for three years, but had not yet been elected, this meant that he could theoretically rule for a total of seventeen years within the terms of the constitution. Following the presidential vote, within 30 days elections were to be held for an assembly to be composed of 80 deputies who were to serve a five-year term. In addition, a 26-member senate would be appointed in part by the main political parties themselves, in part by key interest groups and also by the personal selection of the president.

From Consultation to Candidacy

After nine years in power for Rwanda's transitional government and over three years for Paul Kagame as its president, the moment of truth arrived in August 2003. The long-promised democratic elections were to be held in which he, as yet an unelected head of state from an ethnic group representing no more than 15 percent of the population, would submit himself to the scrutiny of the ballot box in an election conducted by universal suffrage.

How could a president who had gained power through a military invasion win over the support of a majority of Hutu voters, many of whom had supported his rebel army's ethnic adversaries only nine years earlier?

Kagame's advisors, particularly those in the military, believed that there was a risk of the elections becoming a catalyst for further bloodshed. Some pointed to the experience of Burundi in 1993 when President Pierre

Buyoya, also a minority Tutsi in that country, had gambled on the popularity of his relatively progressive policies with the country's Hutu population and lost. Melchior Ndadaye, Burundi's first-ever Hutu president, was elected instead, with 65 percent of the vote, but in the same year he was murdered by army officers, sparking a massive wave of unrest and killing on both sides of the country's racial divide. Another tragic example of an incumbent regime refusing to accept defeat at the polls occurred in 1991 in North Africa. In the ill-fated Algerian elections of that year, a Muslim fundamentalist victory led to the cancellation of the result and the imposition of martial law, in turn triggering one of Africa's most brutal terrorist uprisings in modern times.

In the event of a possible electoral defeat, therefore, would Kagame the incumbent be tempted to use his powers to annul or ignore an unfavorable result as had happened elsewhere, and what would be the consequences for stability in Rwanda?

On the face of it the RPF's control of Rwandan politics could be threatened, especially as the eyes of the world would be fixed closely on the conduct of the campaign. In the wake of the controversy of the Congo invasions, accusations of corruption, human rights violations and mounting donor irritation at what many saw as an increasingly one-party authoritarian state, Rwanda's incumbent president could ill afford any kind of scandal to emerge during the polling.

Paul Kagame declared his candidacy in early June 2003 shortly after the result of the constitutional referendum. Meanwhile, the main representative of the opposition, Faustin Twagiramungu, a Canadian-trained economist who was still in exile in Belgium, prepared to return to his homeland to stand against the incumbent. It was eight years since the MDR prime minister had resigned, following a series of killings inside the country allegedly carried out by the RPA, leading to a clash with Kagame in August of 1995. After citing these issues as well as open threats against him in his letter of resignation to President Bizimungu, Twagiramungu had fled the country while remaining an active voice in opposition from his Belgian base.

However, the 58-year-old moderate opposition leader had also opposed Habyarimana's regime, strongly condemned the genocide and lost dozens of family members himself in 1994. He reportedly only escaped the *interahamwe* by wrapping himself up in a tarpaulin and being smuggled to safety across Rwanda's border with Zaire. Despite these credentials and this personal experience, Twagiramungu was to be tarred early on with the all-encompassing "divisionist" brush by the RPF establishment. This slur was to be a continuing weapon used against him and others who could be accused of reverting to ethnicity as a means of rallying support in their campaign rhetoric.

As early as January 2003, however, Faustin Twagiramungu declared his intention to run for the presidency, seeing himself as leader in exile of Rwanda's largest opposition party and the probable recipient of support from the vast majority of the country's Hutu voters.[3] Shortly after announcing his intentions, he already launched a broadside against the Kigali regime: "The Rwandan people have been disappointed by the RPF," he said. "They were promised a democracy which has been turned into dictatorship.... Newspapers are being closed, journalists are put in jail, people are forced to adopt the words of the president. It is intolerable. Today people are tired of Kagame not only in Rwanda but throughout the region. But he has to give us the means to challenge him and the Rwandan people the right to choose."[4]

Undermining the Opposition

From the standpoint of the RPF, the trump card of incumbency, as in all elections, would prove a major asset in defeating an opposition which could potentially outnumber it many times over. In addition, the policy and indeed strategy of denouncing "divisionism" became a valuable and frequently used pretext for removing potential challengers from the election arena.

In the same way as PDR-*Ubuyanja* had been eliminated using the divisionist charge and its leaders expelled or imprisoned, so in the election year did the MDR, Twagiramungu's party, come under judicial scrutiny for similar reasons. Although the process was far more lengthy, the MDR having been an established political party since Rwanda's independence, the parliament initiated an investigation into the role which it had played in "the divisions which had characterized Rwanda's history." As with other anti-government targets during this period, once the fateful "D" word had been uttered, it was a good bet that the party's days were numbered.

A commission was set up to consult with government and outside experts and to rule on the MDR's future; in April 2003 it found that the MDR was internally split (it had indeed been particularly split in the pre-1994 days of mounting extremism in government) and that it was "divisionist," promoting a pro–Hutu ideology which was illegal under Rwandan law. From there the official banning of the MDR was only a matter of time, but not before several of its other supporters had been harassed, arrested or expelled from the country.

Indeed, the debate on the MDR became an extremely effective device not only to discredit and dissolve the main opposition party, but also to eliminate various individuals who could become strong adversaries of the RPF in the forthcoming elections. Throughout the early months of 2003 various prominent members of the administration, the military and other political parties either fled or disappeared after being cited in the commission's proceedings. In some cases they went directly abroad after just being warned that they might be implicated in investigations related to the anti–MDR vendetta, which was soon expanded into a kind of rolling witch hunt against dissenters from various sections of public life.

Among those who fled was the former minister of defense, General Emmanuel Habyarimana, who left for Uganda and later sought asylum in Belgium after being accused of disloyalty by a government spokesperson. Dr. Leonard Hitimana, another moderate MDR deputy who, like Twagiramungu, had been an active opponent of the genocide, disappeared on April 7 in suspicious circumstances.[5]

Freedom to Join the Party

A further aspect of the pre-election months was the intensive campaign by the RPF to bring as many people as possible into the party, especially members of professions and community leaders, who in Rwanda wield disproportionate influence on the local populace. RPF activists in certain areas were reported to have embarked on a campaign of counseling, persuading, soliciting and coercing influential and respected Rwandans to join the party. Meetings were held at which pressure was reportedly put on people to join the RPF as well as to encourage others to join. Accusations were made that party officials often approached prospective members repeatedly until they agreed to join and that the aim was to give the impression that to not join would be to identify oneself with the opposition, which in turn was likely to be a sign of advocating "division"—with all the possible implications which that highly loaded term carried in the political and legal contexts of the moment.[6]

RPF officials countered these charges by claiming that there was a spontaneous desire on the part of many people to join the party in the run-up to the elections and it would have infringed their rights to prevent them from doing so. Whatever their true motivations, the pre-election months saw a sharp increase in membership of the RPF and unquestionably contributed to the overwhelming performance which the party was ultimately able to record at the ballot box.

A remarkable aspect of the election preparation process which surprised outside observers was the manner in which part of the necessary funding for the conduct of the polling was raised. Although Rwanda had asked its backers in the international community to provide the necessary financing, not all of the funds had been made available in time for the ballot. The European Union, for example, financed and conducted operations for the monitoring process but, after earlier committing to fund the elections as well, it held back the funds originally earmarked for financing the administration of the polling itself.

In response to this, certain communities set about raising money from voters themselves, in an unprecedented show of determination to carry out the country's first democratic elections. In Nyamirambo, Kigali's most populous district with over 100,000 inhabitants, Mayor Dusabamungu set about mobilizing to raise the necessary financing through a series of measures intended to secure small contributions from the largest possible number of citizens.

First, all civil servants on the district's payroll were asked to contribute 20 percent of their salaries in two consecutive months. This measure raised 2.5 million francs, or about $4,500. Then the ordinary population was asked to give voluntary contributions of at least 300 francs, or about 50 U.S. cents each, which raised a further 1.3 million francs. Finally a series of events such as public concerts was planned to raise the balance of the 5 million francs required to fully underwrite Nyamirambo's elections.

It was against this background that Faustin Twagiramungu returned to Rwanda in June 2003, a leader without a party, preparing to face a well-financed and well-established RPF incumbent. Furthermore, the dates of the presidential elections, which had originally been foreseen by the Constitutional Commission as taking place in November 2003, had been moved up to August 25. Whatever the official justification for the change in the timetable, it was easy to see that this measure left Twagiramungu and the other independent candidates almost no time to organize a local support base, hire campaign workers and organize rallies in the country to bring out voters to support them.

Although Twagiramungu initially sought to establish a new party, by the time of going to the polls, the embryonic Alliance for Democracy, Equity and Progress (ADEP), the potential successor party to the MDR had yet to receive governmental approval. Because of this and with the small amount of time remaining, he ultimately decided to run as an independent, while at the same time calling the elections to be postponed. The other two independent candidates, Nepomuscene Nayinzira and Alvere Mukabaramba, also demanded more time to establish their candidacies.

Twagiramungu's main election policies consisted of accelerating the process of democracy, ending what he called "one-party dictatorship," returning the monarch, Kigeli V, from the United States as well as improving efforts towards regional peace and returning Rwandan refugees from neighboring countries. Interestingly, in pre-election interviews he also spoke of a need to "free the minds of Rwandans," a pointed reference to the all-pervasive influence of the government on civic activity, access to information and freedom of association which he believed had increasingly characterized Rwandan society in the years immediately prior to elections.

In the wake of the disappearances of opposition leaders and the recent passage of the laws allowing the dates for elections to be set, Kagame's opponents called for the donors who were funding the process, principally the European Union and the Netherlands, to insist on a deferral of the polling date. In early July Twagiramungu complained that it was unfair "that Kagame had already been able to campaign for many months," adding that "the EU should not fund the elections in the current circumstances."[7] Ultimately the Dutch Ministry for Development Cooperation did cut its financial support for the elections, but probably more because of lingering disapproval at the controversial departures of opposition leaders and less on account of the timing of the elections themselves.

In response to the postponement calls, President Kagame, however, stood firm: "Faustin Twagiramungu, some years back was making noises that we were delaying bringing about elections. So I'm surprised that when elections come he starts asking for a postponement … we have been making it clear at every stage that we have been heading for elections." Regarding opponents such as Twagiramungu who were only just returning to the country, he continued: "…many of them are worried because they have spent a lot of time staying outside Rwanda. The fact is that some of us stayed in Rwanda trying to solve the problems and if there is an advantage in that, so be it. It's not our fault that we stayed in the country…"[8]

With weeks to go before the poll, Twagiramungu therefore prepared to take on the formidable RPF electioneering machine with a total of two cars, one computer and 12 volunteer regional representatives. State-run radio continued to blast out accusations of his opponent's divisionism, while emphasizing Kagame's slogan: "*Ubumwe, Demokarasi, N'Amajyambere*" (Unity, Democracy and Development). The president moved around the country from one well-attended rally to another underlining his message and cementing his popularity. At his opening rally in Kigali's Amahoro Stadium, Paul Kagame addressed a crowd of 50,000 enthusiastic, cheering supporters.

Achievement Through Authority Wins the Day

There can be little doubt that by August 2003 the vast majority of the Rwandan electorate associated their president closely with the recent years of security and stability that their country has known since the end of the insurgency in the north and west of the country. Despite continuing poverty, the tentative economic recovery was beginning to be felt by the ordinary peasant as well as the party leadership. Most importantly, the RPF's efforts at rebuilding a devastated and traumatized society, towards the reconciliation of the survivor, victim and perpetrator communities, *génocidaires* and orphans, returnees and rapists, allowed Kagame to establish his image as the unique unifying force against a return to ethnic confrontation and killing.

In a country with a high illiteracy rate — many voters chose their candidate at the ballot box by thumbprint — and where people are used to being told what to do by their leaders and then doing it, there could have been little prospect of any other outcome than a win for Kagame. The tactics used during the election run-up by the RPF would not be acceptable in advanced democracies nor against the standards of western civil rights; however, although espousing democracy as an objective, it is important to note that the RPF's leaders never claimed that their country could yet have achieved full democratic conditions due to the traumatic events and insecurity of the recent past. Most have used phrases such as a "transition to democracy" and a "transition process which will take a long time" by way of justification for the less-than-perfect conditions in which the campaigning and elections were conducted.

Memories of the genocide and the fear of a return to ethnic violence still remained the crowning justification for the irregularities which would have been strongly condemned in a western democratic process. Tharcisse Karugarama, vice president of the Rwandan Supreme Court, summed up the position of the country's leadership in the week before the election: "There are still those who would like to finish off what they started," he said, in a barely disguised reference to unrepentant *génocidaires* still at large inside as well as outside the country. "Given our past it is not possible to have perfect elections."[8] What he might have said too was that so soon after genocide, allowing freewheeling debate, unrestricted candidacies and a totally level playing field for a potentially violent opposition to organize and campaign was a luxury which Rwanda in 2003 could not afford.

To summarize the approach and the expectations of the RPF leadership, in a speech given in March 2003 Kagame himself expressed confidence that the process could only lead to one result and gave his reasons why: "I can even say that the outcome of these elections is known. Those elected will be individuals who are 100 percent in line with the current political agenda, aimed at building the country. This will be the case and I am sure that it is also your wish to have national security, unity, development and democracy. Anyone who would bring in division ... will not be elected."[10] The approach seems to have been a mixture of confidence and a determination to win but at the same time an almost casual affirmation that there could only be one possible outcome.

"Tora Kagame"— Vote Kagame

With the process and the preparations all pointing to a Kagame victory, there would be little by way of consolation or encouragement for Faustin Twagiramungu in the final days of his campaign. Just prior to polling day Alvere Mukabaramba, the only female candidate, dropped out of the race and declared her support for the incumbent. The week before

Paul Kagame election banner, August 2003, Kibuye.

the election, the executive secretary of the National Unity and Reconciliation Commission (NURC), Fatuma Ndagiza, accused the challenger of
"spreading negative and divisive ideologies geared at planting seeds of ethnic hatred among Rwandans." At a press conference in Kigali she accused
Twagiramungu and his provincial campaign officers of threatening the
population in rural areas with a return to war if they voted for Kagame.
She went on to tell reporters that the opposition candidate's representatives were "...creating confusion and an atmosphere of fear within the
population. This is jeopardizing what we've already achieved on the
ground. It is awakening old wounds."[11]

The final blow against Twagiramungu came two days before the election when all 12 of his provincial campaign representatives were arrested
for "planning to coordinate acts of violence in all the provinces," according to a police spokesman.[12] The representatives were held in custody but,
up until the time of polling, none of them were charged with a crime.
With his representatives in the provinces eliminated, Twagiramungu's
hopes of any substantial showing in the polls were dashed. Some of his
campaign managers appeared on television and renounced support for
their leader. One former manager wrote to him, apologizing and tender-
ing his resignation; the letter, shown to a journalist in Kigali on the eve of
polling day, contained the words: "I'm sorry, but I have to stay alive."[13]

The arrest of Twagiramungu's campaign agents and the continuing
detention of Bizimungu and disappearances of others became focal points
of pre-election international criticism, but the government defended its
actions according to its laws and the circumstances facing the country.
Charles Murigande, minister of foreign affairs, expressed the frustration
of his leadership with the attitude of some outsiders towards African
nations like Rwanda managing their own democratic processes: "...for
them, during elections, our countries should become like jungles," according to Murigande. "The law should cease to apply during the election
period.... The conduct of politics is governed by laws and these laws do
not cease to apply during elections."[14]

To a people more used to following instructions from their rulers and
culturally indisposed to public displays of dissent, the message from the
government was by then crystal clear. At dawn the following day the Rwandan people began to line up in front of the polling stations to cast their
votes, many dressed in their Sunday best; it was the first time since the
genocide that they had been offered a chance to exercise a democratic voice,
and for the first time since independence there had been an election with
at least some choice of candidates to vote for.

Grim Reminder of 1994

In Kigali, shops observed a day holiday and the streets were empty until 1 pm when the polls closed. Schools, churches and municipal buildings, many of which had been the sites of brutal massacres of terrified Tutsis seeking protection from the genocidal militias who rampaged through the capital in April 1994, were converted into polling stations, in a poignant reminder for some Rwandans of how much their country had changed in nine years.

One of the polling stations in Kigali was the building of the Ecole Technique Officielle (ETO) in Kicukiro, the place where, on April 11, 1994, a contingent of 90 UN peacekeepers protecting over 2,000 terrified Tutsi civilians had received the order to abandon the people they were protecting. Outside the school that day stood a detachment of Habyarimana's Presidential Guard and a swarming mass of Hutu militiamen with guns, grenades and machetes, waiting and shouting threats and insults at their terrified prey. At 2 P.M. that afternoon, the Belgian and French peacekeepers drove out of the school compound for the last time, firing in the air as people tried to cling onto the side of their trucks, begging the UN soldiers to take them along, all in vain.

Even before the dust from the tracks of the peacekeepers' trucks had settled, the militia under the direction of Georges Rutaganda, an agricultural engineer and national president of a Hutu militia group, started to fire at the people and throw grenades into the crowd. Some tried to break through the killers to escape to the UN headquarters, but they were cut down by machetes. The rest were then herded down the road for an hour by the government soldiers and made to sit down by a gravel pit near the Nyanza Primary School, where they were then killed. The few survivors of that day were children who had managed to hide under their parents' dead bodies as the militia came round finishing people off after the slaughter.[15]

One such survivor was the 23-year-old Juvenal Arawujo, who was present again at Kicukiro on election day, but vividly recalled the trauma of that afternoon nine years ago: "The Belgian soldiers abandoned us. They did nothing to protect us," he said. But then he was able to continue on a more positive note, even disclosing Kagame as his choice of candidate. "It is he who has got rid of all these painful memories," he said, "coming here to elect our president fills me with hope."[16]

Constructive but Questionable

The final result showed a vote of 95 percent of the electorate in favor of Kagame, with Twagiramungu managing 3.7 percent and Nayinzira 1.3 percent of the total. Although the criticisms that were leveled and to some extent were accepted by the government side indicate a barely credible margin of victory, Rwandans in the main could probably declare their satisfaction with the achievement which election day 2003 marked. Since their country's independence, there had only been showcase elections in Rwanda, with the sole purpose of confirming an absolute ruler's absolute control on power.

In 1978, five years after the *coup d'état* in which he took power, Juvenal Habyarimana held an election in which he was the only candidate; in 1983 he was re-elected with 99.98 percent of the vote and five years after that, he was once again reelected with 99 percent casting their votes in his favor. People who campaigned in elections in those times didn't work to elect a candidate; rather they strove to achieve what is called in the Kinyarwanda "*Ij'ana, Kw'ijana*"—meaning "One hundred percent."

By such standards, the 95 percent gained by Kagame could be seen as modest; however, although undoubtedly popular with much of the population, the margin looked high when compared to, for example, the landmark 1994 South African elections in which even Nelson Mandela could only manage to receive around two thirds of his country's vote.

Some ordinary Rwandans remained skeptical too. One voter, an educated Rwandan from Kibuye who frequently visited the capital, declined to say whom he had voted for. However, in the same breath, he denied the possibility of the achieved result. "Maybe it was about 40 percent for Twagiramungu and 60 percent for Kagame," he said. "But not 95 percent."[17]

Perhaps with remarks such as these, made by a Rwandan voter only weeks after the landslide at the polls, the seeds of a new revisionism were being sown. This time it was not a case of dissenting Rwandans trying to mislead foreigners about the causes and casualties of the genocide. Rather it seemed as if some were already trying to rewrite the history of the elections, perhaps in the hope that one day the "real" result might be achieved.

Tempers Frayed with European Observers

Overseas observers had differing opinions of the outcome, too, largely depending on whether they judged the polls by the standards of the "bigger picture" of a developing African country recovering from a uniquely traumatic experience, or whether they took western democratic standards as their benchmark for comparison.

Thus observer teams from South Africa, *Francophonie*, the association of French-speaking nations, and the African Union pronounced the polls as "free and fair and a reflection of the will of the Rwandan people," while others took a more critical view of the election's conduct.

The European Union's Observer Mission, led by the Luxemburg official Colette Flesch, noted that the vote took place in an atmosphere of calm and without violent incident. However, her EU monitoring teams also reported ballot stuffing, irregular handling of ballot boxes, misuse of government vehicles and buildings by the RPF, lack of transparency at the vote consolidation stage and vote-buying with gifts of goats and cows as an incentive to voters to endorse Kagame.

There were also reports of intimidation at the polling booths and people being instructed to recast their votes when they had initially marked their ballot papers in favor of Twagiramungu. Since the opposition's representatives had been arrested or prevented from being present at polling, the reported "massive presence" of Kagame or National Electoral Commission (NEC) representatives at the urns could do little but contribute to the "climate of intimidation" which the EU mission said characterized much of the election process.

Kagame, however, denied charges of an unfair campaign, finally calling the EU reports "ridiculous" and hailing the outcome of the voting. "You go to villages and ask them: if you find any district that says it predominantly voted for Twagiramungu, if you find a village complaining 'how did we lose?,' then you have a reason to suspect something ... and that can be investigated. So for me, it's a very straightforward thing," the president declared. "It is a victory which brings hope," he also said, "a victory to show all those who think they know Rwanda that they don't."[18]

Another critic of the attitude, if not the substance, of the EU's monitoring reports was journalist and publisher Privat Rutazibwa, head of the privately operated Rwanda News Agency.[19] In a letter addressed to the European monitoring mission's deputy chief, Marie-Violette César, Rutazibwa accused the EU of omitting any attempt at "analysis of Rwanda's political social and historic context" which he felt could "permit honest observers to appreciate with clarity and the nuances ... of the democratic process underway in the country." Describing the EU's judgements of Rwanda's institutions as "systematically negative," he went on to question why so much criticism was directed at Kagame's Rwanda, "which, after all was not the Rwanda of Habyarimana, nor the Zaire of Mobutu nor the Togo of Eyadema" of which the EU had never made such harsh condemnations.[20]

The difference between the European and various African observer missions' conclusions may have been more one of emphasis and culture rather than of actual observations. African critics of the EU stance could reasonably point to the continued dominance of certain major European countries who remained perennial critics of the RPF and would never grant a fair election as having occurred no matter what the actual conduct of the polling had been. Others cited the tendency for the opposition to play to the international media, as their only real form of leverage over the government, since they had no serious power base inside the country.

One South African media representative recalled returning from the Kagame victory rally in Kigali on election night and turning on CNN to see reports of controversial elections marred by irregularities and wondering if he had observed the same electoral events. "The EU observers who came to Rwanda with a negative picture in mind are obviously the voices CNN is listening to.... Some elements of the Hutu diaspora community do not want to see peace in their country. These are the other voices that CNN is listening to.... The sad thing is that [opposition candidate Faustin Twagiramungu] is the voice that the west is willing to listen to because he confirms the stereotypes of Africans incapable of running elections without rigging and intimidation...."[21]

Landslide in the Lakes

Five weeks after the presidential elections, the final stage in Rwanda's nine-year transition to democracy took place, with a series of elections and nominations for the country's 80-member national parliament. Although voting was organized essentially along party lines, 17 independent candidates ran for election and provision for representation of special interest groups was made by reserving a quota of seats for their candidates.

The process began on September 29, 2003, with elections for three seats reserved for youth and the disabled; the following day the main 53 deputies to the legislature were elected, and on the final day, 24 women representatives were elected, completing the 80 parliamentary seats. Also on the final day, the president selected 8 of the 26 senators provided for in the new constitution, with local government officials, college representatives and political parties choosing the balance of the members of the upper house. The initiative developed previously through the constitutional consultations aimed at achieving a large proportion of female parliamentarians was a success.

In the end, as a result of the ballot, women had gained more seats than their allocated minimum quota. In addition to their 24 reserved seats, women won a further 15 seats in the open portion of the election, giving the new assembly no less than 48.8 percent women, 39 out of a total of 80. On the day when the parliament's new deputies were sworn in, they were called to take their oath of office in batches of ten at a time and the chamber responded as one particular group approached for installation, composed of one male and no fewer than nine female parliamentarians, stepped forward to take the oath amid loud applause from the assembly.

Rwanda now has a higher proportion of women in its parliament than any other country in the world, even outpacing Sweden's 45 percent and well above the 14.3 percent which women hold in the U.S. House of Representatives or the 17.9 percent female representation in the UK parliament.

Polling for the parliament was again heavy, despite expectations of apathy following the landslide result in the presidential ballot. However, in the end, the outcome was almost a carbon copy of the previous month's election, with the RPF and its allies the Liberals and the Social Democrats polling 95 percent of the total. No independents were elected and many of the smaller parties failed to obtain the necessary 5 percent of the total required to secure parliamentary representation. The EU election observer mission once again cited cases of intimidation and lack of transparency at the consolidation stage, but these were denied or dismissed in similar fashion to the accusations leveled the month before.

On the opposition side, there were also cases of irregularities leading to controversy just prior to the time of the legislative balloting. According to the electoral law, independent candidates must submit a total of 600 names of supporters in order to be eligible to run in the elections. Célestin Kabanda and Jean-Baptiste Sindikubwabo, both founding members of ADEP-Mizero, the would-be party of Twagiramungu which had by now been banned, were caught providing false signatures and misrepresenting their political affiliation before voters. Exposed before a press conference in Kigali, Kabanda, a former MDR president, accused the authorities of mobilizing the police against his campaign and "intimidating [this] electorate." However, he lost credibility when, shortly afterwards, at least one of his assistants publicly testified to simply copying names off a local register and getting people to fraudulently sign against them.

For the EU observers, a bitter postscript to the controversy over the conduct of the elections raised by their findings came the week after the legislative elections, as Belgian foreign minister Louis Michel visited Kigali for discussions on a range of issues, including a new package of Belgian aid money for the country. After his meetings with government officials, Michel, who in the past had been a vocal critic of Rwanda's actions in neighboring Congo, came out to meet the press. He proceeded to describe the result of the elections as "incontestable," dealing a devastating blow to some of his fellow Europeans who had been on the ground through the arduous observation process.

President Kagame at election victory rally, Amahoro Stadium, Kigali, August 2003. (Courtesy the Rwandan Presidency, Kigali, Rwanda.)

Unacceptable Irregularities or Good Practice for Next Time?

Defenders of the conduct of the presidential and parliamentary polls have pointed to their critics' absence of specific evidence of irregularities, which are typically what election monitors are supposed to observe and comment on. However, the most serious charges made by the EU in its report on the Rwandan election probably relate to those stemming from pre-election day activities, designed to make party representation, campaigning and candidacy itself unusually difficult by western or even other African standards.

Where imprisonment or disappearances of potential opponents, banning of parties and other specific instances of obstructing democracy can be verified, only the cultural interpretation issue or the "uniqueness" of the Rwandan situation can be invoked in defense of the government's running of the process. The EU was the only monitoring group to deploy teams of so-called long-term observers, who arrived well over a month before polling to take up positions in every district of the country.

Other monitoring groups, albeit with fewer resources at their disposal than the EU, generally arrived a week before or in some cases only days before the polls and could not be in a position to observe any actions much beyond the voting itself. Against this, in making their reports and assessments, the African and Third World observer teams might be more likely to understand the context in which the ballot was being held and not see the exclusion of certain kinds of behavior in the same light as the Europeans did.

Without the experience of living in a climate of absolute insecurity in the very recent past and knowing the imperative of preventing its recurrence, it becomes harder to tolerate only relative transparency and liberty in the running of an election. It is on this gulf of experience that much of the initial ill will between the European Union observers and the Rwandan electoral authorities may have been based.

In many western societies and elsewhere in Africa, ethnic divisions are a cause of antagonism and resentment, and political parties often gain many of their supporters because of their attitude to racial issues, if not because of the racial identity of candidates themselves. They do this in order to gain strength and representation for the concerns and needs which they feel affect their group within society and the democratic system allows them to seek representation accordingly. However, even in the west there are few major national parties who seek to gain power with race as their primary *raison d'être*.

A Divide Too Far

In Rwanda, things really are different from other countries, even if they cannot be described as "unique." Ethnicity has been identified incontestably as the source and cause of the worst assault on humanity in the country's history and as such it can no longer be tolerated as a basis for political representation. This goes beyond merely legislating against "racism" as is common in western democracies. In Rwanda it is no longer legal to form an association which has the promotion of an ethnic group's interests as one of its objectives, either explicitly or, as in the case of the MDR moderates, implicitly. Protection against a return to this practice, referred to as "divisionism" in the context of Rwandan transitional politics,

President Kagame (right) at his inauguration, Amahoro Stadium, September 12, 2003, with President Yoweri Museveni of Uganda. (Courtesy the Rwandan Presidency, Kigali, Rwanda.)

President Kagame at his swearing-in ceremony, receiving the spear and shield, traditional symbols of his pledge to protect the country from its enemies. (Courtesy the Rwandan Presidency, Kigali, Rwanda.)

is the motivation as well as justification for measures which are considered by others as being repressive, especially when viewed in the context of their own culture and experience.

In accepting the uniqueness of Rwandan politics and the importance of eliminating ethnicity and division from society, the uncomfortable question remains: how far can this be justifiably extended to depriving fellow citizens of their liberty or other fundamental rights? Is the fact of being a former president or prime minister legally brought into power in compliance with internationally agreed treaties to achieve racial balance in government a reason for banning individuals from political activity today? The difficulty with Rwanda's form of democracy as evidenced by the campaign of 2003 is the uncertainty about where the cause of barring ethnically based political association ends and where rule by arbitrary authority begins.

For the troubled European observers on their way home from the tiring Rwandan election season there was no quick answer to the uncomfortable questions raised by the entire process whereby the RPF fully legitimized its dominance of Rwanda's political life. For many supporters of Rwanda in diplomatic circles, the flaws were overlooked and the fact that the elections passed peacefully was cause for satisfaction. Even if things weren't done quite right, "it's a good start and we expect that things will be conducted properly next time" seemed to be the prevailing sentiment among allies and friends abroad.

At his victory procession in Kigali, Kagame appeared triumphant before the massive crowd that waited to greet him. Although he waved from an armored car as he basked in his supporters' adulation, he appeared casually dressed, as he had been for much of the campaign, rather than in the formal western business uniform which many of his country people had become accustomed to seeing him wear. Observers of the campaign also noted how his speeches and general demeanor had become more relaxed and his prose more flowing, a change from the rather stiff appearances which had been his hallmark in the past.

In the wake of the euphoria of the election result, ordinary Rwandans at home and the country's supporters abroad could only speculate as to whether the new relaxed outward style of the president seen in mid–2003 would be matched by a relaxation of control within the country and its institutions. What was already clear in September 2003, however, was that some key backers of Rwanda on the diplomatic scene, while willing to overlook the irregularities of a campaign set against the events of an exceptional decade, would soon expect to see more rapid progress in other areas of the country's government and political institutions. Hints that greater liberalization and steps towards more openly democratic government would be needed in exchange for their continued support for the coming seven years of Kagame's presidency were becoming noticeable even as the international congratulatory messages were arriving in Kigali.

11

RECOVERY AND RECONCILIATION

Starting from Scratch in a New Century

The effects of the massive devastation of Rwanda's economy which began with the invasion of 1990 and accelerated with the genocide and civil war of 1994 took many years to reverse. With over three million of the population outside the country until 1997 and many of those who were left inside unfit or unable to work, the downward spiral of dislocation continued for several years after basic security was reestablished. Rwanda's gross domestic product (GDP), which totaled around $2 billion in 1990, fell steadily until 1994, then plummeted following the genocide to $585 million, according to World Bank estimates.

Efforts at recovery, constantly hampered by continuing security concerns and faltering foreign aid flows, took time to have any impact and it was not until the end of 2001 that the Rwandan government finally could announce that the GDP had once again reached pre–1990 levels. By this time, however, an estimated 3.2 million people had returned, for the most part with no resources to offer other than their labor, and GDP per head remained stubbornly at one of the lowest national levels in the world, at around $20 per person per month.

Looking for a Place to Call Home

Rebuilding the shattered Rwandan economy presented a daunting enough challenge in itself, without first having to deal with the enormous social problems plaguing the country, which included mass homelessness caused by wartime destruction of housing, followed by the land and property disputes between surviving and returning populations. Balancing the interests of the "old" refugees, mostly Tutsis who had been in exile since

the 1960s and the newly returned Hutus who came back from camps in
Zaire and Tanzania beginning in late 1996, presented a special problem in
itself.

The transitional government made a statutory commitment to the
recently returned Hutu refugees that they would all get their homes back,
as part of the commitment to rehabilitation and reconciliation of the communities. A September 1996 order issued by the Ministry of Rehabilitation and Social Development (MINIREISO) laid down the procedures for
repossessing property, which the authorities then struggled to implement
when the first wave of 1.3 million returnees arrived from Zaire starting in
November 1996.

Many Tutsis had occupied the homes left vacant when their Hutu
occupants had fled in 1994, the former's houses often having been
destroyed in the genocide. The "old" refugees had also taken up residence
in empty homes upon their return, and these people then had to be resettled in order for the government to honor its commitment to the recent
refugees. Initially, a large amount of temporary shelter was constructed
with donor help, while the authorities battled to adhere to its principle of
rights of repossession for those coming back.

Controversial Resettlement Strategy

In response to the need for accommodating returning refugees and
also to further the long-term development goals of the economy, a new
government initiative on the reorganization of rural life was announced
in December 1996. The stated objectives were to create non-agricultural
employment, improve transport and distribution networks and counter
the dispersion of the population, which, according to the initiative, "makes
sensitization of the people more difficult."

Five years later, in 2001, a National Habitat Policy was launched with
two principal aims. The first was the task of rehousing the (mostly Tutsi)
returnees, who had either lost their homes in the war or had been displaced
by more recent returnees from the refugee camps. The second goal was to
regenerate economic activity by ending the geographic dispersal of the rural
poor. The policy involved the movement of large numbers of people into
imidugudu, or "protected villages," which were often distant from the affected
residents' communities of origin. Critics claimed that while the majority
moved willingly and were found new housing, some were forcibly resettled
and threatened with punishment or prison if they refused to relocate.[1]

By the end of 1999, an estimated 94 percent of the population of
Kibungo and 60 percent of the population of Mutara in the north of the

country had moved into protected villages. In addition to pointing out the inhumanity of forcing people to leave their homes, some outside observers also claimed that rural food production dropped sharply as a result of the policy's implementation. According to one estimate, farmers in Ruhengeri were cultivating less than 60 percent of the land in the area in late 1999 due to the removal of much of the population.[2]

The government refuted this, and pointed to the need for creating the necessary critical mass of population in outlying communities to restart meaningful economic activity. The other aspect to the policy, however, was the need to address continuing insecurity, since up until late 1999, insurgents based in the DRC were still managing to carry out massacres in Gisenyi and Ruhengeri; in December of that year, for example, over 300 residents were killed in Tamira, Gisenyi Prefecture. It was easier for the security forces to look after people inside protected villages than when they were living in scattered places of resettlement over a much broader area in the open countryside.

Taking the Road Home at Last

At the height of the political controversy at home and mounting opposition from the new diaspora overseas, in October 2000 President Kagame called a national Summit on Reconciliation and Unity, with the aim of underlining his government's core objective of bringing Rwandans back together inside their homeland. Although the initiative yielded few immediate results, the policy continued and the Government of National Unity went on to try to weather the storms that were brewing both inside and outside the country's borders.

Reconciliation did not come easily for many, however, and the road to forgiveness was a harder one to take in many cases than the way to revenge. The returning refugees, among them suspected *génocidaires*, were easily recognized on arriving in their communities, and for some of their former neighbors the temptation to take the law into their own hands was too great. Referring to the rehabilitation of former killers into Rwandan society, Kagame stressed the need for patience in dealing with such people: "I think you can't give up on that — on such a person ... they can learn," he said. "I'm sure that every individual, somewhere in his plans, wants some peace, wants progress in some way, even if he is an ordinary peasant. So if we can present the past to them and say, 'this was the past that caused all these problems for you and this is the way to avoid that,' I think it changes their minds quite a bit. And I think some people can even benefit from being forgiven, being given another chance."[3]

In 2001, an estimated 55,000 Rwandan refugees still remained outside the country, the majority of whom were in Tanzania (30,000) and Uganda (15,000). In addition, an estimated 30,000 Rwandans remained in the eastern DRC, living in conditions essentially the same as those of refugees. A more worrying statistic was the flight of approximately 10,000 new refugees from Rwanda in 2000, suggesting that the government's proclaimed reconciliation measures had yet to inspire the confidence of many of its own people.

While poverty and economic migration remained factors in the continuing exodus, such a large departure six years after the end of the genocide and during a period when security was ostensibly returning to nearly all of Rwanda tended to support those who criticized the government's human rights record. Mass killings of civilians and other abuses were reported, as the RPA carried out reprisals for the continuing attacks by reformed ex–FAR and *interahamwe*. In their defense the Kigali authorities pointed to the need to curb the resurgence of latent genocidal actions against Tutsi civilians, particularly in the northwest, where insurgent forces based across the border with the DRC were still managing to operate.

In the late 1990s, the government established the Rwandan Human Rights Commission, a national body aimed at monitoring and reporting on the progress to achieving acceptable standards of human rights inside the country.

During this period the authorities also revived the para-military corps known as the "Local Defense Forces," a group that had been created in the wake of the genocide in late 1994 to enhance security at the local level as a supplement to the presence of the RPA. Welcomed in the community by some but accused of abuses and arbitrary arrest or assassination by others, the lightly armed local militias, clad in their distinctive dark maroon uniforms, initially added a presence of some 7,000 men to the manpower available for policing at the community level.

Although human rights groups and political opponents continued their criticisms during the early years of the transition, Rwanda's main international supporters remained on the scene, and conditions slowly began to show signs of improvement.

By 2003, internal conditions had improved markedly, and tens of thousands of Rwandans were returning voluntarily from neighboring countries as the improving internal climate raised the confidence of those who had previously considered the prospect of return with trepidation. According to the UNHCR, over 10,000 Rwandans returned voluntarily from the DRC in 2002, while in the last three months of that year over 23,000 came home from Tanzania.

The UN body declared a change in its own policy in response to easing conditions inside Rwanda, officially altering its stance from one of mere "facilitation" to that of "active promotion" of the repatriation of refugees. In a report justifying the change in policy, the UNHCR cited its "examination of the prevailing conditions in the country, positive political and social developments such as the release of 40,000 prisoners ... and the installation of the Gacaca system."[4]

Ambivalence Towards Amnesty

The massive release of low-category offenders from Rwanda's prisons which began in January 2003 may have won the Rwandan authorities praise from outsiders and eased the huge burden on the country's justice system, but at the community level the impact did not always inspire confidence, often quite the opposite. One problem was an informational one on the part of the authorities, as the release into the community of many known killers took place with very little advance notice. Most of those who got out were freed because the state had been unable to collect sufficient evidence against them, and in any case many had already been in detention for seven years or longer.

However, for local residents who had witnessed the killings and for survivors of the *génocidaires'* actions who often remained in a state of suspended trauma, the possibility of imminent release of the killers into the community revived their worst nightmares from the genocide. Sister Pauline Habarujira, a trained psychologist working in the town of Kibuye, one of the communities most intensely affected in 1994, described the impact on some of the residents she knew: "Some widows in the town were just recovering from the trauma of the genocide [and] could not deal with seeing their husbands' killers at large in the town again. One woman told me that if the killers came back, she would leave the town.... Others who learned that those without criminal dossiers could be released hurried to the authorities to lodge their accusations. When these people were also released their accusers fell into a state of terror that the detainees would seek to exact revenge on them."

Sister Pauline, who had lived in the western lakeside community since 1994, went on to describe other psycho-social conditions affecting members of her local community, particularly the youths who had been orphaned in the genocide and were now growing up, unable to comprehend their parentless, abandoned situation:

> "For the young men there is no work and no sense of attachment to family and society. They cannot cope with the world they are now

growing into and they are dropping out. Many are addicts, they go around intoxicated on *urumogi* [marijuana].... Here it is not like in Kigali, in the big city people didn't know each other, it was easier to forget. In Kibuye everybody knew everybody, we have to look at each other in the face every day.... If we had received more warning, people could have prepared themselves mentally, but for some it is too much to have to confront the killers again.[5]

HIV Epidemic Adds to Survivors' Plight

Amidst the enduring hardships which the genocide imposed on many survivors, the additional burden of living with HIV/AIDS adds an extra cruel dimension. Many widows of men killed by the militias were rape victims themselves in the genocide, and those alive today are struggling with the disease in conditions of poverty. Access to anti-retroviral drugs and other treatment is limited, especially in rural areas, and the cost remains prohibitive for most.

Genocide survivors in Kibuye Province, where an estimated 50 percent of all young people are affected by the disease, have additional difficulties to face due to the extreme poverty of their region. Due to high hospital costs, most patients stay at home in their beds until they die. Many are afraid to find out their HIV status, which compounds the problem further. Genocide orphans are often driven to prostitution by their extreme circumstances and their clients, mostly truck drivers and soldiers, frequently do not use condoms.

One resident of the town lamented an additional aspect of the HIV/AIDS scourge which is now becoming apparent as the new generation grows up: "Here in Kibuye never fool yourself into thinking that young kids of 10 or 11 are safe. Things have changed. Most of those primary school kids are HIV positive."[6]

Rwandan rape victims living with HIV/AIDS have intense psychological scars to live with as well as their physical ailments. Many have seen the *interahamwe* kill their husbands and other family members before being raped themselves. Furthermore, they have children of their own, and are often looking after others, already orphaned. They must explain to their children that soon there will be no one to look after them.

Avega Aghozo is a national organization representing an estimated 25,000 genocide widows in Rwanda. A study conducted by the group in a quarter of the country's 12 provinces showed that 66 percent out of the 1,200 widows sampled tested HIV positive and an estimated 80 percent of those surveyed were psychologically traumatized.[7]

The stigma of rape victims and reticence about coming forward for testing is another factor compounding the health authorities' battle against the disease as well as making accurate estimates of infection rates hard to calculate. According to 2003 statistcis, 13.5 percent of the population was HIV positive, but the real rate could have been much higher and in certain areas it is almost certainly at least twice that level. Rose Musana, a project leader for the Avega Aghozo organization, described the health workers' dilemma: "It is not until conditions worsen that they turn up for testing," by which time the infection may have been spread to others and the victims' condition may be beyond care.[8]

Another group, People Living with AIDS (PLWA), began a campaign for cheaper and more readily available treatment, setting up a network of patients numbering over 20,000 by mid–2003. PLWA also began working with the Ministry of Health to improve distribution of anti-retroviral drugs. In late 2003, the government launched a scheme to make retroviral treatments available to vulnerable patients for the cost of 14,000 Rwandan francs ($24) per month, against the usual cost of up to FrR 40,000 or almost $70 per month.[9]

Rwanda's first lady, Jeanette Kagame, is active in the struggle against HIV at both the national and regional levels. Known internationally in African circles for her work with HIV/AIDS advocacy groups, she personally founded or was involved in a number of initiatives to combat the disease since her husband took over the presidency.

Making Money Work

If the ravages of the genocide and wars of 1990–94 left lasting wounds in Rwandan society, the impact on the country's economy was equally severe. The political and military challenges of the transition left insufficient resources to re-launch the economy in any meaningful way, and at the dawn of the twenty-first century Rwanda remained very much a poor, mostly agricultural Third World economy facing many of the familiar barriers to development known to nearly every sub–Saharan African country.

The Rwandan economy was still based on subsistence agriculture, largely reliant on extractive industries and a few cash crops such as tea for export earnings, and it remained saddled with the trademark developing country obstacles to progress. Insufficient and expensive power supplies hampered the development of industry and a lack of basic infrastructure held back the revival of Rwanda's embryonic manufacturing sector. On a more positive note, by the late 1990s the Dutch-owned national brewer

BRALIRWA was once more exporting its popular Primus brand to the DRC, while within a few months of the end of the genocide domestic production had restarted and the premium brand Mützig had recovered its status as a favorite in the capital's neighborhoods and restaurants.

In education, the newly founded Kigali Institute for Science, Technology and Management (KIST) produced its first graduating class in 2002. A university intended for the grooming of Rwanda's future elite, KIST's 3,300 students receive their training in English, but the agenda is one of distinctly Rwandan orientation. With financial help from the UN, Japan and the Netherlands, the establishment of KIST as the country's second university, after Butare, is aimed at addressing the enormous deficit in trained personnel which inhibits Rwanda's progress.

In the provision of more basic services, however, the country continued to struggle. Water shortages presented problems both in the provinces and the capital and until as late as 2001 it was estimated that over 250,000 of Kigali's residents still had no regular access to safe drinking water. A long-term project to address this deficit was planned by the Ministry of Water and Energy, aiming to divert the waters of the meandering, omnipresent Nyabarongo River to boost the capital's supplies.

Rwanda has reserves of cassiterite (a tin-bearing ore) and columbite-tantalite (coltan) which is found, for example, near Gitarama in the west of Rwanda, for which the price rose sharply after its value as an essential input in mobile telephone hardware was discovered. Exports of coltan quadrupled between 1995 and 1998, providing evidence of likely re-export of ore from the DRC, the legitimacy of which has been contested by international critics, such as the UN panel of experts in its report on the exploitation of Congo's minerals.[10]

A more encouraging development was the discovery of methane gas in Lake Kivu, which will offer the prospect of cheaper and more plentiful energy supplies in the near future. Rwanda's excellent road network, much of which is tarmac surfaced, is one of the best in Africa and could contribute importantly to the establishment of a more active commercial life in the future.

For the ordinary citizen, however, little in the way of visible improvement in standards of living was achieved in the last five years of the political transition. Major projects were slow in beginning, there was little money to buy much more than the basic necessities, bars and cafes in the capital remained quiet except for a few hours on weekends, and foreigners were far less numerous than in the early days of the transition. Men queued in the hope of finding casual work in the early morning at the few major construction sites in the capital. Unemployment remained intractable and the small amount of money flowing through the economy stayed in the hands of the business elite and a restricted group of foreign traders.

Rwanda may have a new constitution, a new government and a new flag, but some of the nation's other symbols give away the fact that there is still a lot to be done. In 2003 one of the main streets in Kigali near to the state house still showed the blurred blue sign for *Boulevard du Roi Baudouin II*, the Belgian king whose colonial envoys oversaw the seeds of Rwanda's later agony being sown. Just next to that still stands the sign for *Boulevard de l'Umuganda*—"community labor street," more a reminder of Rwanda's traditional rural past than an advertisement for the new agenda of the nation.

Jacky Kayiteshonga, operations manager at Bancor SA, one of Rwanda's seven commercial banks, summarizes developments since the late 1990s: "For a few years there was easy money to be made from the UN and the NGO community, renting houses and cars and bringing in supplies. But in 1998 those people all left and there was nothing to put in their place."[11] Furthermore, there were few tools at the government's disposal for reviving the economy, other than accumulating more debt to spend on infrastructure. For the most part, foreign aid flows continued to be the lifeblood of Rwanda's economy, a welcome source of support but also a potential vulnerability, given the unpredictable behavior of foreign donors in response to political developments. In late 1995, external assistance was estimated at $56 per head, almost one quarter of average annual income, while foreign aid accounted for over 90 percent of public investment.

Rwanda became eligible for Heavily Indebted Poor Country (HIPC) relief in December of 2000, which alleviated its external debt estimated at $1.32 billion or 73 percent of GDP in that year.

With no domestic capital markets and an economy of subsistence consumers, the concept of stimulus through the banking system remained largely meaningless in the Rwandan economy. Any saving in the private sector was on a purely short-term basis, and with interest rates at around 18 percent even those with the ability to borrow were unlikely to take on any significant debt. Debit cards were introduced in 1997 and the first ATMs appeared in 1999, although not all banks deemed it worthwhile to offer them to their customers. International money transfer by telex was replaced by the standard SWIFT (Society for Worldwide Interbank Financial Telecommunication) in 1999, finally bringing Rwanda into the modern banking era. Under the Système National de Paiement (SNP) a fully electronic western-style funds transfer system was to be launched in January 2004, ending the dreary but still commonplace Third World necessity of queuing for hours to pay utility bills in crowded city center banking halls.

At Rwanda's stage of development, the need was for a different approach to getting money circulating around the country. For rural farmers, the most promising route tried during the transition was the extension of micro-credits, a revolving loan technique used with considerable success in southern Africa, west Africa and some of Asia's poorer economies.

Bancor's Jacky Kayiteshonga feels that micro lending is probably the way ahead for an economy at Rwanda's stage of development. He cited the success of one non-governmental group, World Relief, who in 2003 reportedly had over 20,000 members in the country accessing micro-credit facilities. "Each member is borrowing short term, in amounts of $200–$1000 at a time, and rates of non-performing loans are only 3 percent," he said. "Rural workers, especially women, have taken to this type of financing which they can immediately put to work to increase their business."[12] With easy access to markets through the Rwandan road system, this avenue offers some hope of stimulating the otherwise bare-bones level of economic activity which remains the reality for the majority of Rwandans.

At the other end of the spectrum, the authorities were working to revive tourism, which was once an important earner for the country, largely based on Rwanda's countryside environment of lakes, mountains and national parks. Perhaps the single most famous tourist attraction are the rare mountain gorillas which roam Rwanda's Virunga National Park. In 2003, two new international-class hotels were under construction, one of which was the five-star Intercontinental Hotel in Kigali, the first of its kind in the country, with another four-star facility underway in Gisenyi, catering for the hoped-for northern parks tourist traffic.

For the fortunate few residents of Kigali, the possibility of a western lifestyle does exist, as in capital cities throughout the developing world. However, around the turn of the new century, as thousands of people in the countryside were moving to their protected villages under the National Habitat Policy, another kind of residential development began to spring up, in this case to cater for Rwanda's new moneyed classes. Most notably in the elegant suburb of Nyarutarama, not far from the parliament and government ministries district, dozens of elegant villas were erected, Santa Monica–style, complete with spacious garden compounds, marble exteriors and double garages.

At a bend in the road on the suburb's perimeter is the entrance to a country club based on the American model, offering golf and tennis to its members. Not far from there is the prestigious Green Hills Academy

Paul Kagame (second in line) gorilla trekking in Virunga National Park, northwest Rwanda, with German minister of foreign affairs, Joschka Fischer, 2000. (From the personal collection of President Paul Kagame.)

where the community's younger residents can receive their schooling, paying each trimester in fees only a little less than the average Rwandan can expect to earn in a year.

A leafy haven for foreigners and the governing elite or a residential retreat for Kigali's new business classes? Salaries of government ministers in a country like Rwanda can only go a part of the way to explaining the demand for a luxury construction boom. At the time the business aristocracy of Kigali could have lived comfortably together in one long street, but still the villas were built, bought and quickly occupied. Perhaps part of the answer to the enigma, "Whence the new wealth?" can be spotted under some of the garage doors and on the registration tags of the 4x4 vehicles purring down Nyarutarama's driveways: in addition to the ubiquitous national "RAA" license prefix, a visitor to the area could note the evidence of vehicle tags from Rwanda's resource-rich neighbor and sometime economic province to the west — the unmistakable "NK" registration of vehicles hailing from Congo's North Kivu Province.

Prosperity and Security in a Uniting Africa

Once referred to as the "Switzerland of Africa" because of its hard-working people, a landlocked geographical position and its relative prosperity in the region, Rwanda's image as well as its involvement with the outside world have been turned upside down by the events of 1994 and the subsequent turmoil inside and around its borders. No longer able to act politically in isolation nor to achieve economic self-sufficiency through traditional economic means, the eight million people living in the *Pays de Mille Collines*[13] are bound to look outwards for their future survival, even if the experiences of the past are driving them to look inwards at themselves in search of understanding and reconciliation.

With rivals and opponents still lurking in nearby nations, prone to offering criticism as often as extending the hand of cooperation, the road to regional reconciliation was ever an uphill one but still a road which had to be taken. At the end of 2003, relations were once more on the mend with the DRC; although Joseph Kabila did not see fit to attend President Kagame's inauguration that September, Foreign Minister Dr. Charles Murigande traveled to Kinshasa shortly thereafter for talks with his counterpart She Okitundu and the Congolese president, to spell out the newly reconfigured foreign policy aims of the incoming government in Kigali.

With the formal ending of nine years in transition, "normalization" became the catchphrase of the moment in Rwanda, while the Congo itself was only just embarking on a political transition of its own. In regional affairs, revival of old relationships and consolidation of new ones were at the heart of Kagame's thinking for the post-transition era. After decades of neo-colonial patronage, economic reliance on Europe and financial assistance from international institutions, Rwanda's newly elected president favored stronger and more effective ties with his African neighbors in the years ahead. "It is indispensable that Rwanda and other countries on the African continent speak with a common voice in dealing with different parts of the world," Kagame said, "...rather than if each speaks only with its own voice. So integration is paramount and Rwanda wants to join in that integration process."[14]

Steps in that direction were already taken in mid–2003 when Rwanda assumed the vice-chair of the African Union, sending full-time emissary Patrick Mazimhaka to take up the role of Rwanda's representative to the AU in Addis Ababa, Ethiopia. An AU-sponsored conference on good governance was planned with Kigali as the host city, both as trial and testament to the standing which Rwanda hoped to cement among its continental neighbors, while the warm glow of Kagame's election victory was still burning in the capital.

Rwanda is also a member of the Community of East and Southern African States (COMESA), the East African Community and NEPAD, the New Partnership for African Development. Furthermore, with improving ties between the DRC and Rwanda and hopes of greater stability in Burundi, the prospect of reviving the CEPGL is very much on the government's agenda.

The tri-nation economic and political community, which once brought together the three central African nations that had formerly been under Belgian colonial rule in a common economic space, was a vehicle for regional integration before the wars and ethnic strife which exploded in the region. Foreign Minister Charles Murigande is a strong advocate of relaunching the CEPGL if and when conditions across the region would permit. He explained how things used to work: "The people of Rwanda, Burundi and the Congo could move freely among the three countries, establishing themselves and undertaking professional activities wherever they chose. It used to be a dynamic community thanks to its many assets: an agricultural research institute, a regional bank, a joint hydroelectric dam project on the Ruzizi, an energy agency...." While lamenting the unrest that forced the suspension of its activities, Murigande expressed optimism. "I think that following the unhappy recent history of our three countries, the CEPGL provides exactly the required forum for political dialogue."[15]

Changed Times at Urugwiro Village

The reaffirmation of presidential power from the ballot boxes in September of 2003 and the renewed appetite for regional diplomacy stemmed from a presidency quite unlike those that had preceded it in Rwanda. Indeed, the style and routine of the incoming administration might have surprised those familiar with the workings of other political leaders and their cabinets around the globe. The image of the indolent and despotic equatorial ruler making occasional forays into the bush to elicit awe from his subjects, or indeed that of the golf-playing Texan governor managing no more than a few hours a day at his desk in the state house, would be almost the antithesis of the Kagame executive ethic.

Installed in the tranquil, white-walled estate of the presidential compound known as Urugwiro Village, the Kagame team and presidency support staff became used to the long hours and exacting work habits of their

leader. But the pace had not always been so demanding at the chief executive's offices. Presidential communications advisor Alfred Ndahiro recalls
how things were in the earlier days: "Nothing much used to go on here,"
he said, in a blunt reference to the administration of predecessor Pasteur
Bizimungu. "Now all of us in the staff are in here in the evening, sometimes until nine, ten o'clock at night."[16]

The president drives himself hard in working habits but also favors
informality when he can. Often at work casually dressed in open shirt and
boots inside the presidential office or when outside in the country, he
sometimes prefers to drive himself to and from the presidency to his home,
the lavishly refurbished and closely guarded state house, located over-
looking the Kiyovu quarter on the fringes of Kigali's commercial center.

Although the chief executive may often favor informal attire, the uniform of his cabinet is invariable. Ministers and top advisors respect the
dress code of dark suit and tie, not forgetting the ubiquitous Rwandan
national flag lapel pin, worn by all senior politicians, in the style of the
George W. Bush administration, both to the office and when appearing in
public.

Off duty, Kagame enjoys playing tennis, but above all in sport his first
passion lies with soccer. A frequent spectator at matches of *Amavubi* (the

**President Kagame playing tennis. (From the personal collection of President
Paul Kagame.)**

President Kagame at his farm in Kibungo, eastern Rwanda. (From the personal collection of President Paul Kagame.)

Wasps), the Rwandan national team, President Kagame also turned sponsor in 2002 when the financially strapped Confederation of East and Central African Football Associations (CECAFA) was on the point of collapse and unable to run its annual regional tournament. After an appeal from CECAFA Secretary-General Nicolas Musonye, the Rwandan president stepped in with a personal contribution of $60,000 to save the tournament, adding several thousand more for a trophy, and the organizers in turn gratefully renamed the event the "Kagame Cup."

Across the Language Barrier

Despite popular participation in such activities by their head of state, ordinary Rwandans still had reason to feel the distance of the Kagame presidency from their own lives. Being ruled by a president who had only lived full time as an adult in the country for under ten years remained a factor in the minds of some, while for others, his rudimentary command of one of the nation's three official languages, French, was a barrier to closer identification. Just after election time, Paul Kagame declared himself to be working on the language which is still the most prevalent among the country's population after their own Kinyarwanda.

While some hailed the increasing use of English as a sign of change for the better, harboring bitter associations with the role of the French in their country's recent dark past, others took the president's linguistic deficit as a reminder that he and many of the RPF ruling inner circle were raised and culturally formed in English-speaking Uganda. The president preferred to leave these issues to one side. "There is no particular preference for me between French and English. I am unfortunately not able to speak French, not because I hate it.... I am able to speak English better than French because of historical circumstances.... I know that people have tried to politicize that ... this should not have implications beyond simply communicating."[17]

The association between language, education and Rwanda's new overseas allies may not be as easy to shrug off, however. Certainly there is a style as well as a means of communication which others have found admirable in Paul Kagame's dealing with his country's affairs. In the United States, this helped him win support and respect since the early days of his training at Fort Leavenworth. Among those who trained the young Ugandan army major in 1990 in the Joint Combined Exchange Training (JCET) course in Kansas was Major Anthony Marley, who was later to join the United States team in the Arusha peace negotiations. After a 1998 symposium on peace and security in Africa, Marley wrote: "One reason why American officials are enamored with Rwandan Vice President Paul Kagame is that he knows how to communicate with them in a quintessentially 'American' way. He is blunt, direct and conveys an air of simplicity and sincerity."[18]

Another American military officer, Colonel Jim McDonough, who commanded the U.S. special forces who later went to Rwanda in 1996–97, simply described the Rwandan commander in chief as "... an intellectual figure. I would rate him as a first class operational fighter."[19]

After assuming the presidency, Kagame maintained close ties with the Anglo-Saxon allies who offered development funding as well as military support. President Kagame staged a successful state visit to the United States in March of 2003, including high-profile visits to the Bush ranch in Texas and addresses before academic and public affairs bodies as well as members of the diaspora in major U.S. cities.

Meanwhile, the United Kingdom stayed an unquestioning ally of Rwanda. Development Minister Clare Short was an uncritical supporter of President Kagame until her resignation from the Blair cabinet in the summer of 2003. By that year, the UK had become the largest bilateral donor of development aid to Rwanda, giving official assistance totaling some £30 million ($50m) to the country.

In and Out of Uniform

If the confidence of Anglo-Saxon military commanders has been an asset to Kagame in the testing years of the civil war and campaigns against insurgency which followed, Rwanda's president is mindful of the fact that he is, for now at least, no longer a soldier. Rwandan law prohibits a person from being an active serviceman as well as a politician at the same time; the options are either to retire from the military or to suspend active service with the option of going back later. Which option did Rwanda's ex-commander in chief choose?

"I put it in writing to stop being referred to, being known as an active serviceman," Kagame said in an interview for *LeSoft-Grands Lacs* published on September 27, 2003. "It is different from retiring. That is what I did and that is what the law prescribes."

Nevertheless, the sense that comes across is very much of a man who understands intimately the military world and relishes the recollection of past campaigns. Indeed, Kagame perhaps felt more comfortable initially in that capacity than in handling some of the onerous and often frustrating duties that befell the head of an African state struggling to move forward.

However, the reality of the conflict-riven African continent is that the need for military preparedness will continue to be felt. Although part of Rwanda's own armed forces have demobilized, reflecting reduced outside security threats since 1999, there will be a clear need for effective peacekeeping in future situations not far from Rwanda's borders.

Doubtless influenced by the tragic experience of his own country during the presence of the UN system in 1994, Kagame believes that African countries, his own included, should play a greater role in handling their own conflicts in the future. "I fully subscribe to the countries of the region or sub-region to having that capacity," he said. "I don't see why we don't achieve that. Continentally, under the AU, or regionally, we should have that capacity when the situation demands it ... we can handle it. The western countries shouldn't have to come and do it for us ... they can do it partially by providing the resources ... which we don't have."[20]

President Kagame is a strong believer in African countries doing things for themselves, managing their own affairs without interference, and his approach to governing Rwanda has been based on this belief. He feels that things have gone wrong in the past, with certain countries and organizations who have wanted to try to run Africa in their own way and got it wrong. He has said that these outsiders are afraid of what they call "this dangerous development, Africans trying to do things their own way."[21] Whether in the historic decision to invade Rwanda in October of 1990, in the struggle to end the genocide in 1994, in the Congo campaigns of 1996 and 1998, or in the drafting of the constitution and the running of the elections, he has been willing to risk criticism and face unpopularity with world opinion to get things done in his own way.

The RPF has been both the vehicle and the backbone of Kagame's success since the first campaign to take back Rwanda that began in October of 1990. Following his election victory in 2003, Rwanda's president described the fundamentals upon which his movement's success was built: "First of all we had a belief in the RPF, and based on that we had our philosophy and our strategy for the country over time. The RPF had this idea that really worked politically to remove the dividing lines that have been created by colonialism and the political forces that took over in our country."[22]

By late 2003, with the presidency secured and the military struggles at an end, Kagame also remained positive on the prospects for reconciliation in Rwanda. He also believed that change for the better was occurring and he remained confident that it could heal the country's wounds. "We always knew it was possible that Rwandans could very easily live together," he said from his office in the presidency. "...It is like a process, a healing process. I get a feeling that today, when you go to the local people down in the villages, even the old people, there is a sense that they are happier ... I see it working, it is really becoming different in the country, it is happening all over, it is just like magic."[23]

APPENDIX:
THE BANYARWANDA IN
EAST AFRICAN HISTORY

Until the middle of the nineteenth century, much of east and central Africa was ruled by kings, each controlling his own territory, exercising power and seeking to strengthen his domain by conquest or subjugation of neighboring rulers and chiefs. So it was in the region containing Lake Victoria, Lake Tanganyika, Lake Albert and Lake Kivu, known as the Great Lakes of Africa, a region which encompasses modern Uganda, Rwanda and Burundi, as well as parts of the Democratic Republic of Congo, Tanzania and Kenya. The more successful kings of the region in time came to rule over large tracts of mostly rich agricultural land, suitable for cattle rearing as well as cultivation. They jealously guarded their independence and waged war from time to time to defend their kingdoms' boundaries or to expand their rule into their neighbors' hills and valleys.

By the late nineteenth century the European colonial powers had carved up much of the African continent for their own domination, often by drawing approximate lines on explorers' maps and only later visiting the perimeters of their new possessions to discover the imperial treasures that they had acquired. In this way Germany acquired the kingdoms then known by the Europeans as Ruanda and Urundi, the fertile hilly regions bounded in the west by the Belgian Congo and to the northeast by British East Africa, which included Kenya and Uganda. These small kingdoms that had evaded the influence of the Europeans thus far in their scramble for Africa were drawn into German East Africa at the Berlin Conference of 1884 and so were acquired as part of a package which included the much larger country of Tanganyika to the south and east.

During the nineteenth century before the arrival of the Germans, the kings of Rwanda, who came from the ethnic group called Tutsi, themselves had grown steadily in power, successfully suppressing rebellious chiefs in the south of their territory and containing but never fully dominating the powerful northwestern chiefs who were from the more numerous Hutu ethnic group. Expanding westwards into the hinterland of Lake Kivu, a region which the Rwandan kings had long coveted, the Tutsi warriors, armed with spears, bows and arrows, ultimately encountered the Belgian colonial forces with their firearms and quickly realized that they had met their match on the battlefield. It was time to make peace with the colonists or be annihilated.

Demographics of Dispersal

Rwandans are classified racially into three groups: Hutu, Tutsi and Twa, who historically have accounted for around 85 percent, 14 percent and 1 percent respectively of the country's population. However, in broader regional terms, all three groups can also be described as Banyarwanda, people coming from the land of Rwanda and who all speak a common language, Kinyarwanda. The Banyarwanda make up east Africa's largest single tribe and in addition to Rwanda itself, they historically lived principally in southwestern Uganda, the eastern Democratic Republic of the Congo (DRC) and western Tanzania.

Until the late 1950s, the turbulent period of Rwanda's history just before independence when Paul Kagame's family and tens of thousands of other Tutsis like them fled their homeland, the differences between the three groups were thought of by Rwandans themselves more as class distinctions rather than ethnic differences. Ethnicity nevertheless played a major part in determining people's role in the economy and society and for a long time the relationship between the different groups was a stable and working one. The country was a monarchy until 1959, the *mwami* or king was a Tutsi and the aristocrats and the upper classes in society were also Tutsi. The Hutu were mostly agricultural workers, and the Twa were primarily a hunter-gatherer tribe.

A feudal system was in operation, but unlike the European feudal system of centuries earlier, economic and social status in Rwanda was based largely on ownership of cows. The cattle owners were mostly Tutsis and their "clients" who gave their labor and crops in exchange for one or two cows were either Hutus or sometimes poorer Tutsis. While Hutu-Tutsi intermarriages were one means through which class boundaries became blurred, an important additional means to class mobility was that

Hutus who managed to acquire larger numbers of cows were able to become Tutsis. (The process by which this happened was known as *kwihutura* or literally "shedding Hutuness.") The process occurred in the same way as "social climbing" in western society occurs when an individual succeeds in moving upwards in society through marriage or material success.

Beyond the boundaries of the kingdom of Rwanda, Banyarwanda of both Tutsi and Hutu background had been settling long before the waves of persecution that forced Paul Kagame's family to flee from their homeland. Some had always lived outside the country's modern borders and became administratively separated from their compatriots as a result of the arbitrary drawing of lines on the map by the Europeans. Later, a second group had moved outside Rwanda's borders voluntarily, seeking a better economic situation than their own poor and crowded countryside could offer.

In Uganda, the Banyarwanda who had settled prior to the drawing of the colonial boundaries lived in the southwestern part of the country, principally in the border region around Kabale as well as in Ankole and Toro districts. Similar groups of Banyarwanda had lived in Zaire's North and South Kivu provinces and the immediate hinterland, as well as in neighboring parts of Burundi and Tanzania where they were integrated with the local economy and society but often continued to speak Kinyarwanda. The total of such Banyarwanda in the early twentieth century was estimated at 500,000 in Zaire (then Belgian Congo) and 200,000 in Uganda.

The second group were the economic migrants who went to Rwanda's neighbors in the mid-twentieth century, arriving from their overpopulated homeland as laborers to meet the shortage of manpower as the British colonists in Uganda began to cultivate a new cash crop, cotton. A further incentive to migrate were the periodic famines which ravaged a country struggling to feed its people from a limited amount of land under cultivation with too much allocated to the production of cash crops for export rather than those suitable for the subsistence of its own peasantry.[1] But perhaps the strongest motivation of all to emigrate from Rwanda was the increased imposition of the system of community development labor, the *umuganda*, on the peasants by the colonial administration. The requirement to give two or more days a week in unpaid communal labor was often backed up with beatings of ordinary workers who showed reluctance to comply or who wandered away from their assigned tasks to catch up with the backlog of work needing to be done on their own land from which they subsisted.

Thus the influx of the third group, the Rwandans fleeing persecution at home who left from 1959 onwards, were only one last phase in a larger historical presence of Banyarwanda, and even at the peak of their numbers in 1990, in the case of Uganda, this group of "'59ers," as the refugee group came to be known, probably comprised no more than 15 percent of the total ethnic Rwandan population in Uganda at the time.[2]

Delegation of Dominance

Rwandan society was traditionally built around the monarchy, with the *mwami* at the top of a structure based on the triple foundations of the army, the clientage system in the countryside and the political institutions, all of which were Tutsi dominated. The ranks of the army were formed from Tutsi recruits and Hutus were used only as auxiliaries, while remaining under the protection of their army chief. The *mwami* appointed two chiefs to each district, one a cattle chief and the other a land chief, each collecting dues from the proceeds of ranching and agriculture, respectively. On appointment each chief himself received a gift of a large number of head of cattle, cementing his position and authority indisputably within the territory for which he was responsible.

Poorer Tutsis became the "clients" of wealthy Tutsis, supplying services in exchange for cattle, and Hutu laborers in turn became clients of the less-elevated Tutsis, paying dues and providing labor, often in exchange for rights over some of the same cattle which the higher Tutsis had in turn made available to them. In this way a complex but well-defined structure of society was in operation, built around and cemented by this clientage, or *ubuhake*, which defined economic and social relationships among Rwanda's different castes.

The arriving German colonists, unlike their British, French and Portuguese counterparts, had only become turned on to the idea of an African empire late in the day, but by the end of the 1800s the idea came to be accepted as a necessary and desirable extension of nationalist expansionism in Europe. As the new colonial rulers of Ruanda and Urundi, they sought to control and administer their outlying territories with minimal expense of manpower and resources. They maintained the structure of the Rwandan monarchy and aristocracy and adapted the existing feudal system in an attempt to produce revenue for their new east African empire.

Indeed, they supported the Tutsis as their preferred caste in administrative positions, adopting a policy of replacing the relatively few Hutu chiefs with Tutsis and favoring the latter in other administrative roles and access to education. The act of carrying out one such replacement of chiefs with Tutsi substitutes in 1910 in northwestern Rwanda, a dynastic Hutu stronghold, led to a popular revolt by the Hutus, which the Germans put down by force.

Although the Germans supported the Tutsis in their domination of society in internal administrative and political matters, the German presence and that of other European colonists in the neighboring countries eventually began to undermine one of the traditional sources of power of the *mwami* and his aristocracy as well as dismantling an essential aspect of historical Rwandan culture. The warrior tradition of the king and his chiefs, their pride in the conquest of neighbors and gaining land, symbolized by the sacred *kalinga* drum, *intore* dancing and other rituals, was all coming to an end as a practical component of dynastic life. With no means to wage war successfully against European-controlled territories protected by soldiers equipped with modern firearms, one of the three operating organs of Rwandan society, the military power and prestige of the *mwami*, would soon be rendered impotent and later became more an item of historical and cultural interest rather than an essential element of power in the kingdom.

Following the East African Peace Settlement of 1919, Ruanda and Urundi came under Belgian administration and the two kingdoms were transferred to them under a League of Nations mandate in 1923. The practice of the German colonists in reinforcing the dominance of Tutsis as the administrative class of their colony continued after the handover to the Belgians and indeed, as colonists who sought to be more involved than their predecessors, they intensified their intervention in certain key aspects of Rwandan politics and society.

Although only a minority of around 15 percent, the Tutsis held 80 percent of school places, as well as nearly all posts in government ministries and other positions of civil and economic power. Although primary education through the religious missions was available to Hutu as well as Tutsi children, higher and professional education was reserved for Tutsis. An official school of administration at the city of Astrida, later renamed Butare, was set up and places were reserved exclusively for the sons of Tutsi chiefs. At the Group Scolaire, technical training for the running of agriculture, medicine, veterinary work and higher administration was given to Tutsi students while the only professional careers open to Hutus were teaching posts in the religious seminaries.

To cement this feudal delegation of colonial power, in the 1930s the Belgians instigated a formal registration of every citizen with an identity card clearly marking the holder by *ubwoko*, or ethnicity, a measure which was to have drastic consequences for the minority Tutsi population of the country over half a century later. The Belgians also continued to bring

Catholicism to much of the population and over time the influence of the priesthood (the *pères blancs*, or "white fathers") on educational and civic life became all-pervasive.

However, although political and administrative power was confirmed unassailably in the hands of the Tutsis, the Belgians continued the dismantling of the military power of the king and the aristocracy which the Germans had begun. The existing military structure was abolished and soldiers from the Congo were brought in to form the new *Gendarmerie Nationale*, the Rwandan police force. In 1931 Mwami Musinga was deposed by the Belgians and replaced, not by his hereditary successor and according to the Rwandan custom of *abiru*, but by colonial administrative selection, with support from the church rather than the chiefs and the aristocracy.

A core motivation behind the colonists' decision was the slow rate of conversion to Catholicism among Tutsis which was occurring under Musinga. The new king, Mutara Rudahigwa, was much more pro-conversion and it was during his reign that the majority of Rwandans became Catholics.

Nevertheless, the sidestepping of the monarchy and traditional constitutional provisions for the succession further undermined this central aspect of Rwandan life. The *mwami* was weakened as a symbol of power and unity in the country and the common loyalty shown to him by both Hutus and Tutsis became harder to maintain. Mass conversions by Tutsis to the Catholic church took place, confirming the power of the Belgians over the power structure in the country.

Following World War II, Rwanda continued under Belgian rule, becoming a United Nations Trust territory in 1946. As the international movement towards independence in former European colonies began in the 1950s, the majority at the UN generally supported the birth of new countries free from colonial domination and in Africa in particular, a new breed of young leaders with aspirations for their countries' freedom and embracing a Pan-African ideology was emerging. Julius Nyerere of Tanzania, Kwame Nkrumah of Ghana and Kenneth Kaunda of Zambia were among the most prominent of those who led the first wave of countries gaining their independence. Each of these aspired to a greater or lesser extent towards replacing the colonial economic model with a socialist one as the means towards the development of their countries' potential.

New Emphasis by Priesthood

Also, beginning in the early 1950s, a change in attitude to the status quo in Rwandan society came about on the part of the priesthood. The Catholic church, which had until then solidly supported the primacy of the Tutsis in administrative and political life, now increasingly began to favor equality for the hitherto lower-class Hutus. On the one hand the Hutus had shown greater willingness to convert to Catholicism; but on the other hand the forces of change came from within the ranks of the priesthood itself.

Starting around this time, more and more emancipation-conscious Flemish missionaries were arriving in Rwanda and the new arrivals were more inclined to be sympathetic to the underprivileged Hutus. The Flemish as an ethnic group in Belgium were struggling to break out from decades of dominance under a French-speaking Walloon hegemony of power in Belgium, and so they supported the cause of those who were starting to call for an elevation of the Hutus in Rwandan society.

On the hillsides of Rwanda, another of the three pillars of traditional society began to break down during the interwar period: the rigid system of clientage and economic dependence which, as well as keeping them in a subservient role in society, had also provided both protection and an element of stability for the Hutu peasant laborer class. Beginning in the late 1920s, the economic opportunities in the British colony of Uganda drew workers away from their traditional roles and relationships in the struggling Rwandan economy. As the colonists tried to extract more surplus from agriculture in Rwanda, through an intensification of *umuganda*, they helped drive labor northwards to take advantage of kinder working conditions and better compensation in the Ugandan cotton and coffee plantations.

This process, together with the arrival of the monetary economy, was the beginning of the end of *ubuhake*, the bond between patron and client which had been the glue of economic life in Rwanda for generations. As money from cultivation of cash crops grew in importance, cattle-based clientage diminished in its role at the center of the Rwandan society and economy. Finally, in 1954, *ubuhake* was formally abolished, with cattle being redistributed between patron and client. There was no redistribution of land, however, and the client still had to pay his patron for the land he grazed the cattle on, except that now the obligation was fulfilled with money, not labor. There was no true realignment of economic power, only a replacement of the traditional service and patronage relationship with one of monetary obligation.

Another change initiated by the colonists in the 1930s was the ending of the practice of giving new chiefs a gift of cattle upon their appointment. This tradition had previously ensured that newly appointed chiefs had not only political but also economic power in the districts which they governed. However, the new system only gave the appointees the salary and administrative authority that went with their position, but not the additional economic power formerly invested in them by the *mwami*. The former chiefs who had been deposed were allowed to keep the cattle which they received, but the new ones only received individual financial and material benefits, giving them a much reduced role in society, no matter how much power they still might wield in the politics of the country.

The ending of cattle clientage, economic migration, the rise of the monetary economy and the separation of social from economic functions of the chieftaincy all served to erode the role and functioning of another element of stability in pre-colonial Rwanda. The social responsibility of the chief towards his subjects disappeared and individual interests became a more important motivating factor in economic relationships. This, combined with the rapidly growing population and the continuing inequalities of the land distribution regime, which had not been addressed in the same way as the cattle ownership issue, led to rising tensions in Rwandan society.

In summary, as a result of the changes brought about by colonial administration and regional economics, traditional Rwandan hierarchical ties were replaced by those of self-interested economic exploitation against a background of scarcity of the factors of production. Tutsis held the land rights as well as the higher-status and better-paying jobs in a modernizing society where there was no longer a social responsibility to accompany their monopoly of privilege.

Pressures for Democracy

Under the terms of its agreement with Belgium, the UN Trusteeship Council sent periodic missions to monitor developments in Rwanda. Beginning with one such mission in 1950, the UN increasingly called for more rapid progress towards change and the development of democratic institutions in the country. By the late 1950s the politics of the times were inevitably leading the country towards independence, which, while much remained uncertain about the country's future, served to accelerate the climate of change and fluidity inside Rwanda.

This new character and mobility of Rwandan society, together with the influence of the Catholic church, anticipation of independence, pressure resulting from the criticisms made by the UN visiting missions and a reactive colonial administration now favoring democracy, all led to a growing momentum for the political mobilization of the Hutu community.

Because of the restrictions on educational opportunities for Hutus in the Rwandan society of the 1950s, the national champions of Hutu emancipation came from the seminaries, among them a priest from the south of the country named Grégoire Kayibanda. Kayibanda came from the seminary at Nyakibanda, the country's leading institution at the time for the education of the aspiring Hutu elite. A schoolteacher and later an administrator in TRAFIPRO,[3] a coffee cooperative established by Paul Kagame's father and the first of the parastatal organizations to be opened up to non–Tutsi nationals, he was also the chief editor of *Kinyamateka*, a church magazine and the main vehicle for the publication of emancipationist ideology.

Kayibanda was also one of the authors of the key document in the evolution of the struggle for the rights of the ordinary Hutu. The publication, in March 1957, of the so-called Bahutu Manifesto, set out the historical grievances, rights and reparations (to be claimed) and aspirations of the country's majority ethnic community. Its proclamation provided the intellectual basis for the political movement that was growing for the launch of a Hutu ascendancy in the management of Rwanda's affairs. In a characteristically Rwandan example of manipulation by the competing interests of outside actors, it was also produced to coincide with the arrival in the country of one of the UN Trusteeship Council's periodic missions.

Political parties began to be formed across Rwanda's regional and ethnic spectrum. After some initial mergers and modifications, the largest of the Hutu political groups which emerged was the Mouvement Démocratique Républicain — Parti du mouvement de l'émancipation des Bahutu (MDR-PARMEHUTU), which drew its support from the north and west of the country and of which Kayibanda was the leader. Another essentially Hutu party, APROSOMA, was launched by the businessman Joseph Gitera, who initially sought broad support but ultimately became leader of a Hutu party drawing its support from the Butare area in the south.

Gitera's other major claim to fame was his vociferous lobbying of the colonial administration for the removal of the *kalinga*, the traditional court drum, which was a symbol of the historic supremacy of the Tutsis. The drum was reputedly adorned with the testicles of Hutu chiefs whom the *mwami* had defeated in battle and therefore its preservation represented an obstacle to the development of a democratic society. The impact of this demand on the Tutsi elite was highly inflammatory, akin to a Northern Irish Republican leader demanding the abolition of the Loyalist annual Apprentice Boy's March through the city of Londonderry, symbol of the pro–British faction's traditional dominance in that province's society.

Independence and the Hutu Revolution

With the death of the *mwami* Mutara Rudahigwa, the Tutsi king, in July 1959, further changes were set in motion. Because of the emerging realignment of the colonists with Hutu power interests, the Tutsis soon began to revile the foreign rulers who had long underpinned their dominance in Rwandan society. They resisted the reversal of allegiances by the colonists and sided with the UN, whose Trusteeship Council at that time was strongly influenced by the socialist ideals which many newly independent African member states were embracing. The Tutsis therefore sought to end Belgian colonial rule as it was clear that their traditional European backers, after underpinning Tutsi dominance for half a century, had now decided to align themselves with the underprivileged majority.

Although not all Tutsis favored an immediate end to Belgian rule, in August 1959 the more radical among them formed the Union Nationale Rwandaise (UNAR), a pro-independence movement dedicated to supporting the accession of Kigeli V, the new *mwami*, maintaining the monarchy, and of course protecting the societal status quo which had cemented the Tutsis at the top of the pyramid of Rwandan society. In a further snub to the Belgians, Kigeli was appointed clandestinely, according to the traditional *abiru* ceremony, as if to ensure that their traditional system which had been circumvented by the colonists in 1931 would be preserved this time around.

Paradoxically, in the context of Rwanda in 1960, a group which was socially very conservative in its own national context was also capable of identifying with a seemingly left-wing agenda in regional political terms— namely the replacement of colonial rule with an independent national leadership modeled upon socialist principles. UNAR received financial and diplomatic backing from the socialist members of the UN Trusteeship Council, further pigeonholing their movement as a potentially pro-communist African leadership.

During the same period, the emerging Hutu elite for their part sought to achieve the establishment of democratic institutions before independence, concerned that an early handover by the colonists to the Tutsi-dominated establishment while it still held power could waste the huge opportunity which was now within its grasp. The Tutsi establishment, including the *mwami* and UNAR, however, sought to achieve the opposite, to achieve independence as quickly as possible so as to maintain its legal hold on power at the time of effective independence.

The timing of the date which the UN would confirm for Rwanda's independence took on enormous significance as tension grew rapidly inside the country, and the tendency of the Hutu leadership from late 1959 onwards was increasingly towards violence. However, the Belgians were also under pressure from the Tutsis, still in control of the country's army and local administration and who were also becoming more inclined towards violent protest in support of their demands.

In October 1959, the Belgian administration removed three northern Tutsi chiefs from power after accusing them of inciting violence at UNAR rallies. Tutsi protest against the administration led to riots in Kigali with hundreds participating and the Belgians dispersing the crowd with tear gas. Tension was mounting and fears of an armed Tutsi backlash against PARMEHUTU and pro-democracy Hutu activists increased. One such attack by a Tutsi mob against a Hutu abbot sparked further social unrest and on November 3, 1959, a Hutu peasant revolt broke out, with waves of attacks against Tutsis in the countryside. The king in return organized armed commando attacks against the most extreme of the Hutu activists.

In the general atmosphere of confusion and violence, many among the peasantry believed that the attacks against Tutsi chiefs and their subjects were being carried out on the orders of the king, who they thought must have sanctioned the arson and evictions of the Tutsis in revenge for their oppressive abuse of power. Moreover, demonstrating that traditional grassroots loyalty to the monarchy had still not yet been destroyed, some Hutus actually rallied in support of the king when he sent troops to attack APROSOMA elements during the early outbreaks of fighting. However, the bands of suddenly radicalized peasants who performed the destructive work across the country were mostly crazed drunken youths, roaming the hillsides, destroying their neighbors' properties and chasing Tutsis off their land. The ugly revolt of November 1959 and the confusion of its actors has been summed up by an observer of the times as an insurrection which was "...monarchist in ideology, anarchic in conduct."[4]

This reversal of fortunes of Rwanda's two groups, accelerated by the influence of the ruling foreign power, led to the waves of attacks on Tutsi civilians such as Paul Kagame's family and thousands of others like them. The Belgians and the United Nations struggled to restore order, although each had its own agenda: the UN sympathizing with the pro-independence cause of UNAR and the Tutsis, while Belgium increasingly leaned towards the Hutus, urging them to assume greater power and condoning the militias' actions of terror and eviction in the countryside.

In a decisive move at the moment of rising tension, Belgium sent troops to help restore order and assumed control of the army. With other, bigger problems to deal with at around the same time in the Belgian Congo to the west, Brussels had no desire for a messy engagement in another complex African civil uprising. Sending the crusading and ideologically inspired Colonel Guy Logiest to take charge of their reinforced military presence, the Belgians suppressed Tutsi protest and proceeded to oversee an increasingly aggressive upsurge in violence on the part of the Hutu community against their ethnic neighbors.

Logiest was detached from his post in the Congo in November 1959 and stayed in Rwanda for three years. Among his earlier actions, he replaced the Tutsi-controlled *gendarmerie* with Congolese draftees. From his earliest involvement, Logiest believed that the moment of destiny for Rwanda was at hand and that his forces had to take sides. Although he was a military man, the Hutus could not have had a more ardent supporter of their radical social cause. Logiest truly believed that he had been sent on a mission to ensure the liberation of the oppressed peoples of Rwanda, and in his own account of his mission, he later summed up his actions: "...the time was crucial for Rwanda ... its people needed support and protection. My role was crucial ... what it was that made me act with such resolution ... the will to give the people back their dignity."[5]

Against this violent backdrop and the rapidly changing allegiances of the colonists, Belgium proceeded to organize local elections in Rwanda starting in late June 1960. The outcome was a landslide for the PARME-HUTU, who took 2,390 seats against 233 for APROSOMA and a derisory 56 for UNAR. The result gave massive political power at the local level to the Hutus for the first time and in many areas the newly elected *bourgmestres* set about using their power to continue and step up evictions of Tutsis in the areas under their control.

The UN Trusteeship Council was following events in Rwanda with increasing disquiet, and Logiest and Grégoire Kayibanda, now leader of the country's largest political party, were nervous about possible intervention over the heads of the Belgian administration, who were still officially administering the country under trust from the UN. To preempt such an intervention, in January 1961 Colonel Logiest convened an extraordinary council of all the *bourgmestres*, in Gitarama, Kayibanda's natal town. Jointly, the two men proclaimed the "Sovereign Democratic Republic of Rwanda," in a bold move which challenged the UN but which the international body ultimately proved powerless to resist.

From that time onward, with the Hutus now "legally" in power, per-secution gained momentum and was condoned if not supported outright by the Belgian authorities, in turn underpinned by Logiest's military com-mand. Further waves of Tutsis fled Rwanda, the majority going to Burundi, but many also fleeing to Uganda, Tanzania, Zaire and some who could, even further abroad, to Europe or to North America. In education and gov-ernment, over the coming months and years, quotas were established and enforced to reflect the proportion of Hutus as against Tutsis in the pop-ulation. This meant that from being in the position of holding most of the prestigious positions in the economy and society, Tutsis were now legally restricted to holding no more than 9 percent in any institution, reflecting their official demographic representation in Rwanda.

In September 1961, legislative elections were organized, with the PARMEHUTU gaining 35 of the 44 total seats in the country. The UNAR won only seven. Politically it was all over for the Tutsis. The UN Trustee-ship Council, outmaneuvered, could only bleat, albeit with prescience, that an old oppressive regime had just been replaced by another one and that "future violent reactions on the part of the Tutsi" could not be ruled out.[6]

Despite the efforts of the United Nations, who initially wanted to merge Rwanda and Burundi at independence to form a single state and recognizing the distasteful *fait accompli* which had occurred under their trusteeship, on July 1, 1962, the Trust Territory of Ruanda officially became the Republic of Rwanda and Urundi became Burundi. The leader of the PARMEHUTU, Grégoire Kayibanda, became the first president of Rwanda at independence without being elected. Due to an outside-encouraged democratization of society and institutions, legitimized and imposed by the outgoing colonial administration, Rwanda was at last dominated by its Hutu majority.[7]

GLOSSARY

abakada: RPF irregular/vigilante soldiers dispensing justice after the genocide

abakonde: regional power group indigenous to the northwest of Rwanda

abiru: traditional rites of coronation of Rwandan kings

akazu: *lit.* "little house," usually referring to the inner circle of Agathe Habyarimana or other governing clique

amavubi: "the Wasps," nickname of the Rwandan national soccer team

bashingantahe: elders of the rural community or "wise men"

ibyitso: collaborators, term referring to all Tutsis inside Rwanda after 1990

igihango: blood pact, also name of the ADNR, a post-genocide opposition movement

imidugudu: "protected villages" used for resettlement under the National Habitat Policy

impuruza: "the mobilizer," name of a traditional war drum in ancient Rwanda

impuzamugambi: "those with a common purpose," a militia closely allied to the CDR

inkotanyi: struggling fighters, name of the RPF soldiers and later of the political party itself (historically, with royal regimental connotations)

interahamwe: "those who work together," militias supporting the MRNDD party

intore: traditional warrior dancers

inyenzi: cockroach, Hutu Power propaganda name for any Tutsi

itsinzi: victory

kadogo: child soldier

kalinga: the traditional mystical war drum of the mwami

kitenge: multicolored tunic and trousers worn by the interahamwe militias

kwihutura: "shedding Hutuness," process by which upwardly mobile Hutus became Tutsis

muyaga: literally a gusty, turbulent wind, used to refer to the civil disturbances of 1959

mwami: king

mzee: Congolese word for ruler, used to refer to, e.g., Laurent Kabila

nyarwanda: local Ugandan expression for the people in the southwest of their country, where there were many Rwandan migrants; derogatory especially when applied to Ugandans

ubuhake: clientage, the system by which access to cattle was given to peasants in exchange for manual labor

ubwoko: term used for ethnic designation, notably on compulsory identity cards in use until July 1994

umugabo: "macho" man

umuganda: unpaid community work obligation

umwuga: profession

urgwagwa: banana beer

urumogi: marijuana

wakimbizi: local Ugandan word for refugees, meaning "those who ran away"

CHAPTER NOTES

Chapter 1

1. President Paul Kagame, interview with author, October 2003.

2. UNHCR *Banyarwanda Refugee Census*, 1964.

3. Estimates of populations and refugee numbers from Catherine Watson, *Exile from Rwanda*, U.S. Committee for Refugees, 1991.

4. Refugee interviews appear in Watson, op. cit.

5. The king had planned to go to the U.S. and went to see his Belgian doctor in Burundi before departure. As his physician was unavailable that day, a substitute administered the requested injections, after which the *mwami* collapsed and died.

6. Interview with François Misser, in *Vers un Nouveau Rwanda?: Entretiens avec Paul Kagame*, 1995.

7. In Kinyarwanda, the letter pair "ri" in a word is not used, hence "Kigeli" and not Kigeri, which can often be seen in texts. However, Habyarimana, as opposed to the correct "Habyalimana," is so universally used in English and French literature on Rwanda, it is also retained here for conformity.

8. Gérard Prunier, *The Rwanda Crisis: History of a Genocide*, 1997.

9. Interview with author, October 2003.

10. *Le Monde*, October 7, 1982, in Prunier, op. cit.

11. Interview with author, October 2003.

12. Quoted in R. K. Nyakabwa, *Statelessness and the Batutsi Refugees' Invasion of Rwanda, 1990–94*. Ph.D. diss. University of London, Institute of Commonwealth Studies, 2002.

13. Interview with author, October 2003.

Chapter 2

1. The name stuck and would later be used by the extremist Hutu propagandists to describe Tutsis in derogatory terms, with the objective of dehumanizing and discrediting their ethnic rivals.

2. Vatican Radio broadcast, February 10, 1964, in Ian Linden, *Church and Revolution in Rwanda*, 1977.

3. W. Cyrus Reed, "Exile, Reform and the Rise of the Rwanda Patriotic Front," *Journal of Modern African Studies*, 1996.

4. Rwigyema joined Frelimo, the anti-colonialist Mozambican movement, for a year before returning to Tanzania.

5. In Philip Gourevitch, *We wish to inform you that tomorrow we will be killed with our families*, 1998.

6. An area of some 4,500 square kilometers stretching to the north and west of Kampala, bounded by the roads running north towards Gulu and northwest to Hoima and marked on its northern side by the Kafu River.

7. Pascal Ngoga, "The National Resistance Army," in *African Guerrillas*, ed. Christopher Clapham, 1998.

8. Yoweri Museveni, *Sowing the Mustard Seed: The Struggle for Freedom and Democracy in Uganda*, 1997.

9. Ngoga, op. cit.

10. Interview with author, October 2003.

11. Interview with author, October 2003.

12. Interview with author, October 2003.

13. Prunier, op. cit.

14. Interview with author, October 2003.

15. Interview with author, October 2003.

Chapter 3

1. The acronym RPF strictly refers to the political arm of the movement, while the RPA (Rwandan Patriotic Army) refers to Rwanda's military, particularly since 1994. However, in the early days of the movement, the military and political leadership were effectively one and the term RPF may refer to both the military and non-military wings.

2. Interview with author, October 2003.

3. Rwandese, still commonly used, is derived from the French "rwandais," although the word "Rwandan" is used throughout this text.

4. Prunier, op. cit.

5. Prunier, op. cit.

6. RPF intelligence officer interview with author, Kigali, 2003.

7. Although a major in the Ugandan army, Kagame had now assumed the title of Major-General of the RPA, more appropriate for his status as the force's commander in chief.

8. Linda Melvern, *A People Betrayed*, 2000.

9. Interview with author, October 2003.

Chapter 4

1. Linda Melvern, Rwanda Genocide Archive.

2. Interview with author, October 2003.

3. Melvern, in *A People Betrayed*, 2000.

4. Interview with the author, October 2003.

5. Interview with the author, October 2003.

6. Lt. Gen. Roméo Dallaire, *Shake Hands with the Devil*, 2003.

7. Interview with the author, October 2003.

8. Prunier, op. cit. Prunier was an advisor to the French Defense Ministry in Paris during the preparations for *Opération Turquoise*.

9. Reported by Agence France Presse, July 12, 1994, in Prunier, op. cit.

10. Interview with author, October 2003.

11. Interview with author, October 2003.

12. African Rights, *Resisting Genocide: Bisesero, April–June 1994*, 1998.

13. Interview with author, October 2003.

14. Ministry of Local Government, March 2001, *Census of Persons Who Lost Their Lives During the 1994 Genocide*, total deaths documented as 1,074,017. UNREO, Charles Petrie, Kigali, 1994.

15. Even in 1994, many jobs in businesses, embassies and international organizations still went to Tutsis, despite the Hutus' grip on senior positions in politics and the administration.

16. Prunier, op. cit.

17. René Lemarchand, *Rwanda and Burundi*, 1970.

18. Ahmedou Ould Abdallah, with Stephen Smith, *La Diplomatie Pyromane*, 1996.

19. *Notes on the Social Aspect of the Racial Native Problem in Rwanda* was the document's full title.

Chapter 5

1. Interview with author, October 2003.

2. Despite the RPF's hopes that they would be welcomed by ordinary Rwandans, the fighting in 1990–92 caused an estimated 350,000 people to flee their homes to displaced persons' camps.

3. Herman J. Cohen, *Intervening in Africa*, 2000.

4. Allison Desforges, *New York Times*, April 18, 1994.

5. Presidential Directive 25, May 1994, in Linda Melvern, *The Ultimate Crime: Who Betrayed the UN and Why*, 1995.

6. Christine Shelley, U.S. State Department spokesperson, press conference, in the International Herald Tribune, June 10, 1994.

7. Linda Melvern, *Conspiracy to Murder*, 2004.

8. Quoted in Linda Melvern, "Britannia Waived the Rules," *African Affairs*, January 2004.

9. The euro became the common currency for commercial transactions in 11 countries of the EU on January 1, 2002. Prior to that international transfers and non-cash payments could be made through the medium of the ecu, the euro's institutional predecessor.

10. Reported in the *New York Times*, September 18, 1994.

11. Colette Braeckman, *Terreur Africaine*, 1996.

12. Braeckman, op. cit.

13. Norman Finkelstein, *The Holocaust Industry*, 2001.

14. Colette Braeckman, *Les Nouveaux Prédateurs*, 2003.

15. "Aid Into Africa," *The Economist*, February 24, 2001.

16. UN estimates as of July 21, 1994 (Inter-Agency Appeal for Rwanda).

17. U.S. Doc. background paper for U.S. mission, USUN, *Former Rwandan Army, Ca-*

pabilities and Intentions, September 1, 1994, Linda Melvern, Rwanda Genocide Archive.

Chapter 6

1. *New York Times,* September 18, 1994.
2. Médicins sans Frontières/Doctors Without Borders USA Press Release, November 14, 1994.
3. Donors' Round Table for Rwanda, United Nations Consolidated Appeal Process, Geneva, January 1997.
4. The U.S. had ratified the 1948 UN Convention on the Repression of Genocide only in March 1986, much later than most western nations and after many years of debate and opposition from key members of the Senate. Signatories committed to intervene to prevent any act of genocide known to be perpetrated with the means at their disposal.
5. A report was finally issued in December of 1999: *An Independent Inquiry into the Conduct of the United Nations During the 1994 Genocide in Rwanda,* UN Document A/54/549, December 15, 1999.
6. Gourevitch, op. cit.

Chapter 7

1. Braeckman, *Les Nouveaux Prédateurs.*
2. Interview at Kennedy School of Government, Harvard University, 2001.
3. The first of the UN Security Council reports was rejected by the U.S. and the UK, among others, for not including criticism of the looting activities of two of Kinshasa's allies, Zimbabwe and Angola.
4. Barbara Crossette, *New York Times,* February 5, 2001.
5. Braeckman, *Les Nouveaux Prédateurs.*
6. *UN Security Council Report of the Panel of Experts on the Illegal Exploitation of Natural Resources and Other Forms of Wealth of the Democratic Republic of the Congo* (S/2001/1072).
7. UN Panel of Experts report, S/2002/1146, October 15, 2002, paragraph 68.
8. Joseph Bideri, Rwanda Bureau of Information (ORINFOR), interview with author, October 2003.
9. Q & A session at Kennedy School of Government, Harvard University, 2001.
10. An excellent account of the exploitation of the Congo during this period can be found in Adam Hochschild's work *King Leopold's Ghost,* 1998.

11. James Bacque, *Crimes and Mercies: The Fate of the German Civilians Under Allied Occupation, 1944–50,* 1997.
12. John Gimbel, *A German Community Under American Occupation: Marburg, 1945–52,* 1961.
13. UN Panel of Experts Report on the Illegal Exploitation of the Democratic Republic of the Congo, October 20, 2003.

Chapter 8

1. Urasa to Edoukou Aka Kablan, April 4, 1996, in *Human Rights Watch, Rwanda Report,* 1999.
2. Chris McGreal, "Tutsi Soldier to Lead Rwanda," *The Guardian,* March 25, 2000.
3. *Defense and Foreign Affairs Strategic Policy,* April 2000, International Strategic Studies Association (ISSA), Washington, DC.
4. Thomas Ofcansky, *Africa South of the Sahara,* 2003.
5. *Ubuyanja* also contains the meaning of recovery or convalescence in Kinyarwanda.
6. Interview in *Jeune Afrique,* July 3, 2001.
7. Named as Michael Hourigan, a researcher for the ICTR, in a Canadian *National Post* article of March 1, 2000. The "report" which his three pages of findings led to was subsequently transferred to the ICTR in Arusha on instructions from Kofi Annan, but it was not made publicly available.
8. Interview with author, October 2003.
9. Mgr. Aloys Bigirumwami and Bernardin Muzungu, *Imigani "Tima-Ngiro" Y'U Rwanda: Les contes moraux du Rwanda,* 1989.
10. Misser, op. cit.

Chapter 9

1. Gourevitch, op. cit.
2. Colette Braeckman, *Terreur Africaine,* 1996.
3. In Gourevitch, op. cit.
4. In Gourevitch, op. cit.
5. ICTR website, *Status of ICTR detainees,* September 1, 2003.
6. Interview with author, October 2003.
7. Prunier, op. cit.
8. Gerald Gahima, "Prosecuting Genocide in Rwanda," paper given at Irish Centre for Human Rights, June 2003.
9. Zuroff himself visited Rwanda in 1995, going to the church at Ntarama after which he expressed his emotion and evoked the paral-

lels between the Rwandan Tutsis' plight and that of eastern European Jews.

10. Organic Law 8/96, August 30, 1996: Organization of Prosecutions for offences constituting the crime of genocide or crimes against humanity committed since October 1, 1990.

11. In Gourevitch, op. cit.

12. Former detainee interview with Andrew Harding, BBC News, August 2003.

13. Gerald Gahima, address to the Royal Institute for International Affairs, London, 2003.

Chapter 10

1. Tito Rutaremara, president of the Constitutional Commission, interview with author, October 2003.

2. Constitution of the Republic of Rwanda, *Official Gazette*, Kigali, June 4, 2003.

3. Early in the campaign, the Liberal Party, the Social Democrats and two smaller parties declared that they would not field candidates and endorsed Kagame's candidacy for the presidency.

4. Interview with IRIN, UN Office for the Coordination of Humanitarian Affairs, May 16, 2003.

5. Human Rights Watch, "Tightening Control in the Name of Unity," background paper, May 2003.

6. Ibid.

7. IRIN News, op. cit., July 7, 2003.

8. Interview with Reuters, BBC, etc., at the AU Summit in Maputo, Mozambique, July 2003.

9. William Wallis, *Financial Times*, August 25, 2003.

10. Paul Kagame, speech in Byumba on March 31, 2003.

11. IRIN, UN Office for Coordination of Humanitarian Affairs, August 19, 2003.

12. Reported in *Agence France Presse*, August 23, 2003.

13. *The Economist*, August 28, 2003.

14. *Le Soft des Grands Lacs*, September 27, 2003.

15. African Rights, survivor interviews, 1995, in Melvern, *A People Betrayed*, 2000.

16. *Agence France Presse*, August 23, 2003.

17. Conversation with author, Kigali, October 2003.

18. Interview with *The Monitor*, August 27, 2003 (privately owned Ugandan daily).

19. Rutazibwa received a religious education in Zaire before being ordained as a priest in Rwanda in 1990. He joined the RPF in 1992 during their underground struggle against the government of the day.

20. Letter dated October 2, 2003, from Rutazibwa to Marie-Violette César, Observer Mission of the EU, Kigali.

21. Makola, Africa Institute of South Africa, *CNN Listened to the Wrong Voices*, August 2003.

Chapter 11

1. Human Rights Watch, *Uprooting the Rural Poor in Rwanda*, June 2001.

2. Ofcansky, op. cit.

3. Gourevitch, op. cit.

4. *Enhanced Repatriation and Reintegration of Rwandan Refugees*, UNHCR, Africa Bureau, February 2003.

5. Interview with author, October 2003.

6. Damascène Ndaruhutse, interviewed in *The New Times*, Kigali, October 16–19, 2003.

7. IRIN News, *Focus on Genocide Widows*, UNOCHA report, October 2003.

8. IRIN News, op. cit., October 8, 2003.

9. James Munyaneza, *New Times*, September 18–21, 2003.

10. UN Security Council, Panel of Experts "Report on the Illegal Exploitation of Natural Resources and Other Forms of Wealth of the DRC," 2002.

11. Interview with author, Kigali, October 2003.

12. Interview with author, October 2003.

13. Rwanda's traditional French nickname: "The Land of a Thousand Hills."

14. Interview with author, October 2003.

15. Interview in *Le Soft*, Kigali, September 27, 2003.

16. Interview with author, Kigali, October 2003.

17. Interview with Tryphon Mulumba, *Le Soft*, September 19, 2003.

18. Monograph no. 35: *Peace and Security in Africa*, Symposium on International Peace and Security, September 23, 1998.

19. *Washington Post*, April 27, 1994.

20. Interview with author, October 2003.

21. In Gourevitch, op. cit., p. 341.

22. Interview with author, October 2003.

23. Interview with author, October 2003.

Appendix

1. Manioc (cassava) was introduced as a staple crop around this time by the Belgians.

Tea and coffee were the colonists' preferred cash crops for export.

2. A comprehensive diplomatic attempt to resolve the nationality issue of the Banyarwanda was made with the Dar es Salaam declaration of 1991, which gave theoretical options of return, nationality without return or naturalization outside Rwanda to the Banyarwanda diaspora in the Great Lakes region.

3. Established in 1957, the name is derived from the French "*Travail, Fidelité, Progrès.*"

4. Linden, op. cit.

5. Guy Logiest, *Mission au Rwanda*, 1988, in Prunier, op. cit.

6. UN Trusteeship Council report, 1961, in Prunier, op. cit.

7. In Burundi, the Tutsis remained in control of the army and government although numerically the Hutus held a similar majority of the population as in Rwanda.

BIBLIOGRAPHY

Abdallah, Ahmedou Ould. *La diplomatie pyromane: Burundi, Rwanda, Somalie, Bosnie: entretiens avec Stephen Smith.* Paris: Calmann-Lévy, 1996.

Bacque, James. *Crimes and Mercies: The Fate of the German Civilians Under Allied Occupation.* London: Little, Brown, 1997.

Barnett, Michael. *Eyewitness to a Genocide: The UN and Rwanda.* Ithaca, NY: Cornell University Press, 2002.

Bigirumwami, Aloys (ed.), and Bernardin Muzungu (tr.). *Imigani "Tima-Ngiro" Y'U Rwanda: Les contes moraux du Rwanda.* Butare: Université Nationale de Butare, 1989.

Braeckman, Colette. *Les nouveaux prédateurs: Politique des puissances en Afrique Centrale.* Paris: Fayard, 2003.

_____. *Rwanda: histoire d'un genocide.* Paris: Fayard, 1994.

_____. *Terreur africaine: Burundi, Rwanda, Zaire, les racines de la violence.* Paris: Fayard, 1996.

Clapham, Christopher (ed.). *African Guerrillas.* Oxford: James Currey, 1998.

Cohen, Herman J. *Intervening in Africa: Superpower Peacemaking in a Troubled Continent.* New York: Palgrave-Macmillan, 2000.

Dallaire, Lt. Gen. Roméo. *Shake Hands with the Devil: The Failure of Humanity in Rwanda.* Toronto: Random House, 2003.

Desforges, Allison. *Leave None to Tell the Story: Genocide in Rwanda.* New York: Human Rights Watch, 1999.

Doyle, Mark. *Captain Mbaye Diagne.* London: Granta, 1999.

Finkelstein, Norman. *The Holocaust Industry.* London: Verso, 2001.

Gimbel, John. *A German Community Under American Occupation: Marburg, 1945–1952.* Stanford, CA: Stanford University Press, 1961.

Gourevitch, Philip. *We Wish to Inform You That Tomorrow We Will Be Killed with Our Families.* New York: Farrar Straus & Giraux, 1998.

Hochschild, Adam. *King Leopold's Ghost.* London: Houghton Mifflin, 1998.

Human Rights Watch. *Preparing for Elections: Tightening Control in the Name of Unity.* May 2003.

Human Rights Watch Arms Project. *Arming Rwanda: The Arms Trade and Human Rights Abuses in the Rwandan War.* 1994.

International Crisis Group. *Rwanda at the End of the Transition: A Necessary Political Liberalisation.* November 13, 2002.

Keane, Fergal. *Season of Blood: A Rwanda Journey.* New York: Viking, 1995.

Khan, S., and M. Robinson. *Shallow Graves of Rwanda*. London: Tauris, 2001.

Lemarchand, Réne. *Rwanda and Burundi*. New York: Praeger, 1970.

Linden, Ian. *Church and Revolution in Rwanda*. Manchester: Manchester University Press, 1977.

Mamdani, Mahmoud. *When Victims Become Killers*. Kampala: Fountain, 2001.

Melvern, Linda. "Britannia Waived the Rules: The Major Government and the 1994 Rwandan Genocide." *African Affairs*. January 2004.

_____. *Conspiracy to Murder: The Rwanda Genocide and the International Community*. London: Verso, 2004.

_____. *A People Betrayed: The Role of the West in Rwanda's Genocide*. London: Zed Books, 2000.

_____. *The Ultimate Crime: Who Betrayed the UN and Why*. London: Allison & Busby, 1995.

Misser, François. *Vers un nouveau Rwanda? Entretiens avec Paul Kagame*. Brussels: Luc Pire, 1995.

Museveni, Yoweri. *Sowing the Mustard Seed: The Struggle for Freedom and Democracy in Uganda*. London: Macmillan, 1997.

Nyakabwa, R. K. *Statelessness and the Batutsi refugees' invasion of Rwanda, 1990–94*. Ph.D diss., University of London, Institute of Commonwealth Studies, 2002.

Ofcansky, Thomas. *Africa South of the Sahara*. Europa Publications, 2003.

Onana, Charles, and Deo Mushayidi. *Les secrets du génocide rwandais: enquête sur les mystères d'un président*. Paris: Editions Minsi, 2001.

Power, Samantha. *A Problem from Hell: America in the Age of Genocide*. New York: Harper Collins, 2003.

Prunier, Gérard. *The Rwanda Crisis: History of a Genocide*. London: Hurst, 1997.

Reed, W. Cyrus. "Exile, Reform and the Rise of the Rwandan Patriotic Front." *Journal of Modern African Studies*, 34(3), Cambridge UP, 1996.

Ropa, Denis. *L'Ouganda de Yoweri Museveni*. Paris: l'Harmattan, 1998.

United Nations Security Council. *Independent Inquiry into the Actions of the Security Council During the 1994 Genocide in Rwanda*. December 15, 1999.

United Nations Security Council, Panel of Experts on the Democratic Republic of the Congo. *Report on the Illegal Exploitation of Natural Resources and Other Forms of Wealth of the Democratic Republic of the Congo*, S/2001/1072; S/2002/1146.

Vassall-Adams, Guy. *Rwanda: An Agenda for International Action*. Oxford: Oxfam, 1994.

Watson, Catherine. *Exile from Rwanda: Background to an Invasion*. Washington, D.C.: U.S. Committee for Refugees, 1991.

INDEX